365
FLY-FISHING TIPS

For Trout, Bass, and Panfish

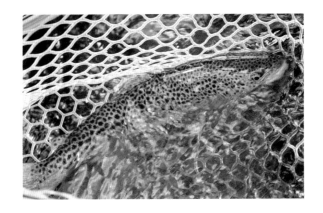

365
FLY-FISHING TIPS

For Trout, Bass, and Panfish

SKIP MORRIS

STACKPOLE
BOOKS
Guilford, Connecticut

Published by Stackpole Books
An imprint of The Rowman & Littlefield Publishing Group, Inc.
4501 Forbes Blvd., Ste. 200
Lanham, MD 20706
www.rowman.com

Distributed by NATIONAL BOOK NETWORK
800-462-6420

Illustrations by Carol Ann Morris
Photography by Carol Ann Morris unless otherwise credited
All flies tied by Skip Morris

British Library Cataloguing in Publication Information available

Library of Congress Control Number Available

ISBN 978-0-8117-3785-2 (paperback)
ISBN 978-0-8117-6774-3 (e-book)

The paper used in this publication meets the minimum requirements of American National Standard for Information Sciences—Permanence of Paper for Printed Library Materials, ANSI/ NISO Z39.48-1992.

SYMBOLS

Tr-S   Trout in Streams

Tr-L   Trout in Lakes

Lg-L   Largemouth Bass in Lakes

Sm-S   Smallmouth Bass in Streams

Sm-L   Smallmouth Bass in Lakes

Pf-L   Panfish in Lakes

Contents

Introduction

If you're new to fly fishing and you read through this book—just one time through—you'll turn the last page a much better fly fisher than you were when you turned the front cover. You'll have improved, I'd estimate, by half again. And that . . . is huge. An investment of only a few pleasant hours for a leap of *half*. (I hope and pray they're pleasant. I did everything in my power to make this book an enjoyable read.)

Imagine how much you'll improve if you read through it twice. Imagine . . .

Even if you've fly-fished for decades, I believe you'll still pick up a heap of fresh, practical information and ideas here.

These are bold claims, indeed. But in case you mistake my boldness for arrogance: nope—it's just me being realistic. Look, I've spent several decades making a living in fly fishing—writing about it (this is my 19th book, and I've published over 300 articles in the fly magazines), teaching it, speaking about it at fly clubs and events, and also fishing with many fly-fishing writers, guides, and experts while asking them lots of questions. I'm bound to be loaded with great information.

If you did all that, don't you think you could come up with a few hundred excellent tips, many that would give even a seasoned fly fisher a happy surprise?

Bet you could.

I believe I did.

The tips, all of them, are tips you'll actually *use*. The kind that, once you apply them, make you blink and go, "Wow—why didn't I think of that?"

The illustrations and photos make this book much better than it would be without them—some things just show better than tell. And for many things, a combination of telling and showing is ideal. This book contains lots of telling-and-showing tips.

When the book was finished, all 365 tips researched, written, and polished, I had some left over. The leftovers were excellent tips, but they could be expressed well in so few words that they didn't fit in with the others. Besides, the other, longer tips were gems—I couldn't let any of them go. So I checked with my editor and she let me add these dandy little leftover ones in, here and there, and call them "Bonus Tips." That's right, they're extras, a gift to you.

There's stuff in here on selecting flies wisely and making sense of all the various fly types, on improving your casting and adding new casts (casting—so important. How else do you get your fly out in front of a fish?). There are deadly fishing techniques of all sorts clearly presented, there's info on how to find fish (usually fish gather only in certain places), there's instruction on how to make up effective rigs, and on and on the list goes. As I said: stuff you'll use.

So read, learn, understand, improve, and, most of all, enjoy. Enjoyment: that's really the main reason for taking up fly fishing. These tips will make your fishing go smoothly, provide insight so that you know what to do and why, and put more fish on your line—what's more enjoyable than that?

CHAPTER 1
MEET YOUR FISHES

Before you go out to catch them, you need to know the fishes this book will help you catch. Here's an introduction.

Tip 1 Meet the Trouts

 Tr-S, Tr-L

All trout are similar, but definitely not the same. The brook trout isn't actually a trout at all, but a close relative called a char. There are more trout (and char) species than the four below, but these four are by far the most common in North America, and the rainbow and brown are now common all over the world.

RAINBOW
Almost as inherently cagey as the brown, and just as cagey when conditions are right. Loves streams, including quick water, but like all trout loves lakes too. Often a wild leaper and heavy on speed and stamina. Green back, silvery flanks. A red stripe may run broad and vivid down each of its flanks or be entirely absent.

BROWN
Born smart, then grows smarter. Tends to like quiet currents but will hold in swift ones. Loves lakes too. A fair to good fighter. Truly brown (to tan) along flanks and back, some red spots, belly is yellow.

CUTTHROAT

Slow learner (but it *can* learn), prefers moderate to slow currents or the still water of lakes. Good fighter. Green back and gray or yellow flanks. Always some sort of orange, pink, or red slash along both sides of the jaw, sometimes faint but sometimes a big, vivid splash.

BROOK

Sometimes moody. Under the right conditions, perhaps even cagey. Prefers lakes and slow water in streams. Modest fighter. Its fall spawning colors are striking. Green back and flanks. There are always wormwood markings on a brookie's back.

Tip 2 Meet the Basses and Panfish

 Lg-L   Sm-L, Sm-S   Pf-L

The basses and panfish (with a very few exceptions) prefer warmer to much warmer water than trout can tolerate. And don't think that warmwater fishes are just misshapen trout—you can be a fine trout fisher yet fail to catch many, or any, bass and panfish.

LARGEMOUTH BASS
Found in every state but Alaska, and in Mexico and Canada. Loves warm water but does fine up north thanks to summer water temperatures. Leaps and fights hard (though briefly). Tolerates only very slow currents—a true lake fish. Has a smudgy black horizontal stripe along each flank.

SMALLMOUTH BASS
Looks something like a largemouth, but has vertical stripes (if it has stripes at all) in place of the largemouth's horizontal band. Likes quick, rocky streams but does just as

well in slow, weedy ones and in lakes. Needs warm water at least a fair chunk of the year but can't handle the largemouth's upper limit. Fights hard and long, and sometimes leaps. All over the United States and well up into Canada.

PANFISH

Bluegill
The most common and beloved panfish in North America. Fights hard for its small size (a 10-incher's a dandy), rarely jumps. Prefers lakes but does fine in lazy currents. Needs warm water. Often schools. Does have powder-blue gill covers.

Crappie
Crappies, both black and white, really bunch up (especially black crappies) for mating in spring. Run large for sunfishes (often a pound and a half, even two pounds). Crappies are rounded and flat-sided like other panfish, but silvery with dark markings.

Other Panfish

The list is long: redear, pumpkinseed, warmouth, green sunfish. . . . They're all well worth knowing and seeking. Use the bluegill as your model, or at least your starting point, for exploring most of the panfish. A few (yellow perch, rock bass, etc.) don't follow the bluegill model.

A yellow perch

Fish Don't Like Meeting Expectations

Tr-S,Tr-L   Lg-L   Sm-L, Sm-S   Pf-L

Fish often act out of character. Brown trout are supposed to be smarter than rainbows; rainbows are supposed to fight harder than browns. Yet for three days on a creeping stretch of Montana river, I watched rainbows turn down flies and presentations the browns happily accepted, and watched the browns outleap and outrun the bows. All were wild fish. So although the descriptions in tips 1 and 2 are solid, don't expect fish to always adhere to them.

CHAPTER 2
STRATEGIES AND TACTICS

Now that you've made their acquaintance, it's time to learn how to catch trout, bass, and panfish.

Tip 3 Know How Fish See and Hear and You'll Fish Unseen and Unheard

 Tr-S, Tr-L   Lg-L   Sm-L, Sm-S   Pf-L

Question: How do you sneak up on a fish when you don't understand how it sees and hears? Answer: Poorly. So . . .

Fish see in nearly every direction but mostly seem to pay attention to what's in front and to the sides of them, not behind. In a current, they're forced to face upstream. So, for example, if you approach a trout or smallmouth bass in a river from downstream, angling your cast upstream and across, *and* if you're far enough away, you won't likely be seen. If you need to present the fly downstream, so that you're upstream of the fish, you'd better be *well* upstream, and probably crouching.

The underside of water is a mirror. Fish see things above the water through a clear little circle in that mirror. Draw two lines down from the opposite edges of the circle to the fish's eyes, and you have a near right angle. Immediately above the water, the angle changes to low: just 10 degrees. Both angles are consistent, so the deeper the fish holds in the water, the wider its view—a fish holding 3 feet down will have a better shot at seeing you than a fish holding only inches below the water's surface. (Don't get cocky,

Casting upstream and across presents your fly to a rising trout without presenting yourself.

Crouching, in a spot close enough to this tree trunk that I could blend in with it, hooked me a 14-inch cutthroat trout rising only a rod's length from my feet.

My wife, Carol, cast with her eyes barely topping that pale boulder to hook a rising trout that was facing upstream. Had she stood tall, she'd have ended the rising, and with it her chances of a hookup. SKIP MORRIS

How fish see above the water.

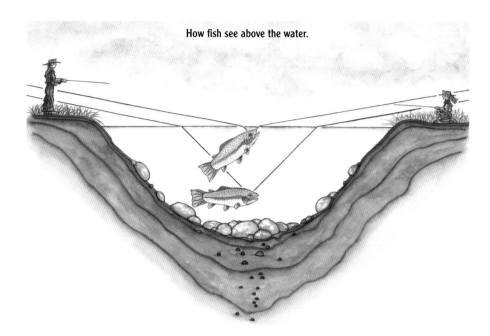

A trout sees above the water within two angles: a medium-wide angle from eye to surface, and a much wider one from the surface out. Note how the deeper trout sees the entire head and shoulders of the angler on the right bank, while the trout holding very near the surface of the water sees only her hat. And note that the angler standing tall on the left bank may as well be carrying a hello-there-I'm-here-to-hook-you sign. (And, since you're already busy noting anyway, note too the size of these trout—they're freaks. Personally, I never wade in water where the average trout exceeds my body mass.)

though—the fish inches down is also extra *skittish*, knowing it's up where predators can snag it.)

How well a fish can see you, of course, also depends on how flat or choppy the surface of the water is. Smooth water's like a window of very clean glass.

Fish *hear* vibrations in the water, and vibrations—sound—travels much better through water than through air. The crunch of a wading boot on gravel, a dropped pop can in a boat: These and more are heard by fish as noisy alarms.

Bonus-Tips **Pick Your Fly Up Quietly**

 Tr-S,Tr-L   Lg-L   Sm-L, Sm-S   Pf-L

If you try to yank line, leader, tippet, and fly off the water all in one violent motion, you might succeed, but you'll also panic every fish nearby. (Yes, I'm referring to the fish you intended to catch.) So instead of just heaving on everything, get the line moving slowly, pick up speed until the line is coming up off the water and everything following it is in motion, and only *then* pick the fly off the water in a backcast. (Or use the roll-cast pickup—see page 120.)

Tip 4 Beware the Full Moon

Tr-S, Tr-L   Lg-L   Sm-L, Sm-S   Pf-L

Carol and I returned just a few days ago from a glorious fishing trip. The weather was mostly mild and pleasant; the rivers and creeks were easy to work, running clear and unhurried in their light autumn flows—and mayflies hatched for hours each day as trout rose steadily to them. Well, not every day. Not that angry day of wind and downpours, which makes sense. And not on our last day.

That few trout rose on that final day, it just didn't add up. It was a calm day of sun mixed with happy white clouds, the same conditions that had brought us good fishing all along. And on water that by then we knew well.

Then we got home.

I looked at my calendar, sighed, and slumped: Our last day of the trip fell on a full moon.

The theory I've heard most often about full-moon fishing is that the fish—trout, bass, whatever—use that soft illumination to feed all night, then relax throughout the following daytime with full bellies and shut mouths.

Look, you're going to run into all sorts of opinions about full moons. Some anglers will even tell you they improve daytime fishing. I can only tell you that the majority of seasoned anglers seem to agree with me that a full moon (and sometimes the day or two before or after one) typically offers slow fishing days.

There's night fishing, of course, where it's legal.

A full moon . . . uh-oh

My solution? When I get my new annual wall calendar each year, I find the full moons and write "full moon" in pen on each date, then swipe the letters with a yellow highlighter. Then I find something other than fishing to do around the full moons.

Tip 5 Fish the Close Water First

Tr-S, Tr-L   Lg-L   Sm-L, Sm-S   Pf-L

I once watched a man wade straight out into Colorado's South Platte River, right through the calf- to knee-deep water I knew the trout were holding in, until he was up to his waist. He then made some long casts to the center of the river and, finally, left—to my utter disbelief—without hooking anything.

My point, though, isn't that you should try the shallows before you cast your fly farther out (though that's related to my point, and an excellent strategy). I want to talk here about not letting some seeming-fish-magnet foam line or downed log keep you from first fishing all that potential holding water between you and it. A matter of restraint.

You want to work the nearest water of any promise first, then the next farthest such water and on out in this way. You do not (or at least *should* not) drop your alarming line over a fish you could have caught, or scare off nearby fish with a hooked fish going wild way out there and then thrashing its way in.

Sometimes, of course, there really is dead water between you and the fish, as when you're working a lake shoreline with a floating hair bug for largemouths, and the fish are in among weeds and fallen timber and such. The water between your boat and the shoreline cover is fishless, or at least too deep for a floating fly. So in this case you shoot straight for the shallows.

It's all quite logical.

Tip 6 Big Fish Prefer Big Prey

Tr-S, Tr-L   Lg-L   Sm-L, Sm-S   Pf-L

The logic is inescapable: A 22-inch smallmouth or brown trout going after a mayfly nymph may wind up with little or no profit in terms of fuel invested versus fuel acquired, while a 9-incher grabbing that same nymph hits the jackpot—to that youngster, the nymph is a mouthful; to the big boy, it's barely a taste. But a meaty 3-inch sculpin? That 22-incher can chase it down, burning off considerable fuel while doing so, and still close the deal with a hefty payoff.

These Morris Minnows imitate little trout (specifically, a rainbow and a cutthroat) to catch big trout.

I offered this juvenile largemouth advice that, thus far, I've never given a human: Beware your parents, your grandparents, your aunts and uncles, all their friends, and all members of your species bigger than you are—they're out to eat you! Flee!

A baby trout—an enticing bellyful for an adult trout

Consequently, size 8 and 6 nymphs and dry flies tend to hook bigger trout than 14s, size 2/0 hair bugs and streamers tend to hook bigger largemouths than 8s. Smallmouths, panfish, same deal.

Of course, big flies also tend to cut average and small fish out of your catch—large hooks, and the flies tied on them, make a difficult fit for little mouths. So if you like lots of action, don't fish big flies (at least not the *biggest* flies).

As I said, exceptions to this rule are legion. For example, sometimes (more than sometimes in certain places) big fish will focus on small feed (feed, usually, that's easy to catch or that drifts right up to them), ignoring mouthful-size prey nearby.

Still, in the end, a small fly will likely catch you small to medium-size panfish, bass, and trout, while a big nymph or streamer will provide the best odds you'll hook a giant.

Tip 7 Big Fish Do Take Smaller Flies

 Tr-S, Tr-L   Lg-L   Sm-L, Sm-S   Pf-L

A 20-inch rainbow taking a size 12 nymph or size 4 streamer is common enough (where there are 20-inch rainbows), but a 20-incher on a size 22 dry fly? Well . . . it happens. Mostly, it happens on a relative few very rich rivers with heavy hatches of tiny insects. And there's the rub: Big trout take modest-size flies with fair regularity, but it usually requires a special situation for them to take tiny flies (or just luck).

So why does a big trout take a middling-size fly? Because it's so close and so easy that the trout will expend little energy to do so. Why does a big trout take a *tiny* fly? Usually because the fly imitates one among *hordes* of tiny insects also close and easy. As usual it's about fuel spent versus fuel gained—with bitsy midges coming down the river in helpless abundance, our 20-incher can hold easily in a soft current and shovel them in. A hundred midges is a bellyful of protein.

All fishes, including the basses and panfish, are looking to come out ahead when it comes to feeding. But it can go beyond that.

In waters where fish are constantly pestered with flies, or lures, they can grow suspicious of the big stuff. On a gravel-pit pond near my college, I finally convinced the big largemouth who hung out in a particular corner by showing it not a big streamer but a dinky bluegill fly. Big fish do prefer big prey, and therefore big flies, but you always have a shot at big fish with smaller flies. And sometimes, little flies are your best shot.

Tip 8 Don't Just Fish for Fish—*Hunt* Them

Tr-S, Tr-L   Lg-L   Sm-L, Sm-S   Pf-L

Your average fly fisher goes to a largemouth lake and looks for docks and fallen timber and fishes them dutifully. Your average fly fisher goes to a trout stream and looks for riffles and runs for the dry fly or nymph. But don't be average.

Those are examples of standard-procedure fishing, following the rules, doing everything correctly. That's fine, but you can do more. I find that I increase the action when I think of myself as a hunter of fish.

Recently, after tramping down a dusty fishing trail by a bridge by a Montana trout stream, I noticed some deepish slow water back up almost under the bridge. I gave it a long look, and then tossed my big dry fly up where the slow water rubbed against the quick. Up came my biggest trout of the day.

Easy spot to miss but, obviously, *not* to be missed. There are lots of such places most fly fishers never notice because they're looking for standard holding water. You'll tend to notice them when you're looking for fish.

I take my time to give each piece of water a long look, letting my understanding of what fish seek—cover, comfort, food—and my experience and my gut, reveal fishy spots anglers seldom bother.

It's not just about trout either. A couple of years ago I pulled my drift boat over to investigate a seemingly too-slow, too-shallow channel off a large smallmouth stream. Nothing much at first. Then it deepened . . . Smallies were all through it, wherever

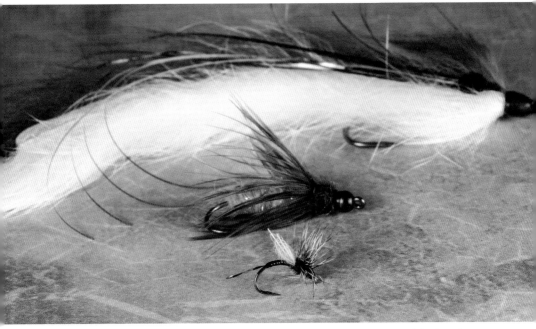

You're more likely to hook a 22-inch brown on the huge Double Bunny streamer at the top of the photo than on the much smaller Brick Back October Caddis in the center. But the Brick Back certainly could hook a trout that large. A 22-incher on the Dinky Smith's Black Cripple at the bottom? Could happen . . .

A hefty Lahontan cutthroat trout showing off the little chironomid-pupa fly it couldn't pass up.

weeds made shade, wherever the bottom dropped off a little. My best fishing of the whole day.

Trout, bass, panfish: Don't be average, do more—*hunt* them.

Tip 9 Read Those Rises

 Tr-S,Tr-L Lg-L  Sm-L, Sm-S Pf-L

A slash at a caddisfly scurrying across a lake; a soft dimpling rise in the calm of a pool; a trout's dorsal fin, but not its nose, showing above the water—if you wisely play the fly-fishing detective (as I suggest elsewhere in these tips), these all become valuable clues. Stream or lake, doesn't matter—the way a trout rises can suggest a lot, and help you determine how to catch it.

Fuel is the key: Trout burn it in the effort of feeding; the things they eat replenish it. No sane trout expends fuel unnecessarily—that's the path to starvation. So our rise-clues are based on the principle of minimal feeding effort.

Smallmouth, most panfish, and even largemouth will feed on top, so all of this can apply to them too. Here are the four basic rise types (according to the author):

THE QUIET RISE
When trout make hardly a stir while gently nosing down insects, those insects are likely tiny, helpless, or both: dying mayfly spinners, miniscule just-hatched midges, and such.

(Note: In quick stream currents or choppy lake surfaces, trout never rise too calmly, regardless of bug size or bug behavior.)

THE EARNEST RISE
When trout take insects with a mild fuss on top, neither manic nor solemn, the insects are probably of at least fair size, matching, say, a size 16 hook or larger.

THE SLASHING RISE
The wild charges of trout are for scurrying caddis, darting water boatmen, mammoth stoneflies—for something big, vigorous, or both.

THE NEAR-RISE
Looks like a rise, but it's really not. See tip 10 to learn how to identify near-rises and what to do about them, and also to see one.

Tip 10 A Trout Rise Isn't Always a Rise

 Tr-S,Tr-L

Once, I watched cutthroat trout rising all over a lazy stretch of an Idaho stream, considered, and then proceeded with beaming confidence. Yellow Sally stonefly adults were fluttering all about, and I caught samples and matched them very closely with dries on size 18 hooks. Then: nothing (or maybe one strike in an hour). When those failed I tried other sorts of floating fly patterns. Again, nothing.

A quiet rise

An earnest rise

A slashing rise—see the water it splashed up to the right?

The dorsal fin of a trout that's not quite rising. When trout feed this way, the best approach is likely a fly fished below, but not far below, the surface of the water.

Finally I stopped, watched again—closely. Moments later I groaned and slapped my cheek with a palm. The trout weren't rising. They were taking something down just short of the water's surface. Anything floating, an insect or artificial fly, was of no interest to them. The light nearly gone, I put up a little nymph and swung it quietly across the fish. In a dozen swings, I hooked eight fish.

It's easy to mistake a near-rise for a rise, but it's important you don't—otherwise, you'll squander a fine evening as I did.

I look first for a bubble left by a rise to determine if it really is a rise; no bubble suggests it's not. No exposed trout nose confirms it's not. Ed Engle, in his book *Trout Lessons*, says that "porpoising riseforms where you can see the trout's back, dorsal fin, and tail" are "a surefire sign" that trout are "feeding on emerging nymphs just under the surface." He adds that "the key is to watch the newly hatched adults on the surface and see if the trout are consistently taking them."

A dry-and-dropper rig can work on near-risers, as can a nymph just below a small indicator. A swung soft-hackle or wet fly, though, is the standard solution and a fine one.

Tip 11 Hook More Smallmouths

 Sm-L, Sm-S

Of all the fishes covered in this book, the smallmouth is the quickest at taking in and expelling a fly. I've watched them do it in both streams and lakes—fly in, a flutter of the jaws, fly out, all in a heartbeat (my heartbeat, not the smallmouth's) or even quicker. I've never seen or sensed that largemouths or trout or panfish come even close to such efficiency and speed. This makes smallmouths tricky to hook.

Trickier yet because they like to grab a sunken fly on the *pause*—that moment when your connection with your fly is light or nonexistent. You needn't trust my experience. I read that this annoying smallmouth personality defect has been confirmed—in a laboratory study.

Here's how I've learned to deal with the smallie's inconsiderate fly-taking habits: (1) keep the rod tip to the water, so there's no line sag to kill your sensitivity to the fly;

(2) always keep at least a *little* tension on the fly—never a tug on the fly followed by a fully limp line; (3) stay alert, reading every nuance you feel or sense; and (4) if you even suspect a take, *set*.

Of course, sometimes a smallmouth just slams your streamer or crayfish fly. That makes hook setting a cinch.

None of this applies to floating flies, obviously. Smallies take them in plain sight, so you know exactly what's going on and when to set the hook.

Tip 12 Low Light = Good Fishing

 Tr-S,Tr-L   Lg-L   Sm-L, Sm-S   Pf-L

The terrifying awareness that a loon's beak or an otter's jaws could clamp onto their fleshy bodies at any moment provides fish with excellent incentive to avoid bright sunshine—sunshine illuminates their meaty, delectable selves in the water, inviting predators to take a bite. Consequently fish tend to stay hidden, inactive, or both during bright daylight hours. But when the light's dim and predators can't get a good fix on prey—game on!

Under cloudy skies or around sunrise or sunset—low-light conditions—trout, bass, and panfish often make up for lost feeding hours by loading their stomachs. This loading they may accomplish as daintily as a debutante nibbling on a tea cake, as when trout

A trout stream running a good level and dense, still clouds overhead—a combination that can drum up serious action

gently sip down floating insects, or as violently as a cage fighter slamming his shin into an opponent's neck, as when largemouth bass slam down hair bass bugs in the shallows.

Bass can feed quietly too, of course, and trout can really slash at insects—low light isn't really about *how* fish feed, it's about how *earnestly* they feed. Expect fish feeding from calmly and steadily to straight-up ravenously when cloud cover, sunset, or sunrise frees them to do so (often, your expectations will be met). And if you can, *fish* at those times.

Tip 13 Low Light = Good Hatches

 Tr-S, Tr-L   Lg-L   Sm-L, Sm-S   Pf-L

There's another angle to that fish-like-low-light business we explored in the previous tip: Insects like low light too. Caddisflies, mayflies, midges, and other freshwater bugs that swim to the surface of the water or climb out of it along shore to hatch, hatch best on cloudy days.

This strikes me as a bad choice for the bugs—they wind up exposing themselves to trout when trout are really out on the prowl. Sunshine, often driving trout back under banks and down into the depths, seems a wiser time for an insect to hatch. Still, for us fly fishers, the bugs' folly and the trout's aggression coming at the same time is a blessing.

Example: a slow-moving Montana trout stream filled with Pale Morning Dun mayfly nymphs and fussy brown trout. I was standing at a promising pool when a dark cloud slid in front of the sun and . . . *boom!* Mayfly duns began popping out all over the water. I hooked several trout over the following 15 minutes or so. Then the cloud slipped away and the sunshine returned. The bugs halted and the trout stopped rising. Until . . . another cloud moved over to block the sun and everything came alive again: mayflies popping, trout rising, me tying into fish. Then sunshine and a lull, then cloud cover and action, and so on, back and forth over the next hour and a half. I've had this same experience on trout lakes with hatches of *Callibaetis* mayflies.

So, hope for strong hatches and surface-feeding trout on cloudy days. It's possible, even likely, you'll get both.

Smallmouths and panfish also feed on hatching bugs, and once in a while so do largemouths. So all this can apply to them too.

Tip 14 The Light's *Always* Low in the Shade   Tr-S, Tr-L   Lg-L   Sm-L, Sm-S   Pf-L

By now you're aware that trout, largemouth bass, smallmouth bass, and most panfish often go deep under bright sunlight but tend to feed in the shallows and on top in the diminished light of sunrise, sunset, and cloud cover. But what about the shade under that tree over there? Isn't *shade* diminished light?

Yes indeed.

Last month I was fishing for large bluegills in a farm pond of around two acres. Its banks were mostly open, just tended lawn, but one tall leafy tree leaned its trunk and half its branches out over the water. I gazed into the shade beneath and eventually made

When clouds showed up, so did these mayflies. That's normally the case with hatching insects: They like clouds, dislike sunshine.

Late-afternoon tree shade—I've seen trout rise in such shade and completely avoid all the sun-touched water.

out the dark bodies of chunky bluegills quietly holding just a few inches down. From then on, one bluegill after another. My friend and I must have caught and set free easily three dozen of them on rubber bugs and poppers before we, and they, tired of the game. Outside the shade of the tree, fishing was slow, one here and, eventually, one there.

Shade isn't just about panfish, though. I've seen trout in a river rise *only* in the shadows of tall trees, and large trout hold in alarmingly shallow water in the shade under grassy banks. Largemouths under docks. Smallmouths under bridges. And so on . . .

Yes, shade is low light, so all the rules about low light apply to shade of any kind. Sometimes, if you're quiet long enough, they apply even to the shade under your boat.

Tip 15 Sunshine Fishing *Can* Be Good

Tr-S, Tr-L   Lg-L   Sm-L, Sm-S   Pf-L

Midday, clear sky, a yellow sun hammering down on you, on the water, on *everything*—if mayflies or caddisflies or midges decide to hatch under these conditions, they'll probably do so briefly, and the trout may not be willing to rise for them. Does this mean the trout are deep in a river or lake sulking and ignoring whatever feed comes along, just waiting for the sun to drop? Perhaps, especially if the water's uncomfortably warm and the day's a scorcher. But most likely, no.

Probably, the trout are down near the bed of the river or lake, feeling comfy there, and happy to grab an errant mayfly or scud. They're feeding down there—they can be caught.

This is not just about trout. Under a high, exposed sun largemouth and smallmouth bass and panfish may go deep, but they too may feed down there. None of this is to say that all these fishes can't be caught on the surface or in shallow water on bright days; it's just that the odds are poor.

The solution, then, is to go down to the fish. A nymph below a strike indicator in a trout stream or trout lake, a nymph on a sinking line for bluegills and other panfish in a lake, a crayfish pattern on a sinking line in a smallmouth stream, a streamer on a sinking line in a largemouth lake—and there are a lot more variations than these. But all are about getting a fly down to fish trying to keep the sun out of their eyes and predators off their backs.

Tip 16 Observation: Make It a Habit

Tr-S,Tr-L   Lg-L   Sm-L, Sm-S   Pf-L

When I lived in Oregon I used to fish the Salmonfly stonefly hatch on a brute of a big desert river, the Lower Deschutes. The Salmonfly is itself a brute, up to two stout inches long. Like all stoneflies, it crawls out of the water to hatch; then, thanks to its scampering and mating and laborious flying, it often ends up, to the delight of trout and anglers, on the water. Fly fishers converge from all over the country to revel in this legendary hatch.

Thing is, it's a tricky hatch. The huge bugs should ignite a flame in the hearts (make that "stomachs") of those stout wild rainbows—and when it does, fishing can be . . . epic. But often, the trout just yawn, "Whatever." I watched a whole lot of fly fishers during the Salmonfly hatch chuck big dry flies and catch nothing. A few, however, were catching plenty of trout. How? Did those few have a magical fly, a special technique, a super-hero ability to communicate with trout and a slick sales pitch? *Nah*—they just had open minds. And open *eyes*.

They watched the water, upstream and down, a hundred feet away and right at their feet; watched the riverbank grasses and brush; watched other anglers, the birds . . . whatever might tip them off. Such observation led them to fish a size 18 midge pupa under a strike indicator or a Pale Morning Dun mayfly-emerger imitation in the eddies—it led them to finding and catching trout.

Two fly fishers observe, point, and discuss. They'll probably find far more success by doing so than by just trudging in and casting.

Close inspection along the edge of a stream or lake can tell you a lot about what the fish are seeing, and eating.
SKIP MORRIS

Just looking around with patient, curious eyes—observation—can work miracles in fishing. There are no really good *un*observant fly fishers. Goes for trout lakes, the basses, and panfish too.

Tip 17 Fish May Be Close to Your Boat

Fish like shade—throughout this book, you'll see that idea presented in a number of ways, because shade plays into fishing in a number of ways. Shade hides trout, largemouth, smallmouth, and panfish from predators; it's kinder than sunshine to their eyes too.

So there you are in a pontoon boat or pram, and what's underneath? Shade.

If you're out on a lake and you move quietly, so your watercraft stays still, the fish you seek will often gather right underneath you. This is one good reason to retrieve your fly until it's right up close to your craft.

Once, on a very clear Canadian lake where I could see trout gliding just over a weedy shoal, I worked my fly ever closer to our anchored boat until the fly was straight down and my fishing partner, Brian Chan (author, fisheries biologist—you'll see his name scattered throughout these pages), noticed I was hooking fish. He eventually wound up on his knees working the line by *hand*, the rod lying on the floor of the boat. He hooked several trout that way—because those trout liked the shade. (And because Brian's curiosity, like mine, is aroused by any new fishing method, especially an oddball one.)

The moral: Work your flies all the way in before picking them up. Let that indicator drift up close when chironomid fishing; retrieve your sinking line and nymph or streamer until it comes up almost alongside your boat. Assuming, that is, it makes it up without a grab from below.

Tip 18 In Fishing, Timing Is *Huge*

Tr-S, Tr-L   Lg-L   Sm-L, Sm-S   Pf-L

So you've done your research—online, with a guidebook, by asking fishing friends or fellow fly-club members or a salesperson at a fly shop, or all or any of these—and you've found a good place to get a good shot at good fishing. Good for you. Well done. But . . . did you ask *when*?

When you fish is half the formula for finding good fishing. Here are just three examples among many: A trout lake that's reliably red hot in May but so warm in August it's useless. A northern-state largemouth lake that turns on in June but is too cold in April for good fishing. A mountain creek that fishes fine all summer but whose trout migrate down out of it a month before the fish and game department closes it and don't migrate back up until a month after they open it—so that in a normal year it's trout-empty at both ends of its fishing season.

In a *normal* year . . . But so many years aren't normal. My wife and I once looked to fish a river that gets a big June hatch of huge stoneflies. But we waited to reserve our cabin, checking the area's snowpack online, checking websites of the area's fly shops for reports on the river's current state and predictions for its fishing prospects in June. We finally reserved our cabin for July.

If we had casually trusted the river's reputation for its big-stone fishing in June and shown up then, we'd have found a river dangerously high, entirely unfishable. July was just right. Missed the stoneflies, but fishing was grand.

Find good water to fish. Then find out *when* to fish it, and then find out how the timing's playing out for this particular year.

Tip 19 Rest Your Fish

Tr-S, Tr-L   Lg-L   Sm-L, Sm-S   Pf-L

Back where Carol and I used to live, I would hike with a float tube on my back into a largemouth bass lake that went wild on muggy, overcast August mornings. I'd fish one downed log or lily-pad cluster along the shoreline to land two, three, even five good bass before the spot went cold, slide over five feet and do it all over again. Being a small lake, almost a pond, its shoreline required only about a couple of hours to cover with a floating hair bug. Once I was back at my starting point, I'd go around again, picking one, two, or more bass from every good spot.

Did you catch that, what happened? I hooked almost as many fish on my second go-round as on the first, fishing the same places in the same way. How? I rested the fish.

Typically, when you catch three fish from a run in a stream or a tight little bay in a lake, be they trout, bass, or panfish, there's another one or two or three—or perhaps way more—in there you didn't catch—they got spooked. So you give them time to forget, at least 10 minutes, at the extreme a few hours or overnight.

That's called "resting fish," or "resting water." It works.

You can rest a specific fish. Say you're working a rainbow trout that's rising to midges and—*oops!*—your fly drags unnaturally across its nose and it stops rising. Rest the fish. Fish on upstream. Then come back. By then, I'll bet your rainbow's rising again.

Tip 20 Here's How I Deal with Cruising Largemouths

 Lg-L

The largemouth bass I see grouped up and cruising around just under the surface of lakes in spring and summer are typically smallish. But they're big enough that I want to catch them—and they're *right there* in plain sight, daring me to catch them. So I have to.

They are, however, tough to catch. Easy to spook too—a fly line sailing out too close or a fly dropping too near, and off they dart, a rush of grouped fish shapes, all aligned and neatly spaced, heading directly, *insultingly*, away from my fly. If I don't spook them, they just refuse my fly, which is, at least, less rude, I guess . . .

I finally found success with these cruisers with one approach only and only one fly. Here's the formula:

Start with a floating line and a leader-tippet combination of at least 11 feet.

Fish the only fly they ever seem to want: a blue adult damselfly imitation in size 12 or 10, a floater. (To see a couple of adult damselfly imitations, go to tip 262.)

Cast the fly out from a distance that won't alert the bass to your presence, perhaps 40 feet, and drop it quietly well ahead of them.

Try to drop the fly where a bass or two on the near side of the school will meet it— you don't want to hook a fish in the middle of the school and panic them all.

As those edge-of-the-school bass near your fly, give it tiny twitches now and then— you really can't *under*do these twitches.

If you hook a bass, try to drag it away quietly from the school. By the time your bass has been played and released, the school's been rested. Hook another one.

Tip 21 Attend the Evening Rise

 Tr-S, Tr-L   Lg-L   Pf-L

You can never count on the evening rise, but just one good one can turn a dedicated pessimist into a bright-eyed optimist, at least where the evening rise is concerned. Here's how good it can be.

A few years ago I fished a Colorado trout stream from 2:00 p.m. on, hard. By late afternoon I'd caught maybe three passable brown trout on a nymph and had yet to see a rise. Finally, the sun touched the mountaintops, and after a bit their shadows began stretching in earnest across the big pool I'd chosen in hopes of an evening rise. A solitary trout made quiet rings on the gleaming black water. Minutes later came another rise farther upstream; scattered rises continued appearing; then the sun was almost gone behind the dusky mountains and things suddenly picked up. I hurried to take down the nymph rig and tie on a length of fine tippet and a size 20 floating emerger fly—the fish

were feeding on something too small for me to easily see on the dark water, so the tiny emerger seemed a sensible choice.

Well, did it happen? Oh yeah. Trout were soon rising everywhere. I hooked . . . *lots*. Bliss.

I've seen the evening rise every bit this good on trout lakes too.

Sometimes, though, after a hot day well into the season, the barometer up and steady, the air still—ideal conditions for the evening rise—it just . . . doesn't happen. But you always have to go prepared in case it does: a light rod and floating line, light tippets and long leader, proper flies.

Though you can never count on the evening rise, you only have to hit it right once to seek it, like a real optimist, for the rest of your life.

Largemouths, bluegills and crappies and other panfish—do they put on an evening rise? Well, sometimes they really binge while the sun drops away and after. Call it an evening rise if you like, but most fly fishers don't. It's grand, though, too. Personally, I haven't observed much of this behavior from smallmouth bass.

Tip 22 Understand the Evening Rise

 Tr-S,Tr-L Lg-L Pf-L

With a little luck you can throw out about any fly and hook trout during an evening rise. The last evening rise I fished on a trout stream was like that—I tried a small half-floating emerger fly, then a modest-size caddis dry fly, and finally a long-shank brute of a dry that resembled a big stonefly adult. They all caught fish.

But how many times at sunset on lakes and streams have I had to match a particular midge or mayfly in order to catch trout? Too many to count.

Yeah, the evening rise can challenge your bug-matching skills. Or not. It's all up to the trout. And the bugs.

Fly size and type aside, is the evening rise on a stream or lake mainly about floating flies? In my experience, yes it is. Sometimes, though, a small nymph dangling from a foot or so of fine tippet tied to the bend of a larger dry fly's hook (dry-and-dropper fishing) is best.

Just choosing a good fly isn't enough. Those surface-feeding trout are nervous, especially when the water's still, as on a lake, or flowing softly and smoothly in a stream. So use at least fairly fine tippets and fairly long leaders, if not *really* fine and long ones. And cast smoothly and drop your fly gently onto the water.

When largemouth bass and panfish feed hard around sunset, the surface stuff (hair bugs, poppers, rubbery floating flies) is too much fun to pass up, and it often kills. Retrieves of such flies can be effective in the conventional tug-pause-tug way, or given a constant, gentle, jerking retrieve. Smallmouth bass? I don't often see them turn on as the sun goes down.

Tip 23 Each Fish Is an Individual

 Tr-S, Tr-L   Lg-L   Sm-L, Sm-S   Pf-L

We humans often flock to the latest blockbuster movie, that lemming sort of urge. But other times we go our own ways to see foreign films, documentaries, peculiar indie flicks. Some never see the blockbusters, others see nothing else. In this way, we're like fish.

A big hatch of mayflies may draw scads of trout up to feed together on the struggling emergers. Nearly all the smallmouth bass in a stream may turn their eyes to crayfish when some part of the crustaceans' mating rituals suddenly exposes them en masse. Fish, like humans, often run with the herd.

But often enough, again like humans, they don't. One trout may spend its life down in a dark narrow slot, feeding on nymphs and larvae, rarely, or never, coming up for a floating caddis or stonefly adult. And when most of its fellow trout are up sipping mayfly duns, there it is, still in shadowed isolation, ignoring their overhead bellies to hug streambed cobble and pick off the nymphs.

It's important you know this, because three rising trout may take your imitation mayfly spinner with quiet confidence while the fourth, hanging close along the grassy bank, may completely ignore it—this trout is waiting for the next fat grasshopper, and you have to figure that out. It's important because although you find some bluegills along the outer weed lines, you may find far more out deeper, or in among shallow lily pads. That's up to you to discover too.

Remember: Fish aren't always all of one mind.

 **Bonus-Tip** Bluegills Get Moody   Pf-L

Bluegills . . . One day they're eager to grab a popper, the next day they're deep. One day they won't touch a popper but will charge a Woolly Worm only a foot down. And *some* days instead of waiting 10 seconds to grab a still popper, they'll wait far beyond fashionably late to make a move, after you've truly given up hope. Keep an open mind when you fish for bluegills. Anticipate attitude. Experiment.

Tip 24 Know Your Largemouth Retrieves and Your Smallmouth Retrieves for Hair Bugs and Poppers Lg-L Sm-L, Sm-S

Largemouth and smallmouth bass are crazy different in many ways. One way: hair bug and popper retrieves.

Though at times I've seen largemouths demand all sorts of retrieves for floating flies, from alarmingly long pauses to quick, constant swimming, here's what works best for me nine times out of ten:

1. Cast the popper or floating hair bug next to cover.
2. Immediately give the fly a sharp jerk to make it gurgle (a gurgle—not a gunshot crack).
3. Let the fly sit quietly for about 10 to 15 seconds.
4. Give it the *slightest* tug.
5. Let it sit quietly for another 5 to 10 seconds.
6. Start swimming the fly back slowly, then ever quicker.

Use that retrieve on smallmouths, and you'll catch few. Like largemouth bass, smallmouths respond to a range of retrieves, but I nearly always do well with this one:

1. On a stream, drop the bug or popper just above the fish so you can give the fly a tug before it's drifted past the lie. On a lake, just cast the fly to land near the lie.
2. Give the bug a sharp tug right away to make it gurgle (just . . . gurgle).
3. After only three or four seconds, make the fly gurgle again.
4. From that point on, make the fly gurgle every three or four seconds.

In *Smallmouth: Modern Fly-Fishing Methods, Tactics, and Techniques*, the authors (Karczynski and Landwehr) say that the *first* pop of a smallmouth hair bug or popper comes "the moment the popper hits the water" and caution that "a premature second pop oftentimes spooks away a fish that was just going to eat your fly anyways." I don't know the authors, but when I read their book, I feel the considerable weight of experience and good sense in it. And my habit of smacking a bug or popper down to attract both the basses and panfish is close to what they describe. So, I'm in.

Tip 25 If You're Not *Certain* Where Your Floating Fly Is—Set the Hook

 Tr-S, Tr-L Lg-L Sm-L, Sm-S Pf-L

Dark dry flies and dark hair bugs, flies that ride half submerged, tiny dry flies, shards of reflected light from the waves of a lake or the currents of a stream—any or all of these factors and more can make spotting your floating fly a struggle. And even if the light's good, your fly is probably out there 30 to 50 feet—that's a long way to keep track of something perhaps the length of a fingertip down to shorter than a grain of rice.

My point: No matter how sharp your eyes or how many hours and years you've fished floating flies for trout, the basses, or panfish or all three, you're going to lose sight of that fly sometimes. Then what? Then this: Watch the *area* in which you last saw your fly (a *moving* area on a stream, of course), or the area experience tells you contains your fly, and when a fish shows at the surface anywhere near there, set the hook.

This really does work—it's my standard way of fishing tiny floating or half-floating fly patterns during the evening rise.

Look, you probably couldn't find your big, bright yellow dry fly 12 feet out on flat water when you first took up fly fishing, yet now you can find a smaller, darker dry 50 feet out. You've developed a sense of where your fly is, and that's how you're finding it. Use that sense when you *can't* find it.

But because that sense is fallible, *assume* any fish that shows within, say, five feet of where you think your fly is, is taking it—and *set that hook*.

Tip 26 Can't See Your Floating Fly? Try This, and This, and This

 Tr-S,Tr-L   Lg-L   Sm-L, Sm-S   Pf-L

Flies are always tricky to spot on water, and sometimes, impossible. (Example: a tiny, dark, half-sunken emerger fly at sunset.) But, you need to know when a fish has taken your floating fly so you can set the hook on cue.

Strategies, you need strategies.

See the white or bright-colored parts of these floating flies? The face of the hair bass bug (bottom); the wing and back of the Humpy (center) made not of the usual somber deer or elk hair but of yellow yarn; the orange end on the dinky foam-ant pattern (upper left, and just below and to the left of the Griffith's Gnat), and the pale wing of the Elk Hair Caddis (far right), tied by its hook bend to fine tippet leading to a little, dark, hard-to-spot Griffith's Gnat—the point of each of those highly visible components is to help you spot your fly on the water, and they do. (The Elk Hair Caddis serves as a sort of strike indicator for the Gnat.)

The previous tip tells you how to determine where your floating fly is when you simply can't see it. Now we're talking about what you can do so that you can see it.

Here's one strategy: Trail your tiny dry fly off the bend of the hook of a bigger, easier-to-see dry fly on a couple of feet of tippet. When the big fly jumps or goes down, set the hook.

Here's another: Fish dry flies that are easy to spot, flies with white or brightly colored wings, or hair bugs with white or bright faces.

And . . . If it's after sunset, fish only in the last gleaming light on the water, where your fly appears as a silhouette.

Tip 27 Fish Should See Your Fly, Not You

 Tr-S,Tr-L Lg-L Sm-L, Sm-S Pf-L

There's "sight-fishing," actually seeing the fish you're trying to catch, and then there's pretty much all the other fishing, just trying in general to get your fly out in front of a fish without it seeing you. Here, we're talking about the latter.

Longish to plain long casts can do it by putting sufficient distance between you and a trout or a bass so that you're out of sight—but the line, the fly, or both had better not slap down and scare that fish off. (Unless a fly slapping is appropriate, as when imitating the sloppy, unplanned water landings of grasshoppers.)

Crouching, even kneeling, can be appropriate when fishing a clear stream, especially if it's in low water, or when casting from the shore of a clear lake. A low posture can keep you outside that little window from which fish see our world of air. (See tip 3.)

Crouching in tall grass, standing behind trees, backing into brush along the edge of a stream—these and other ways of hiding or obscuring yourself from a fish can determine whether that fish takes your fly or flees for its life.

Your shadow is a big deal—if it comes anywhere near a fish, that fish will panic. Shadows, to fish, mean predators.

How carefully you need to hide from the fish you seek to catch varies by water clarity, fish species, current speed, the intensity or lack of light, and probably a dozen or more other factors. Sometimes you can get very close; sometimes you must cast long from a kneeling position. The fish will let you know.

Tip 28 Know When to Look for the Take and When to Feel It

 Tr-S,Tr-L Lg-L Sm-L, Sm-S Pf-L

If you wait to feel a trout suck in your dry fly or a smallmouth bass grab your popper, you'll probably be waiting all day. With floating flies and hair bugs and poppers, and nymphs below strike indicators, you watch—you *see*—the take of the fly (or the dip of the indicator), and *then* you set the hook.

There are other kinds of fishing that aren't about seeing. Czech nymphing is mainly about feeling the take. Streamer fishing with a sinking line is about feeling a trout or

Here I am, trout, all lit up by afternoon light for your viewing pleasure. Hey—where did you all go?

Here I am again, trout, still standing tall—what, you can't see me in the shadow of this high tree trunk? Good!

smallmouth bass clamp on. On lakes, it's *typically* about feeling the fish take (though there are plenty of exceptions).

On lakes, fishing deep, there's really nothing to see, so you retrieve the fly, always ready to tug the hook home if the line tightens or resists even slightly—trout and both largemouth and smallmouth bass can take a fly very lightly, when they're not trying to snap it off your tippet. Trolling is about feeling the take too, unless your hands are on oars—if they are, you jump for the rod the moment its tip jerks.

The logic should be plain by now: Set your hook by sight or feel depending on which is appropriate. It's important.

Tip 29 Know the Length of Your Leader and Tippet Tr-S, Tr-L   Lg-L   Sm-L, Sm-S   Pf-L

Most of us fly fishers (yeah, me too sometimes) just tie on a fly and start fishing it. We don't (though in fairness, I now usually do) first check the length of our leaders and tippets.

We should.

First, they may be too long or too short for the water we're fishing.

Second, if we don't have a clear sense of how long they are, we're inaccurate—we catch our nymph on a low branch of a yellow-leafed aspen tree instead of dropping it next to that deep far bank as we intended; we keep putting our dry fly out a foot and a half short of the current line where a trout is rising.

The wise thing to do is check your leader and tippet both. Then decide if you need them shorter or longer and make whatever changes are in order. Next, plant their combined length in your consciousness, and then practice casting a little to get yourself tuned into that length. After that, go fish, accurately, confidently, successfully.

Tip 30 A Steady Retrieve for Poppers and Hair Bugs Is *Occasionally* Best for Largemouths Lg-L

For largemouth bass, I normally retrieve a floating hair bug or popper with lots of pauses (see tip 24), and I've learned to trust that retrieve—it outfishes every other kind nearly always. But once in a while . . .

A few years ago, on a private largemouth (and bluegill and crappie) lake, managed by The Fly Shop in Redding, California, I was only having fair luck fishing a popper in my usual patient way. So I went to streamers and the gratifying yanks from 2- to 3-pound bass started coming in almost steady succession. But I felt certain the bass were willing to come up, and the fact I couldn't convince them to do it for a hair bug kept pricking the back of my brain like a fly hook. Then I fished the lake with Mike Mercer (author of *Creative Fly Tying*), who'd fished it many times before. Right off, Mike was catching bass with a very busy hair bug—I changed my retrieve to a steady series of tugs, the bug constantly lurching and gurgling ahead. From then on, the largemouths just kept coming. All day long.

I've noticed that largemouths especially like a steady retrieve of bugs and poppers after sunset, in that last 20 minutes or so before true night.

Tip 31 Smaller and Slower Can Be the Answer ![fish] Tr-S, Tr-L ![bass] Lg-L ![sunfish] Sm-L, Sm-S ![panfish] Pf-L

The average fly fisher selects an average-size fly and, if a retrieve is in order, retrieves it at an average pace. On average, that's enough to catch an average number of fish. But sometimes it provides below-average results.

Especially on hard-fished water, catching fish may require flies smaller and retrieves slower than average. Fish wise up, but they always seem to have trouble figuring out the little stuff quietly presented.

I find this especially true of trout. I stood once on a well-trodden trail along a popular stretch of an Oregon spring creek wondering what in this wide world I could possibly show these trout that they hadn't seen a hundred times. No rises, so I went through nymph after nymph without a take. By the end, I had a heavy nymph as a point fly but a *tiny* nymph as a dropper: a size 20 midge larva, looking like just a snip of black thread.

It worked. I hooked several of those obstinate trout.

One spring in college, I spent much of my class time fishing a gravel-mining pond of perhaps two acres until its largemouth bass finally took offense and stopped biting. Eventually, I came around to smaller flies—tiny streamers, wet flies on size 10 hooks—and then to fishing them slowly. In the right light I could watch the bass, and felt I could read their minds: "Fine—another hook all dressed up like a pork chop from that *jerk* who yanks us out just to toss us back in. No . . . wait . . . That little thing looks . . . right." Then a bass would glide up to the fly . . .

It's not just about trout and largemouth bass; heavily pestered smallmouths, bluegills . . . small and subtle often wins them over.

Tip 32 Learn Chironomid Fishing

 Tr-L

If you're even halfway serious about fishing trout lakes, you need to take up chironomid fishing because (1) it's deadly, (2) it often works when other methods fail, and (3) the insect whose hatches it's designed for is the most common of all the hatching trout-lake insects. That insect is the chironomid, of course, which squirms its way slowly to the surface of a lake to emerge as a mosquito-like winged adult. If the trout let it get that far.

When chironomid pupae are rising in a hatch, trout normally cruise the shoals, picking off the helpless insects within a couple of feet of the lake bed (though sometimes higher up). Here's chironomid fishing in a nutshell:

1. Find the hatch by looking for emerging chironomids or their leftover glassy, white bearded shucks.
2. Anchor your watercraft amid the hatch.
3. Find a bead-head fly that imitates the natural's color and size.
4. Rig up a long leader (9 feet minimum, usually 12 feet or longer) and a long tippet (4 feet at least) and a floating line.

Chironomid fishing with a strike indicator in a lively breeze—the pupa imitation's doing the Charleston down there.

5. Tie on the fly with a loop knot.
6. Clamp forceps on the fly's hook bend and lower them to check the depth, and then lock a strike indicator on the leader so the distance from fly to indicator is one foot short of the depth.
7. Cast across the wind and then let the line belly as the waves bounce the indicator and jiggle the fly.
8. Finally, once the line is straight downwind, work the indicator in with short tugs between long pauses (if there's no wind, cast, wait a full minute, and then retrieve the indicator as though it's downwind).

Of course, if the indicator tells in any way—set the hook.

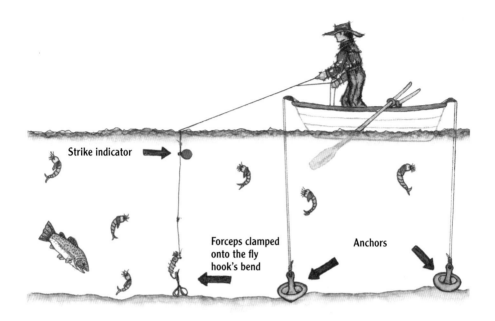

Strike indicator

Forceps clamped
onto the fly
hook's bend

Anchors

1. Find a shoal and a hatch, drop anchor, set fly-to-indicator distance.

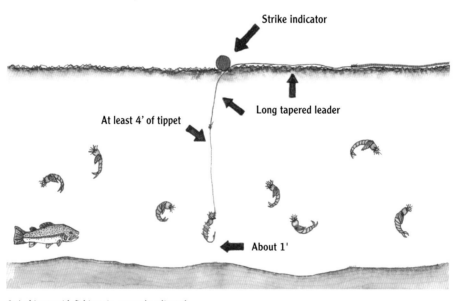

Strike indicator

At least 4' of tippet

Long tapered leader

About 1'

2. A chironomid-fishing rig, properly adjusted.

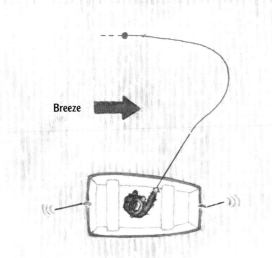

3. Cast across the breeze. Let the line belly.

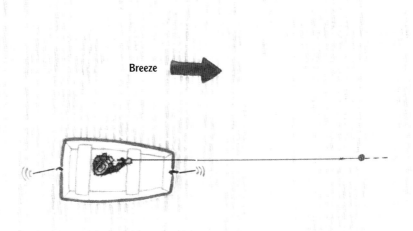

4. Watch, wait, and when the indicator tells—by even the slightest twitch or stall—set!

Tip 33 Try Chironomid Fishing Naked

 Tr-L

"Naked"—that's what I've heard it called. Yes, I used a racy word, so go ahead, get the one-liners and sniggering out of your system.

Chironomid fishing (see previous tip) is a wildly popular and wildly effective method for fishing trout lakes, and its success normally depends on reading a strike indicator. So what happens without the strike indicator? You have to retrieve your imitation of a chironomid pupa while keeping it within a couple feet of that lake bed 6, 8, 15, or more feet down. Tricky? Yup.

That's fishing naked—no indicator. My advice: Get comfortable and confident with indicator chironomid fishing before going naked. The challenges: getting the fly deep enough, not getting the fly too deep, keeping the fly at a constant depth. Experience, skill, and cultivated instinct required.

My friend (and coauthor of *Morris & Chan on Fly Fishing Trout Lakes*) Brian Chan was and is among the chief pioneers of chironomid fishing; regarding that method he's something of a legend. So I asked him about the naked thing.

Brian considers indicator chironomid fishing invaluable, and uses it most of the time. But when it's not working well, yet he's confident the trout want a chironomid, he fishes naked. For one thing, he says, the fly is moving across the lake bed more quickly without an indicator than when dangling below one, thereby covering more water. For another, chironomid-seeking trout sometimes respond best to an imitation moving distinctly sideways. (Why? Who knows?)

My two cents: I usually chironomid fish naked when trout are taking the pupae not near the bottom but at some mid-depth.

Tip 34 Chironomid Fishing Works with All Sorts of Flies Tr-L

When most fly fishers practice the deadly floating-line, long-leader, long-tippet, strike-indicator method for fishing chironomid-pupa nymphs just off a lake bed, they call it "chironomid fishing" and leave it at that. They shouldn't. Chironomid fishing can be just as deadly using imitations of leeches, mayfly nymphs, damselfly nymphs, scuds, and even attractor flies that imitate nothing at all.

Naked chironomid fishing (see previous tip) is also effective with this same string of imitations and attractors. About 20 years ago I was fishing with my friend Brian Chan on a very clear lake in the trout-lake-famous Kamloops region of British Columbia. The light was good, despite a gauzy layer of mayfly-inviting clouds, and a dozen feet down I could see the dark backs of trout cruising in over the bottom of pale crusty-looking patches of marl dappling the yellowy bright green of the chara. I could even, with it all the way down there just over the chara, see my fly. It was an Ultimate Skip Nymph, a proven imitation of the *Callibaetis* mayfly nymph the trout were finding.

Many times that day I watched a stout fish of 15 to 18 inches come slowly in, turn to a side or tip up or down slightly to meet a rising nymph, and then swing easily and confidently toward my fly. Then—blessed havoc. Yes, my fly: not a chironomid but an imitation of a mayfly nymph.

Indicator, naked, shallow or deep, the fly seen (a rarity) or unseen (the norm), chironomid fishing can go well beyond fishing chironomid-imitating flies.

Tip 35 Never Line Your Fish

 Tr-S, Tr-L   Lg-L   Sm-L, Sm-S   Pf-L

A fly line is thick, is cable—might as well be a barber pole if you drop it near or if it drifts over a fish, any fish: trout, smallmouth, largemouth, bluegill, crappie . . . (Well, maybe not a crappie, poor dimwitted creature.) Any fish with an ounce of sense will flee when a fly line drops in close, will stop feeding and slink away if current carries it overhead.

Only makes sense, doesn't it? A fly line, clean edged and constant in diameter, is wholly unnatural. I sometimes think wily fish know exactly what it is. They see it and go, "Oh, fishing a six-weight today, are we?"

With streamer flies for any fish, on dark sinking lines, some fly fishers use short leaders and no tippet; then the fly is never far from the line. These folks seem to get away with it, usually in the turbulence of river currents. I never go really short on leaders and tippets with any fly on any line. Seems too much like warning the fish. But, maybe that's just me.

Most of the time, though, in most situations, letting a fish see your line is a game killer. So make those casts to the shallows short enough to keep your line well away from the largemouth bass you seek; drop your line well inside of that trout rising out in midstream. Cover the near water with your fly before working it out farther and dropping your line over the near-water fish.

Show fish your fly, but never your fly line.

Tip 36 Close Means In *Close*

 Tr-S, Tr-L   Lg-L   Sm-L, Sm-S   Pf-L

I can't tell you how many times I've seen fly fishers, usually casual ones or newcomers, miss out on a whole lot of fish just by failing to get their fly close enough to a bank or weed bed or current seam.

If trout are tucked back in under lily pads and you drop your nymph a foot and a half out from the green disks, you may catch a few trout. But drop your nymph in that slim space between two pads or within two inches of a pad's edge, and . . . *wham*! If your beetle imitation drifts just out from a bank rather than close in along its shadow, or better yet back *in* the shadow under the leaning grasses, well, that can make all the difference.

So get your hair bug not just sort of near but right up *against* that floating log when you're fishing for largemouths, your emerger *in* that patchy foam for rising trout, your popper close behind that boulder in a smallmouth stream, your nymph so close to that bank in a river bend that it ticks the edge—sometimes your fly can drop in a general area and take fish, but often must land right on target to move a fish.

Tip 37 Big Fish Are Often Loners

 Tr-S, Tr-L   Lg-L   Sm-L, Sm-S   Pf-L

If you catch a 4-pound brown trout or a 10-inch bluegill or a 3-pound smallmouth bass, odds are you'll catch it from some spot where you catch few, if any, other fish. I don't mean a big spot, such as an entire pool on a river, but perhaps a dark nook under exposed tree roots or the brush-shaded tip of a tight, deep, little channel.

Sure, you can be out working a lake shoal and tying into 14- or 15-inch rainbows when that 22-incher hits—that sort of thing happens all the time, Godzilla hanging out among the iguanas. Still, it's far more likely you'll find a trophy rainbow defending his hollow under a deep bank rather than out holding with the masses in a thigh-deep riffle.

So go out and fish the lily pad fields of largemouth lakes and the pocketwater of trout streams and have a blast. But keep an eye out for that special spot where the fishing seems to halt even though the water seems ripe with promise, and then spend a little extra time working it hard. Might be a giant in there.

Tip 38 Fish Memory Is Real—Use It to Your Advantage

 Tr-S, Tr-L   Lg-L   Sm-L, Sm-S   Pf-L

Way back in the 1980s, when you may have been a kid (and when I was, in fact, pretty young myself) or just a hypothetical, a fly-fishing guide friend told me, "I hesitate to call it 'memory,' but I've seen fish probably ten days after the bugs were pretty much gone keep going back to the kind of water where they'd found them, water they usually ignore." He was talking about the rainbows of Oregon's Lower Deschutes River and the Golden Stonefly hatch.

He hesitated, I won't: It's fish memory. What else could it be? We know *why* they kept returning—they wanted more of those gargantuan bugs. But *how*? How did they know to go to those spots after the bugs were gone? Well, memory, of course—the fish remembered where to find those huge, juicy, savory mouthfuls of tender meat.

I've seen lots of evidence that trout remember food and where they found it. I've seen them crowd a lake bay an hour *before* the damselfly hatch starts up.

 Cast Low to the Side for Spooky Fish

 Tr-S   Sm-S

When a stream is low, slow, and clear, the trout or smallmouth bass in it feel edgy, exposed—and they can see very well. Best strategy: Put real distance between you and the fish. When real distance isn't possible, as is sometimes the case on streams, crouch. But what's the point of crouching if you're waving your 8½-foot rod and its sailing line way up high? When you need to keep low to avoid spooking fish, keep your rod and line low too, by casting with the rod tipped well off to your side.

Smallmouths, largemouths, bluegills and other panfishes? Not so sure. These aren't normally bug-hatch fishes, so their opportunities for remembering big food-providing events are rare. But they're smart, so I expect they do remember. And they do occasionally feed on hatches, so . . .

If you show up just after a killer hatch, or soon after any big food-providing event on a stream or lake peters out, try fishing as though it's still going on. The fish may remember how good it was and keep feeding as though it still is.

Tip 39 Here's How to Deal with High-Water Streams  Tr-S

In late spring and early summer I sometimes face trout streams running up onto their banks, swollen from melting snow and rain. In uber-wet years I've had to cope with heavy flows as late as—get this!—*August*. So, you'd better learn to deal with high water; it can sneak up on you.

If your trout stream is dangerously high, roaring along at real flood stage, leave it alone; fish somewhere safe (a trout or bass or panfish lake, perhaps?). But if the water's high yet manageable, you may still find good fishing.

I'll start by quoting my friend Ed Engle from his book *Trout Lessons*: "The most important thing to remember about high, off-color water is that the trout probably don't

All the quick, angry water out beyond that flooded line of brush is of no interest to trout—but I caught one on a nymph from the soft water you see right in front of me.

like it any more than you do." Agreed. Ed goes on to say that trout may like it better than early high, *clear* water. Ed again: "I've found that the high, clear water at the beginning of the runoff cycle is often the initial snowmelt from the top of the snowpack." In other words, the water's icy cold, and the cold-blooded trout in it are dazed. Next, the stream warms as its banks thaw and their mud mixes in. After that the stream may remain high but pull ever less color from its banks until it's again clear but *now* with a temperature trout can handle.

That's how that works—but where are the trout with all that racing current? Answer: They're wherever they can avoid it. So they're along the banks, behind boulders, in soft side channels, below islands, in eddies, and in other sheltered spots.

Expect to catch high-water trout on deep nymphs, usually large, heavy nymphs, perhaps with smaller ones as trailers or droppers.

Tip 40 Fishing Can Sizzle Right After a Heat Wave  Tr-S, Tr-L   Lg-L   Sm-L, Sm-S   Pf-L

A few years ago, some friends and I arrived at an Idaho river during a heat wave. Fishing was all sweat and misery beyond lunchtime, but worse, it was nearly useless. Though there was a brief flurry of good fishing most mornings and at sunset, those naive cutthroat trout spent each baking afternoon too uncomfortable to worry about food.

Then a day of heavy overcast came, the predicted high only 74 degrees Fahrenheit. Fishing was fair until about noon, then it dropped off as the cutts braced for another sauna. Twenty minutes later, they seemed to realize it wasn't coming—and they fed for the remainder of the day with a vengeance! The river seemed full of trout begging for us to show them a fly they could charge.

It really was that good.

Sure, the muted light of cloud cover helped. But I've seen trout, and the basses and panfish too, in both streams and lakes, binge feed after a big temperature drop following a heat wave—under sunny skies. Perhaps it's as big a relief for them as it is for us.

When a heat wave really breaks—go fishing.

Tip 41 Sight-Fishing = Bewitchment
Tr-S, Tr-L   Lg-L   Sm-L, Sm-S   Pf-L

If your goal is to catch one fish after another, conveyor-belt style, you may not meet your quota by sight-fishing. But, if for you, fishing means challenge, precision, utter fascination, then you're going to love sight-fishing.

Seeing the signs of fish—the rippled bull's-eye rise of a trout, a bluegill, or a smallmouth or largemouth bass (yes, largemouths *will* rise like trout, though I see it only rarely); the exposing of a dorsal fin, then tail, in the lazy arch of a trout feeding just short of the surface of the water—is perhaps fully as glorious as sight-fishing. But sight-fishing it is not. A cutthroat trout picking its way along the edge of a clear lake in only a foot and a half of water, a rainbow holding in a slot among trailing weeds in a spring creek, a smallmouth bass gliding over a shallow flat, bluegills holding high in the shade of a leafy tree bent out over the water—if you can truly see these fish, *that's* sight-fishing.

This big, dark cutthroat trout, cruising a lake's shallows over a pale bottom, is plain to see (if you're paying attention). But take a look at the next photo.

A light-olive-backed smallmouth bass over green aquatic weeds—how easy is that fish to spot? Both fish and background are, essentially, greens, but at least they're different shades of green . . . (Whoopee!) The point: Sight-fishing demands keen and patient eyes.

Sight-fishing usually requires quiet, accurate presentations of the fly. You must get it out in front of the fish without alarming or even just tipping it off.

Sight-fishing often requires patience: taking the time to determine the best angle for the cast, moving slowly into position, figuring out the currents, whatever.

Sight-fishing often requires stealth: crouching to get close enough to spot the fish, keeping your shadow off the water, casting sidearm. There's an old saying among old fly fishers: If you're seeing the fish, it's probably seeing you. Once a fish sees you, your odds of hooking it are near zero. Use stealth to defy the old saying.

Sight-fishing can help you weed out the big ones. In his book *Sight Fishing for Trout*, author Landon Mayer, a Colorado fly-fishing guide and top-notch fly fisher, describes spotting "a small pod of giants" and then getting his client into a 9-, a 10-, and a 12-pound rainbow. Incentive enough for you?

Tip 42 Nymph Streams Systematically

 Tr-S

Nymph fishing a trout stream—whether indicator or Czech style, hopper-dropper, whatever—is most effective when it follows a plan. That plan: Run your nymph (or nymphs) through *all* potential holding water.

To implement that plan you must fish your nymph systematically—as my friend Dave Hughes says in his book *Fly Fishing Basics*, by covering "the bottom as if the fly were a paint brush," the idea being that you give all the holding water an even coat of nymph paint.

To accomplish this paint job, begin at the lowest point downstream on your nymph water. Drift your nymph through the nearest water of any promise once or twice; then cast up again but *out* a little farther, a foot maybe. Eventually you'll need to wade out to reach water ever farther off.

Just keep doing this until you've covered all the water near and across from you; then wade back to shore, walk upstream a bit, and do it all again.

Another approach: Keep moving upstream and covering all the water you can by wading only the shallows until you're at the top of the holding water—then walk the bank back down to where you started, and wade *farther out* and work the new water you can now reach, again progressing upstream. Then go back down and wade out even farther if need be.

The first way, you cover the water by working all the way across it from each position; the second way, you work a strip of water all the way up, then the next strip out, and so on. Both are fine ways to paint a streambed. Your choice.

Tip 43 Fish Where Your Anchors Were

 Tr-L Lg-L Sm-L  Pf-L

You drop anchor, fish until the fishing slows, and then pull your anchors (or, for a little inflatable craft, your *anchor*, singular) so you can try another spot. So what do you suppose happens down there when your anchors are yanked up from the muck? Right: Silt, maybe torn waterweeds, and *insects* and other trout foods get swept up from the bottom.

What do you suppose the trout do about this? Right: They head over to grab an easy meal. Do you suppose trout in popular lakes get trained to look for pulled anchors? Do you suppose the answer to this last question is obvious?

So after pulling your anchors, move quietly off until you're a good cast away, and then cast back and get your nymph or streamer down where the anchors were. I generally use a full-sinking line and the countdown method.

Do largemouths, smallmouths, and panfish rush over to where anchors have just been pulled? Honestly, I'm not sure. But it sure makes sense that they would.

Tip 44 Plan Your Angle

 Tr-S, Tr-L   Lg-L   Sm-L, Sm-S   Pf-L

You spot a trout rising to mayfly duns in a thread of current near the far bank of the stream, then mark its position against a stump on the far bank—ready to wade out and show the trout your fly?

Hold on.

First, you need to consider this: What's your best angle from which to present your fly? Upstream and across, straight across, or downstream? One of these angles will probably present the least risk of spooking the fish and the best odds of presenting your dry fly to it with a clean dead drift.

You may also have to consider which angle gives you your best chance of landing the fish once it's hooked—if there's a snarl of tree roots just upstream, for example, casting from mostly downstream will help you drag the trout down and away from that tangle.

There may be other considerations: What angle avoids backcast problems? What angle is best if there's wind? What angle will help you avoid spooking other rising fish? There are probably more.

When I see a patch of water I intend to fish, I give it a long look, feel my way through the options, and eventually the best position reveals itself. If you haven't fished long enough to pull that off, look, *think*, and *then* pick an angle.

Picking a good angle, a good position, for approaching a fish isn't just about rising trout in streams. All of this goes for nymphs, streamers, smallmouths in streams, large-mouths in lakes, from foot, from a boat, and so on . . .

Don't just jump into fishing a spot; take a moment, plan your angle.

Tip 45 Try Fishing Around Boat Launches   Tr-S, Tr-L   Lg-L   Sm-L, Sm-S   Pf-L

Human nature: launch the boat, immediately head across the lake or get drifting downstream to reach the "good" water. Consequently, the water fished least is the water around the boat launch. Seriously, it happens.

A few years ago, during three weeks on a big western trout river, the most consistent spot Carol and I and some fishing pals found for rising trout was just around the corner from a boat launch. We could hear the chatter of anglers and the metallic rattle of the boat trailers backing down the concrete slope all day as we cast for hours to rainbows rising all over a great eddy. Despite all the drift boats going in and coming out, we never saw anyone else work our fish. Well, not really *our* fish, but they sometimes seemed like ours.

Once, after hours of searching for big bluegills in a lake well known for big bluegills, I found a heap of them—just as hefty as advertised—next to my beached boat. That's right: at the boat launch.

Fishing streams next to highways and freeways can be very good (though noisy)—the people in passing cars think, Who'd want to fish there? I would, precisely because others wouldn't.

Places rarely fished tend to hold lots of innocent, eager fish. Often, boat launches and stretches of streams along busy highways are rarely fished.

Tip 46 Try Nymphing Just Before the Hatch  Tr-S, Tr-L

Okay, this is mainly a trout thing—I've rarely fished nymphs as a prior-to-an-expected-insect-hatch strategy for the basses and panfish. But where warmwater fishes see big hatches, it could definitely pan out as a bass-and-panfish thing; I just don't know

So here's the thing, or rather, what the thing is, from a trout-fishing perspective: Nymphs of mayflies, stoneflies, and damselflies and pupae of midges and caddisflies get jumpy and active before they actually start heading up, or in to shore, to hatch. So although there may be no bugs showing on top of the water, or along the edges, trout may be gorging themselves down near the bed of the lake or river. Wait for the bugs to actually show, and you miss some excellent nymph fishing.

Chironomids and dragonflies in a trout lake, stoneflies and mayflies in a stream—one way or another, these and other insects may all expose themselves to trout in their underwater forms just before they hatch.

With chironomids, midges, damselflies, caddisflies, and mayflies, this nymphing-before-the-hatch business is normally a short-term proposition: For maybe a half hour to an hour or two before the insects emerge, the deep nymph can kill. With some insects, however, it's long-term: Stonefly and dragonfly nymphs creep from the depths to the shallows and then out, exposing themselves to trout along the way. Fishing nymphs that imitate these creeping-to-hatch insects may hold up for hours, even all day, for a week or longer.

When I ran all this entomology business by entomologist (and fly-fishing author) Rick Hafele, he checked my facts and said, "Correct." (But he asked me to remind you that midges and chironomids are in actuality the same bug.)

Tip 47 Fish Behavior May Change Just Before, During, and Just After Their Spawning—but Should That Matter?

Tr-S, Tr-L   Lg-L   Sm-L, Sm-S   Pf-L

Crappies, which I've found to be loners by nature, will school tightly for spawning around or in flooded brush, around bulrushes . . . fairly shallow stuff. Male largemouth

A brook trout like this one, in its standard soft and lovely colors, will feed and behave normally.

The markings and coloring of a brook trout ripe for spawning explode, as has this love-mad brookie's sanity.

Male bluegills clear patches of a lake bed in shallow water for nests. Once the eggs are down and fertilized, the males guard them as the females recovers at spas. Male bluegills on nests are far more aggressive than usual—they'll smack whatever they reckon an invader.

bass will protect the sand or gravel beds they've fanned out with their tails in as little as a foot of water by attacking anything that comes near. Brook trout in streams will group in shallows with soft currents.

The point is, these fishes are all behaving very oddly: exposing themselves in ways that would normally give them the chills, grabbing flies they'd normally disdain, running on half or less of their usual IQs. And all this while they're bringing us the next generation of their kind—should we anglers just leave them alone to their important business?

The obvious answer is yes, but it's a little more complicated than that. Trout are an easy matter: Beyond a few special exceptions, avoid spawners. Largemouth bass? Depends on whom you ask. I try to avoid spawning largemouths, but many feel catching them is okay provided it's done with care. Working spawning or preparing-to-spawn smallmouth bass in most places is considered respectable enough and pretty harmless when done right. Crappies bunched for spawning are a standard target for all anglers, largely, I believe, because it's the one time they're easy to find.

Fishing regulations often close waters when spawning is heavy, making the spawner-fishing question irrelevant. Otherwise, about all you can do is bone up a little on the debates and facts regarding the specific species you're considering, and then let your own good sense and conscience decide.

Tip 48 On New Water, Consider Hiring a Guide—a *Good* Guide

Tr-S, Tr-L   Lg-L   Sm-L, Sm-S   Pf-L

Water that's new to you, especially water very different from your familiar home streams and lakes, may take quite a while to figure out. Insect hatches, water clarity, where the fish lie, how the fish feed—all of this and a lot more may prove distressingly foreign.

Maybe it's time to invest in a guide.

If you do, make sure you get a *fly-fishing*, not just a *fishing*, guide. You are a fly fisher, right? (You bought this *fly-fishing* book, after all.)

Find a good guide who suits you. I look for one who's patient, respectful—one who will help, not torment. But if you miss your old drill sergeant or the driver's ed instructor who kicked you in the ankle whenever you pressed the wrong pedal, sure, find someone like that.

The matter of temperament aside, you want a guide who really knows their water and knows how to make it give up its fish. Reviews are easy to find online these days, and you can always just ask among your fishing pals or at your fly club.

I like to get a feel for the water before my day with a guide. It helps me ask good questions: Should I fish pocketwater or pools? Big flies or small? Shallow flats or deep edges? So I'll fish a day on my own, then fish with a guide and observe, inquire, and learn all I can, and then finish out the remaining days of my trip on my own—but now, armed with a heap of wisdom and local knowledge, and a new comfort with this intriguing new water.

Tip 49 Don't Always Rely on Guides

 Tr-S, Tr-L Lg-L Sm-L, Sm-S Pf-L

I'm all for fishing with guides (provided they're *good* guides: attentive, professional, knowledgeable, respectful). A guide can get you into lots of fish, teach you new techniques and strategies, and make the fishing more fun and more productive than it would be if you were doing it on your own.

My point is just that if you *always* rely on guides, never picking out flies yourself, choosing where to put them and how to present them, setting up leaders and tippets of appropriate and effective length—all the decisions that come with fishing—you'll never improve very much as a fly fisher.

Going out and getting skunked, finding where the trout or smallmouth hold through determination, trial and error, knowledge, often by plain luck—doing it all yourself instructs and matures the fly fisher in you.

So, sure, fish with guides, learn from guides. But learn on your own too.

Tip 50 Learn the Mega-Drift

 Tr-S Sm-S

Continuing the drift of a dry fly or nymph and indicator until it's way off downstream can offer advantages. A floating fly, or hair bug or popper, simply covers a lot of water this way, increasing the odds of a take. Much of a nymph's drift is spent getting the fly down where the trout hold—once it's down there, why not just keep it drifting and fishing as long as possible?

Another advantage: An uncommonly long drift sometimes allows you to present your fly in water you couldn't otherwise reach. You can just let that indicator or dry or popper glide on down along your bank where thick or overhanging brush or a vertical wall of rock makes it impossible for you to get any closer.

The parachute cast is handy for a mega-drift, or you can strip line off your reel and waggle your rod tip to feed it out, making occasional line mends for control, or you can do both. Do keep in mind, though, that hooking and playing a trout or smallmouth that takes your fly 50 feet downstream can be tricky, as can detecting a take of your fly.

Tip 51 Never False-Cast Over or Near Your Fish

 Tr-S, Tr-L Lg-L Sm-L, Sm-S Pf-L

Fish grow up paranoid. The most paranoid ones make it to adulthood—by fleeing at *any* sign of a predator. Seeing your pal Ben get scarfed up in a yellow beak leaves an impression on you as a youngster.

So a fly line sails in overhead or just nearby and the fish thinks, *Aargh!* Suddenly, that fish is gone—it's now off somewhere deep, dark, and safe. (That's if, in fact, fish do think. More likely a fish just reacts. Same result either way, though.)

So, don't false-cast over or even near a fish you want to catch. Make your false-casts either well off to the side of the fish (downstream of a fish in a current, since that fish must face upstream) or well short of the fish, and then shoot line to put the fly out near it.

Tip 52 Follow the Crowd, but Arrive a Little Late Tr-S, Tr-L Lg-L Sm-L, Sm-S Pf-L

A friend of mine and some friends of his fished a big western river right after a holiday (Memorial Day weekend, as I recall). Starting the first day after the big weekend, they, among the few others on the river, caught trout after trout—after *trout*. A day of wild action. That's a difficult river, too. I know—I've fished it a lot. Seldom have I found fast fishing on it. For three days they fished, and on each day the action was quick and constant.

Here's how I figure it: The trout saw armadas of drift boats passing, all those wadered feet in the water, their trout buddies panicking at the end of fly lines, and they simply went on strike, a hunger strike. They settled down in a safe place and fasted through the weekend, glum and thinking unprintable thoughts about fly fishers.

Then, suddenly, it was all gone. No boats, no anglers crunching around on the riverbed, no fish-pals getting dragged off, all after three days of growling stomachs—and they went, "Whee! Let's eat!"

Hot post-mob fishing is no sure thing, but it's a thing. And it sure can happen.

Tip 53 Learn to Recognize the Come-Back-Around Rise Tr-L

It can drive you mad—a trout swirls on your floating fly, you set the hook, nothing. Again and again. Once, during a post-twilight hatch of huge *Hexagenia* mayflies, I set on eight such swirls before the hatch ended and hooked one trout.

Just one . . . stinking . . . trout.

When big insects—*Hexagenia*s, Traveler Sedge caddisflies, grasshoppers—lie atop lakes, trout will often try to drown them by swirling at them, then swing back around and take them. So if you've got big bugs on top of a trout lake, and you miss a couple of fish without feeling even a touch, try this: Let the fish swirl at your fly as you *do nothing* (impossible? no—you can *do* this); wait; and then if the trout comes back at the fly again, *set the hook*.

I've never seen this come-back-around thing with fishes other than trout, or anywhere other than lakes. So I asked guide and fly-fishing author Ed Engle (*Trout Lessons* and other titles) if he'd seen the come-back-around on trout streams and he said he hadn't. Makes sense, actually: Play with your food on a river and by the time you're ready to eat it, it's already drifted off downstream.

Tip 54 Here's a Stealth Fly-Presentation Trick  Tr-S

It's so easy to put down a rising trout, especially a cagey one rising in slick water, that I sometimes still do, and that's after decades of working slick-water risers. The fly or line comes down a touch too hard or too close to the trout . . . it's gone. So I try to cast far enough upstream that my fly and line won't alarm the fish. But I must make casts that provide slack so I don't put off the fish with fly drag—and that makes putting the fly in the right place more difficult than it already is.

It's that tricky, and it's why I feel no guilt at putting down a wise old riser. No one should feel guilty about that. But it's less tricky if you use the following trick.

Watch your quarry's rises, time them, and *right* after a rise occurs, drop your fly on the water. I've never read or heard about this, and I don't understand why it works, but I know it often does.

Perhaps there's a moment after taking down an insect that the trout is distracted with working the bug down its throat, or maybe the rise obscures the trout's vision or the trout's briefly tipped down and looking down. Maybe, maybe . . . Does it matter why? Just go out and try it.

Does this also work with rising smallmouth bass? I don't know, since I've never found rising smallmouth that were really skittish. But if you do, sure, try my trick.

Tip 55 A Breeze Can Save the Day

 Tr-S, Tr-L   Lg-L   Sm-L, Sm-S   Pf-L

As much as I hate wind of any kind, in certain situations I welcome a breeze. (A *breeze*—not a relentless, soul-numbing *blast*.)

Usually, those situations involve clear standing or flat, slow-moving water and nervous fish, be they trout, smallmouth, largemouth, or panfish—especially if those fish are holding close to the bank or near the water's surface. Then a scuffed-up top on a lake or stream or pond gives the fish a comfy sense of being hidden while you're hidden from them too. They feed freely; you avoid much of the fuss and strain of staying out of sight while still delivering your fly. Your fly's drop to the water is lost among the wavelets too. And it's always easier to let small waves bounce your strike indicator than to tug and tease it across a calm lake when you're chironomid fishing.

So, yeah, I guess wind isn't *all* bad.

Bonus-Tip Try Dry-and-Dropper Fishing on Lakes Tr-L

Though dry-and-dropper fishing is, to most, a method for fishing streams, I use it also for trout that are rising in lakes. When trout wise to the artificial fly come to a twitched dry, let's say an Elk Hair Caddis, and see it for a fake, they turn away and then notice that obviously legitimate little mayfly nymph or chironomid pupa wriggling only a foot or two deeper (that is, they notice my *imitation* of a nymph or pupa). Try this when fussy trout are up at a lake's surface picking through a mix of feed.

Tip 56 Avoid the Largemouth and Smallmouth Bass Post-Spawn Slump

 Lg-L   Sm-L, Sm-S

Prior to spawning, largemouth bass throw a lot of mixers—specifically, boy-girl parties. Once paired up, each couple puts scads of fertilized eggs in gravel, and then the male protects the nest. After both male and female have spawned, though, they spend the next two to six weeks wrung-out and stressed, but they don't stress eat—they fast.

Largemouth spawning starts as early as February in the Deep South to as late as July in the Way-Up North. Such range makes it hard to pin down the post-spawn. Plus, the timing varies from year to year. To avoid the post-spawn, you really need to check around: Ask at a fly shop, research online. Best of all: Get to really know a lake.

I taught some clinics on fly fishing for largemouths and panfish on a private lake in sizzling-hot Northern California one year in late April. Spent two days beforehand learning the lake so I'd do the thing right—and found the bass in post-spawn. Made the classes tough, but I soldiered ahead and my students learned a lot anyway. What I learned was to avoid that lake in late April. Next time it'll be late March or mid-May.

Regarding smallmouths, I've never knowingly had poor post-spawn fishing for them. But Bob Clouser, in his book *Fly-Fishing for Smallmouth in Rivers and Streams*, says, "After the bass spawn and the fry leave the nest, the adult bass spend a week or two recovering." During their recovery, he adds, "Fishing is often subpar."

Tip 57 Make Your First Presentation on New Water Count

 Tr-S, Tr-L   Lg-L   Sm-L, Sm-S   Pf-L

It's never wise to carelessly chuck out a fly and hope you don't scare off the fish you hoped to catch, but it's especially unwise to do so on "new" water; that is, water you haven't yet fished. Unfished water (not yet fished by you nor, you hope, by anyone else today) holds special promise. Don't mess it up with your first sloppy, unconsidered cast and only *then* work on making a clean presentation.

So, you're working upstream with a dry fly on a trout river, or perhaps working around the edge of a largemouth lake, and you're about to drop your fly on new water. Pause, relax, consider where you want your fly to go and how you want it to arrive, *then* make that first cast with accuracy and care. If your dry fly drifts naturally rather than dragging off sideways or your hair bug drops at the edge of a lily pad, congratulations! You're making the most of new water.

Tip 58 Here's the Deal with Selectivity

 Tr-S,Tr-L   Lg-L   Sm-L, Sm-S   Pf-L

There's your trout, rising amid a profusion of tiny upturned wings—hatching mayfly duns. Among them some much bigger duns occasionally appear. Then, down nearly nose to water, you see miniscule midges drifting quietly by. Now what?

You guess. Maybe your fish is on the few big duns. You offer a solid imitation a dozen times, and . . . nothing.

So you imitate the smaller mayfly, then the midge—still not a touch. Eventually you realize the fish is on mayfly spinners with rust-colored bellies—*got 'im!*

That's high-level selectivity, a well-fed, angler-schooled trout. Here's another scenario: All these bugs are on the water, your trout is rising away, you show the trout some fly or another, and it takes it. Despite the hatch, this fish isn't being choosy.

Most of the time, in most streams and lakes, trout feed on what they get: a steady mix of insect sizes and forms. Only when there's a hatch or a fall of flying ants or such—some event that presents a lot of identical bugs at once—does it make sense for trout to turn selective.

So, sometimes trout are open-minded, sometimes they're mildly selective so that just a fly change or two will close the deal, and sometimes they'll make you get the size, shape, and action of your fly just so and make you fish it appropriately on, in, or under the surface before they'll budge.

The point: Anglers often fret over selectivity when there's none and blame it for their slow fishing, *or* they fail to respect it when it's there. So assume trout are not being selective unless you see signs that they are, such as fishing well among plenty of fish but getting no takers. Though it's uncommon, selectivity can also happen with largemouths, smallmouths, and even panfish—trust me . . .

Tip 59 Carry Two Rods, Three, More?

 Tr-S,Tr-L   Lg-L   Sm-L, Sm-S   Pf-L

When I head out onto a lake, I nearly always bring two rigged rods, sometimes three. Here's an example of how that works: After tossing a popper for a while to catch only one runt bluegill, I reel in the line, hook the popper in the rod's hook-keeper, set that rod aside, and reach for my rod with the full-sinking line and a wet fly. By bringing *two* rods already rigged, I don't have to snip my popper off my *one* rod, reel everything in, take out the spool and replace it with one carrying a sinking line, etc., etc. I just set down one rod, pick up the other.

Decades ago I watched a friend go out on a trout lake in his dinky pram with *seven* rigged rods. He fished most of them that day. I knew him as a deadly fly fisher; consequently, I had to consider his strategy. Soon I was hauling around extra rigged rods too when I fished lakes. Extra rods in a boat is pretty easy, though you have to be careful not to set ice chests and anchors on them, or to step on them. Extra rods in a float tube or pontoon boat is a tricky proposition, but there are special rod holders for inflatables.

I carry extra rods on streams (one with a dry fly, one with a nymph rig, one with a streamer, etc.), but it's a practice fraught with problems: finding a safe place to set the extra rods, having to find them when it's time to move on, forgetting I brought extra rods until I'm half a mile upstream . . . My solutions: (1) place extra rods thoughtfully in safe spots; (2) set them angling up, where I can see their tips; and (3) keep reminding myself that I *did* bring extra rods.

Tip 60 Learn the Downstream Presentation Tr-S Sm-S

This isn't about flies that are normally presented downstream (streamers, soft-hackles, etc.) but about a floating fly drifted downstream to a rising (or willing-to-rise) trout.

A downstream presentation of a dry fly, or floating emerger fly, isn't the norm, but it's a killer when conditions are right. I use it mostly (1) when a fish is holding where an upstream presentation will spook it or (2) when a fish is holding just above an obstacle I can't fish around.

Example, situation 1: There's your trout, rising in that quiet seam only three feet out from the bank, your bank, but you can't cross the river because it's too deep. A cast upstream will throw fly and tippet and leader over the trout's head, and the leader will drop right on the fish—game over. So instead, you creep your way well upstream, staying back.

Now, crouched, you cast partway down to the trout, maybe drag the fly in a little to line it up with the fish and to get your fly line in near the bank. Then you let the fly drift freely, feed out line. Your fly's nearly on the fish . . .

If the fish takes your fly, give a good pause before setting the hook, since downstream sets are always dicey. If the fish doesn't take it, let your fly drift past and sweep in near the bank, and only then pick it all up and try again.

Example, situation 2: A smallmouth is rising in front of a log angling out from a steep bank, your bank. How do you cast *up*stream to *that* fish? You don't—you can't. So you make a downstream presentation.

Tip 61 Learn to Tell Selectivity from Moodiness Tr-S,Tr-L Lg-L Sm-L, Sm-S Pf-L

The title of this tip offers sound advice, but telling when trout are locked into taking only olive-colored *Rhyacophila* caddis pupae or are just feeling . . . off . . . is tricky.

So, start by determining if anything is hatching. If there's a hatch going on, odds are high that trout, very possibly smallmouth, and just possibly largemouth and panfish, are on it.

Then try imitating what's hatching.

If nothing's hatching, determine if anything is currently abundant. Do largemouth fry dart in panic in the shallows at your approach? Are dragonfly adults soaring low all over a broad smallmouth pool?

Then try imitating what's in abundance.

No hatches, no abundance? Then it's time to consider: Have your fish simply caught a mood? If so, maybe it's because the barometer's dropping at the edge of an incoming storm. Maybe it's because the mercury's hit 95 to 100 for a week.

Or *maybe* they're just having a bad day.

You can try to shake the fish up with some bright, goofy attractor fly, perhaps fished in some odd way like skidding it across the water. Or you can work the fly intensely, perhaps drifting a nymph and indicator while applying every possible ounce of care and attention until you finally move a trout to yawn down your fly when it comes hovering up. Or you can leave and then come back at sunset, or tomorrow. Or you can just relax and hope the fish mood passes soon—but if it doesn't, you're still out in the clean air and a beautiful place. Fish or no fish, isn't that enough?

Tip 62 Learn to Tell Selectivity from Spookiness Tr-S, Tr-L Lg-L Sm-L, Sm-S Pf-L

In my early years as a fly fisher (which, in fact, were still my early years in general), I often thought fish—trout, largemouth, panfish, others—were refusing my fly because it was the wrong fly. Or because I wasn't fishing it right. It didn't occur to me that trout might just continue to hold in their deep lie in a river, in full view when a window of smooth water passed over them, and ignore every fly I ran past them because they knew I was there and were spooked. Didn't occur to me when panfish lined up to stare at me and sneer at my flies either. Didn't occur to me when largemouth bass and smallmouth did the same.

No, it didn't occur to me back then, but I eventually figured out that that's what was going on.

Stealth can keep you from spooking your target fish into a bad case of lockjaw. (You'll find advice on how stealth works peppered throughout these tips.) Once spooked, a fish needs time alone, 10 minutes, maybe an hour, before you have another shot at it.

The best way to tell whether fish are refusing your fly because it doesn't match what they're eating or because you've tipped them off or altogether freaked them out is to (1) make sure you apply a heavy dose of stealth to ensure you're undetected, and (2) be certain your fly presentations are properly executed on proper rigs. If you cover 1 and 2 and the fish still won't touch your fly—especially if they're clearly feeding on some-thing—you've likely got fish in a selective mode.

Tip 63 Learn to Tell Spookiness from Moodiness Tr-S, Tr-L Lg-L Sm-L, Sm-S Pf-L

The theme of these latest three tips should be pretty clear by now: You'd better learn to identify *why* fish aren't taking your fly if you hope to catch those fish. Until now, you had a choice of selectivity or moodiness, selectivity or spookiness. That leaves spooki-ness or moodiness, of course.

The most straightforward way to tell if fish are spooky is to note how easily they flee at your approach—if easily, they're spooky. Clearly, you need to approach spooky fish with real stealth.

There's no straightforward way that I know of telling for certain if fish are moody. The best I know is to approach them with such high-level stealth that it's almost impossible you spooked them; then, if there are no hatches, and no insects or other feed is particularly available and the fish refuse all your logical flies, they're probably in a mood.

As I say in the previous two tips, spooked fish need some time to forget you. So leave them unbothered for a while and then try them again later if you like. Moody fish? Wait them out, harass them with odd flies or fly presentations, or just fish them hard until they crack under the pressure. Or just quit fishing. Maybe instead of catching a fish, go catch a movie.

Tip 64 Watch the Birds

Tr-S, Tr-L   Lg-L   Sm-L, Sm-S   Pf-L

When birds swoop across and skim the water, there is usually one reason: bugs. Bugs (mayflies, caddisflies . . .) hatching at the water's surface, bugs (mayfly spinners, flying ants . . .) dropping onto the water. Watch the birds at your stream or lake, and if they're working an area, go there and try to find out what's got them excited. If insects have birds feeding on them somewhere, they probably have fish there feeding on them too.

Hatches are typically about trout fishing, yes, but smallmouths, largemouths, and panfish sometimes get on hatches too.

Tip 65 Adjust Your Tactics for Creeks

Tr-S   Sm-S

Be they trout or smallmouth bass, if they live in creeks and you normally fish larger water, you'll probably have to change the way you do things to catch them. First matter: Is the creek open, or is it surrounded by trees or high brush?

If it's flowing through open meadows or hemmed by only *low* brush, no problem—other than approaching with lots of stealth and making short casts, proceed as usual. But if your creek runs though forest or head-high bushes, well, listen up. The heedless backcast is now your enemy. Look behind you—*before* you cast. You may need to angle your backcast below outstretched tree branches or above them, or straight down the bed of the creek. You may even need to find a hole in the foliage and aim a narrow backcast loop at its center. Creek aficionados get very good at all of this.

An alternate is the roll cast, which nearly eliminates a backcast altogether.

Another option: the bow and arrow cast. Point the rod at your target, hold the fly by its bend (don't even *touch* the hook's point because if you do, you'll likely stab yourself with the hook), load the rod by pulling the fly straight back (but not very far, or you might break the rod tip), and then let go. Won't put the fly out very far, but it'll put it out.

Another option, often very practical for creeks: dapping. (See tip 121.)

And, of course, there's that stealth I mentioned—crouching low, staying back, even casting sidearm to keep the moving rod tip from showing against the sky.

Stealth—a quiet approach, crouching, casting gently upstream—is key to successful creek fishing.

Tip 66 Path-Rising Is a Miracle with a Blessing  Tr-L

Trout are always looking to expend minimum energy for maximum gain. That's why they sometimes do something miraculous on lakes: They rise in a predictable pattern.

Swimming at a steady speed is more efficient than slowing, stopping, speeding up; rising in a rhythm is more efficient than rising without one; rising in a line is more efficient than zigzagging and reversing direction. Consequently, if a trout is feeding efficiently, you can often line up its rises on a lake, time the rises, and have your fly waiting where the next rise should occur.

This fishing: captivating.

Demanding too. You watch a trout's rising, catch the time and distance between rises, line the rises up—and you're already almost out of time. But if things go right, you *quietly* (so you don't send out alarming wavelets from your boat) fire that fly out to land where the trout should rise next (and *soon*, so you don't spook the fish with the fly's landing) and wait. No take, such is life. But if your fly lifts on a little swell, circular wavelets spread, and you set the hook to feel a shocked, fiery rainbow on your line: *Oh, sweet God . . .*

I've long referred to this sort of rising as "path-rising." But you can't count on getting path-rising trout. Often, during daylight hours, trout rise randomly, without any pattern, probably to confuse predators. (I call such rises "searching rises.")

At sunset and dawn, though, predators can't see well enough to do much. Then, you may be blessed with path-rising trout.

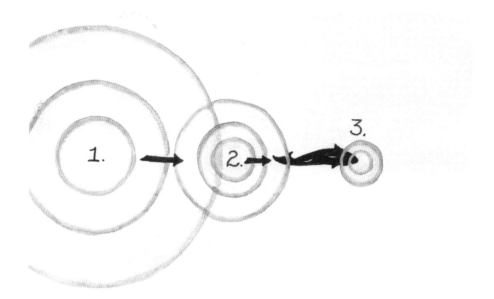

A path-rising trout

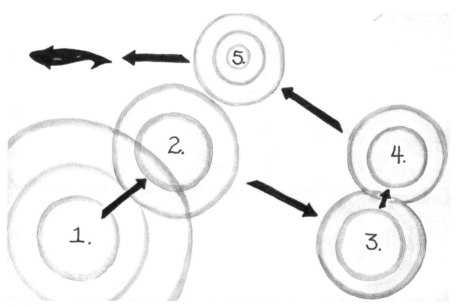

Searching rises

Tip 67 When Trout Don't Path-Rise, They May Still Rise

 Tr-L

When the sun's high, clouds or no, the birds and mammals that prey on trout can see their quarry just fine. So when trout rise on lakes during daylight hours, they tend to rise erratically so those predators can't anticipate their next rise and meet it with open jaws or open talons.

Erratic rising is sort of the opposite of path-rising. But trout rising in any way is always a gift.

A trout, for example, picking off hatching mayflies over a shoal at noon, taking one here, then taking another a minute later 20 feet off, then taking a hard left to snap up two more in quick succession, offers you no pattern, no way to predict where the next rise will occur. But, so what? You have on a fly that looks like those mayflies, a half-floating emerger you can toss out there in the general area of the rising and let rest between tiny twitches. If that trout, and others, are out there working the hatch, one of them will eventually find your fly.

You just need to *keep* tossing it out among the fish and insects until something happens. Be patient; if you're fishing well and presenting a suitable fly, it will happen. And keep happening. If it doesn't happen, try another fly.

Tip 68 Here's the Deal with Fast-Water, Slow-Water Trout-Stream Fishing

 Tr-S

Take a trout that's been rising softly to mayfly duns on a smooth flat, a persnickety trout that's refused your flies over and over, and plant it in a surging bend in a quick stream, the surface of the water a chaotic chop, with that same mayfly hatch in progress—think that trout will still refuse your dry flies? Maybe . . . but not likely. Because now it'll be hard for the fish to get a good look at a fly, amid the turbulence, and find a flaw. Also, because that look will be brief, those quick currents will hurry that fly through and on downstream. The trout won't have much time for making its decision.

The problems trout have inspecting a floating fly in fast water match up neatly with the fly fisher's needs: A bushy, heavily dressed, and therefore especially buoyant dry or emerger will stay stubbornly afloat on the chop, while the trout will tend to overlook its unnatural bulk because they can't get a clear look at it and must decide quickly.

The opposite, of course, is true for slow currents: Lightly dressed flies, especially floating flies but nymphs too, generally fish best.

Tip 69 Got Big Clumsy Bugs? Plunk Big Dry Flies Down Close to Trout Tr-S, Tr-L

I suppose you could read only the title of this tip and get the main point. But you'd miss the finer points if you did. So read on . . .

The big bugs of trout streams—the Golden Stonefly October Caddis, grasshopper— are poor fliers, or maybe competent but careless fliers: They sometimes complete their flights by smacking onto the water. So instead of setting your fly lightly onto a stream far enough upstream to not alert the trout, plunk down a hopper or big-stone dry fly just a foot or two upstream, where the trout can plainly see the splashdown.

A big dry fly carries some real mass (at least for a trout fly) and, consequently, significant weight—it'll hit the water fairly hard no matter what you do. But you want a real commotion. So aim your forward cast low, give it more punch than it really needs, even draw back on the rod a little just before the line loop straightens to snap the fly down— all of this will help make your fly land like a meaty bug out of control.

But don't overdo it either. Watch the real insects and try to match their landings with your fly.

The near-trout fly crash can pay off around the edges of trout lakes too, especially with grasshoppers.

Glad you stuck around for the details?

Plunk! Down goes a big dry fly in a tiny splash. If that's how the real insects are landing, then all is as it should be.

Tip 70 Crazy Can Work (Sometimes, It Works Wonders)

 Tr-S, Tr-L   Lg-L   Sm-L, Sm-S   Pf-L

Honest: The rules and guidelines we fly fishers trust—they work. But they don't work all the time. When they fail, don't give up. Try something crazy.

Those bitsy-bug-loving brown trout in that quiet spring creek, trout everyone goes after with flies of size 20, 22—size *26*—if they won't come near such flies, maybe toss out some caddis-adult dry-fly monstrosity tied on an absurd (absurd, at least, for this refined water and these sophisticated fish) size 6 hook, and then twitch and skid the thing across the soft current. Might fail. But it might kill. I actually did exactly this— tugged a giant dry fly across a famously difficult spring creek where tiny flies are the rule—and caught my biggest trout of the day by doing it.

Illogical approaches—a fish-egg fly called a Glo-Bug hanging unnaturally below a strike indicator in a trout lake, a hair bug worked frantically for largemouth bass that normally demand a patient retrieve—can work. Illogical flies—a little soft-hackle for largemouth bass, a bass popper for trout, a tiny nymph for smallmouth bass—can work.

So trust the standard flies, methods, and strategies, and nearly always they'll get you into fish. But remember that when all that fails, illogical stuff, *crazy* stuff, can be the solution. On occasion, it can work wonders.

Tip 71 With a Floating Fly on Streams, Lead Your Fish   Tr-S   Sm-S

New fly fishers see a trout's rise as a bull's-eye—they aim their dry fly directly at it. But that's a losing strategy. That trout's probably done rising for the moment, and so the fly drifts safely off to nowhere . . .

You should (nearly) always drop your floating fly *upstream* of a rising trout—both so that the trout can see it in time to comfortably begin its ascent to meet it and so that the fly doesn't hit the water so near the trout that it spooks it. On the slowest currents, drop your fly well above a riser; in quicker, choppier currents, shorten that distance. Want specifics? Sorry, I've never been able to measure how far my dry flies land from rising trout; can't get a yardstick out there. After some experimenting, though, I'll say two feet clear up to five feet.

Smallmouth bass in streams will rise to take hatching insects. Then it's the same deal as with trout in streams: Lead your fish.

Sometimes when bugs are buzzing around on the water or plopping down onto it, you want to drop your fly, even smack it down, near the fish. That's certainly not the norm, though. Leading a rising fish *is* the norm.

Tip 72 With Almost *Any* Fly on Streams, Lead Your Trout 🐟 Tr-S 🐟 Sm-S

There's leading a rising trout and then there's leading a trout that's not rising—the previous tip covers the former, but here, we'll consider the latter. Let's say you figure a trout is holding just behind that boulder standing in three feet of lively current. You're fishing a nymph with an indicator. Do you drop your nymph right where you figure the trout is holding?

No. Because if you do, your nymph will barely sink before it's already well downstream of the trout and beyond its view. A nymph must normally drift down near the streambed to be effective. So, you cast well upstream, far enough up that the nymph is down skimming the cobble as it nears the boulder; then it comes around to the trout and . . .

Streamer flies are a different proposition from nymphs: Streamers are sometimes fished deep in trout streams, sometimes fished near the water's surface. In either case, you must still lead your trout, but you'll need to lead it by a considerably greater distance with the deep streamer than with the only slightly sunken one.

Soft-hackled flies are swung softly across streams by the currents alone. This makes for a different kind of leading: tossing the fly far enough out so that it swings *in* to meet that trout feeding just under the surface of the water.

All this applies to smallmouth bass in streams: lead them with your steamers, poppers, crayfish flies, whatevers.

Tip 73 With a Floating Fly on Streams, *Time* Your Trout 🐟 Tr-S 🐟 Sm-S

When you see a trout rising in a stream, don't fish, just watch, so you can catch its timing. The span of time between a trout's rises may not be constant, but it may be nearly so. Especially if the hatch is at least fairly heavy.

During a heavy hatch a trout can afford to rise in a steady rhythm—the most efficient and comfortable way for it to feed—because a bug will always be waiting on the surface, whenever the trout happens to get there. Have your fly just coming down to meet the trout when it gets there.

During a thin hatch, a trout may rise sporadically, since it has to take a bug whenever one shows up. Still, even when hatching insects are few, give a trout a little time after it's risen before showing it your fly.

What you don't want is for your fly to show up a little late behind a natural. The trout will take the natural, and your fly will drift off downstream as the trout drops down to swallow. That's going to happen, of course, regardless of how well you think you've got a trout's feeding rhythm figured out. Just keep doing your best until everything lines up.

Trout feeding rhythms vary. Sometimes trout rise almost constantly, making individual rises difficult to distinguish. Other times they rise so seldom and so inconsistently that there's really no rhythm at all. Regardless, watch, and use what you see.

Smallmouths rise too, so all this applies to them when they do.

Tip 74 Big Fish Aren't Big on Surface Feeding Tr-S, Tr-L   Lg-L   Sm-L, Sm-S   Pf-L

I fished a little round, forest-rimmed, largemouth bass lake for 15 years before I finally caught a lunker there. Oh, I'd caught scads of bass in it, but nothing approaching the mystical 3-pound mark (that's a giant around here). Then, one afternoon, I came to a log I'd never noticed before, apparently pushed out from the shallows by some windstorm, rotted bare of branches, angling up from the silty bottom in about five feet of water.

I stopped rowing to gaze at the log, then tried to understand why I was gazing. Gradually it came to me that a big bass might be holding by it. I still don't know why that particular log stood out—sunken timber is everywhere in my local lakes.

I worked a hair bug on top as usual, keeping my distance. Nothing. I got another nudge from my instincts: Try a big streamer, they said. I dug out my biggest, fattest streamer, a construct of mainly rabbit fur on the hide, tied it on, and tossed it out close to the log. I'd already gotten the message to let it sink.

A few tugs into the retrieve, I hooked the log. But then it wasn't the log and everything was chaos. I felt the living weight of the big bass, and in a lake around here that's a rare feeling. The rest was pretty standard big-fish procedure: panic (the fish's), more panic (mine), tippet on the verge of breaking, desperate lunges (the fish's) for the log, panic again (the fish's and mine).

I got it. It was big. *Easily* 3 pounds.

Bass and trout and even panfish grown large have *survived* long enough to know they're easily spotted by predators, both airborne and swimming, when they go shallow or near the water's surface. So sunken streamers and nymphs trump dry flies and poppers if you're on a big-fish hunt.

Tip 75 Sometimes, When Nymph Fishing a Stream, Linger Tr-S

Nymphing streams is tricky. The fly is normally down well beyond sight over a streambed whose contours and lies are largely mysteries. You plug along on faith, mostly—each strip of holding water gets a few passes of your fly as you study your indicator, and then you cover another strip in hopes you covered the last one well. And you catch some trout. All must therefore be well.

Maybe . . .

I believe that working progressively through holding water in a systematic way is a solid approach to stream nymph fishing, and the best one, normally. But sometimes I finish up a stretch, having hooked a trout or two, and get a feeling: the feeling I missed something. Here's really promising water, and all I've made of it is a meager showing. So I've learned that when I sense I'm on what seems especially good nymph water and I'm not catching much, I should slow down, even go back through it.

If I see the potential right away, I'll go on alert, working each drift of the nymph with special care, experimenting to make sure my fly is truly down close to the streambed among the fish, shutting out everything except my indicator and its every nuance. Working upstream this way, I often make discoveries, discoveries that get me into fish: hidden streambed grooves, lie-protecting boulders, deep slots along steep banks, and such.

When I reach the top of the water, I might go back down and then work up through it all again, perhaps making more discoveries. Perhaps catching more trout.

Tip 76 Know When and How to Sink Your Tippet  Tr-S

If you watch a floating tippet drift under sunshine over calm shallows in clear water, you'll see the problem: The depressions the tippet makes in the water's skin cast shadows on the bottom. Shadows on the bottom, odd patterns on top—there's just too much of the unnatural here to suit a clever trout. So how do you eliminate the shadows and patterns? Sink the tippet.

The tippet's always sunken in presenting a streamer or a nymph, so, problem solved. It's with floating flies that a tippet likes to float. Here's how you can make it sink: Use fluorocarbon.

Fluorocarbon is supposed to really disappear underwater. Many fly fishers are convinced this is true. Some have doubts. But two things are certain regarding fluorocarbon tippet: (1) it costs per foot about the same as spun gold, and (2) it sinks.

Trying to keep a floating fly on top with a sinking tippet is a bit tricky. You have to drop your fly far enough upstream of your fish so that the tippet has time to sink but not so far that it drags the fly down. You'll get it.

Of course, all this is about cagey trout, the spoiled-rotten kind that spend their uppity lives looking for one little excuse to pass up your fly. Innocent trout—or any trout feeding where the current is quick, the surface is rough, or both—don't need sunken tippets. In fact, I often rub floatant on my tippets for choppy-water dry-fly fishing.

I haven't felt the need to fish a sunken tippet for trout in lakes (though on flat water with dry flies I may yet) or for the basses or panfish. It's really a trout-stream thing.

Tip 77 Become a Fly-Fishing Detective

Tr-S, Tr-L   Lg-L   Sm-L, Sm-S   Pf-L

There are two fine reasons for seeing yourself as a detective when you fish: (1) you'll catch more fish, and (2) it makes fishing truly intriguing. Suppose you're *not* a detective, just a take-your-best-shot-and-leave-it-at-that sort of fly fisher. You go to your good old trout stream and start tossing your good old Royal Wulff dry fly around on it exactly the same good old way you always do. You catch nothing over the next two hours, so you reel in and go home. Woo-*hoo*—scintillating! (That's sarcasm.)

Now, suppose you're a fly-fishing detective. You fish your Royal Wulff for 15 minutes without a touch. Woo-*hoo*—detective, you've just been presented a mystery to solve! (Not sarcasm.) You stop, and look around for clues. On that slick water downstream, you finally spot a few rises. A clue. You head down there and find tiny mayflies drifting atop the currents. Another clue.

So you add a length of 6X tippet to the 4X tippet you started with, tie on a tiny dry fly that matches the mayflies, and cast it upstream so that it drifts down into the rises. And catch trout. And it's all based on clues—and on *your* detective work.

Exhilarating, yes? Congrats.

Sometimes clues are broader than this, such as no takes of a dry fly or no rising trout at all. They probably mean you should fish deep, with a nymph or streamer.

Make a habit of watching for clues—bugs, fish behavior, water levels, what's going on with other anglers—and you'll catch more trout, bass (both kinds), and panfish.

So, detective, go solve a mystery.

Tip 78 Detective, Start Looking for Clues Right Away

Don't wait until you're out wading in the river or rowing in the lake to become a fly-fishing detective—watch for clues from the moment you step out of your car. Sharp—and successful—fly fishers take their time on a riverbank or lake edge. They check along the water for insect shucks or grasshoppers, search the water's surface for insects, peer into the water looking for leeches or minnows or dragonfly nymphs, scan *all* the water for rising trout or the dimpling of schooled bluegills. And more.

There's a lot to see. Almost anything you do see may help. Hatching insects may help you determine which fly to tie on and how to fish it on or in a trout lake or trout stream; a crayfish in a stream's shallows suggests an imitation might be killing for smallmouths.

But it's not just about feed. A long look around a lake or upstream and downstream on a river may help you decide where to head first. Distant clouds moving toward you on a light breeze may prepare you for a shift in fishing in an hour. Watching that guy across the lake catch a couple of trout with a brightly colored floating line and equally bright strike indicator suggests that chironomid fishing may pay off.

So don't wait until you're rigged and on or in the water to search for clues to good fishing—start early, detective.

Tip 79 Become a Scientist Too

When I speak at fly-fishing clubs and expositions, I tell anglers to become detectives—to search for clues, to solve the classic Case of the Reluctant Fish. I tell them that when the sensible and established ways fail, to try unlikely, even crazy things. And I tell them to experiment, that is, to become fly-fishing scientists.

Detective work, experimentation, the scientific method—they're all related. (Crazy's different. It's just crazy.) Where becoming a scientist veers off on its own is where it involves theories.

Example: Trout are rising *hard* right in front of you, but you can't get a touch on your fly, a parachute type that matches the size and shape and coloring of those big hatching Western Green Drake mayflies out there. So you try other flies—Green Drake

Though this idea is touched on throughout the main tips, it's really important, and needs to be stated plainly: Despite their resemblance, largemouth bass and smallmouth bass are very different fish. Their lies, their ideal water temperatures, their fondness or distain for currents in streams, their flies and the retrieves for those flies—despite some overlap, these and many other factors differ from one fish to the other. Don't think you know both fishes just because you know one.

Same with panfish—no way are the habits of bluegill similar to the habits of yellow perch.

half-floating emergers, caddis imitations, attractor dry flies—but still no touch. So you wisely stop, and watch (for clues, like a detective).

Then, you reason: The hatch is obvious, and I fished appropriate flies for it without success, so something else is probably going on. Then you *theorize* (like a scientist): Perhaps there's something important that I'm *not* seeing. You get your eyes down close to the water, sweep an aquarium net through the water's surface. You find midges.

Your new theory: The trout are ignoring the few big Green Drakes to take the ample midges. You test your new theory by putting up a fine tippet and a size 22 floating midge fly. And you start hooking those previously disdainful trout. Guess what? You're a scientist!

Tip 80 Half-Disturbed Trout May Move Only Halfway Down Tr-S

So, I was working a deep bank of mild current on Oregon's Lower Deschutes River, a desert monster of a trout stream. A cameraman was there, to shoot for a video (this was back when "video" meant a VHS tape or DVD for sale), and so was one of my friends who'd recommended the spot. "Always a few fish working by the bank there," he'd said. And there were.

We saw their dark forms holding high in the soft flow behind a great boulder exposing its dry, white top. Every few seconds, a trout would tip up to rise. The cameraman was loving the footage.

Then it was time for the catching. I made a dramatic (and, in fact, appropriate) creep into fishing position downstream, bent low. After a couple of practice casts, I dropped my dry fly just above the lowest trout. The fish took it. The cameraman shouted, "Great! Do it again."

So I did. Occasionally I pull off a fish-on-demand.

The cameraman wanted more fish, and so did I. But my friend said, "I can't see 'em. I think they're gone." I'd been through this scenario before, so I put on a nymph just heavy enough to go down three feet and worked my way up to the boulder, putting out the nymph, letting it drift and sink. Casting straight upstream, I was concerned about a strike indicator so instead watched the floating leader.

The trout weren't gone at all. They'd only gotten nervous and moved down two or three feet to safety. Not safe from me, though: I hooked three, landed two.

And that's the whole point: Trout in streams will often stay in the same spot but move deeper when they get a little spooked. You just have to fish deeper.

Tip 81 Here's How to Untwist Your Fly Line and Keep It from Tangling

Tr-S, Tr-L   Lg-L   Sm-L, Sm-S   Pf-L

Fly line likes to mess you up. It'll coil, tangle, catch on your shoes, find a way under foot—and twist. *Twist*—what an asinine thing for a line to do! After each cast, with rod in hand, do I execute a couple of somersaults? *Noooooo*. How and why then does fly line twist? A mystery to me.

Fly line just likes to somehow twist. Here's what you do to untwist it.

In a stream: (1) check to make sure your ferrules are secure and tighten them if they're not; (2) cut off your fly (now there's no fly to stop a rod section that comes loose and slides down the line and off, hence the ferrule check); (3) cast, and then pay out a lot of line so that it streams in the current for maybe a minute; and (4) done.

In a lake: Do steps 1 through 3. But since there's no current you'll need to row around for a bit towing the *un*twisting line behind you.

If a line takes on curls (from the reel's spool), just stretch it firmly between your hands, working down it in yard-long sections.

Tip 82 Bring It All

Tr-S, Tr-L   Lg-L   Sm-L, Sm-S   Pf-L

Without clarification, "Bring it all" could wind up being lousy advice. Say those words to the overcautious type, and she will find a way to justify hauling to the water a mountain of flies and tackle (as will he).

That's not what I'm suggesting.

Example: Three days ago I took an in-law who is new to fly fishing to a lake of large bluegills. Because each of the previous three times I'd fished the lake I caught all the bluegills I could want by plunking a little rubbery floating fly close to shoreline cover, I brought only rods with floating lines. I left at home the rods I nearly always carried along, the ones loaded with sinking lines. Care to guess what happened?

Correct: We needed those sinking-line rods.

The bluegills must have gone deep. We rowed around for three hours and caught a few small ones and a couple of small bass, but compared to my previous visits to that lake, it was dismal fishing; I'd come to expect 30, even 40 bluegills—per angler.

I should have brought the sinking-line rods so we could fish deep. A week later I returned with a sinking line and, again, caught all the bluegills I could want.

So here's what I *am* suggesting: *Do not* bring every possible line and fly and gadget and more, but when you go out fishing, *do* bring all the *standard* stuff. You know, like nymphs and strike indicators to a trout stream even if you plan to fish dry flies, poppers to a smallmouth river where you plan to fish crayfish flies. Never . . . assume.

Tip 83 Get a Fix on a Rising Fish

 Tr-S, Tr-L   Lg-L   Sm-L, Sm-S   Pf-L

Rising trout are the obvious subject here, but rising smallmouth bass, rising bluegills and pumpkinseeds and other panfish, and rising largemouths (I've seen that) are important too. Really, any kind of display—jumping, slashing, slurping—falls under this tip. Goes for lakes and streams both.

The point is, when a fish shows itself, immediately fix its location. *Then* you can go after it. Note its position relative to brush, boulders, trees, weed beds—anything along the shoreline or out in the water you can use as a marker.

Now wade up, row in, make a cast, whatever, and put the fly where it needs to be so that it's presented effectively to the fish (assuming the fish is still there—this is a game of playing the odds).

If you *don't* fix the position of your fish, and you're anything like me, you'll take your eyes off the spot to wade or row or do some distracting thing and suddenly you're going, Now where was that fish . . . ?

Tip 84 Fish the Edges of Groups of Fish

 Tr-S, Tr-L   Lg-L   Sm-L, Sm-S   Pf-L

Fish group. Perhaps it's because they've all bunched into a prime feeding line of current or a swatch of concealing shade or for spawning or just because they like to school. Trout, largemouth, smallmouth, bluegills and crappies and other panfish—I've found each grouped together many, many times.

What do you do about it?

Well, consider this: A dozen good trout are up sipping down Western March Brown mayfly duns along a line of current dappled with white foam. Where do you throw your floating fly? In the middle of the working fish? *Wrong.* Above the fish farthest upstream? *Wrong.*

You drop your fly above the trout holding farthest *down*stream, but below the next one up. When you hook the trout, you try to haul it downstream and away from the others quickly and quietly, so you can play it down where they won't notice. Of course, the trout may have other ideas . . . But you try.

If you get your way and the fish comes in without tipping off the others, you set your sights on the next fish up. If things keep going your way, you might land half those dozen trout before you put the rest down. But if you'd have cast into the center of them, you probably would have had a real shot at only one or two; you'd have scared off the rest.

Where there's current, forcing fish to face upstream, start with the fish farthest downstream and then work on up through the rest (if you can—with some methods and approaches you can't), and try not to let a fish you've hooked alarm the others.

In lakes, cast to the fish along the edges of the group (and, again, try to get your fish in quietly).

Tip 85 With Sinking Lines in Lakes, Keep Your Rod Tip Down

 Tr-L   Lg-L   Sm-L   Pf-L

Washington State, side to side and bottom to top, is loaded with trout lakes. Around here, we *know* lake fishing.

Go to one of our lakes and watch the fly fishers out in their boats and pontoon boats; watch until you pick out the ones who know what they're doing: They'll be the ones catching fish. Now look closer. See how they're angling their rods down, how their rod tips are touching or even just under the water?

That's part of why they're catching fish.

Imagine this: You're anchored out on a lake, your fly deep on a full-sinking line. Your rod tip is up, perhaps two feet above the water, and a trout grabs your fly. Question: What do you do? Answer: Absolutely nothing—because you didn't feel the take! Detecting a take with a deep fly on a sinking line is about *feeling* the fish sail off with, grab, or just stop your fly.

That short stretch of line hanging limp from your rod tip to the water is your problem—there's no possible way it'll communicate a take of your fly to your line hand so you can set the hook.

So as soon as you've cast out a full-sinking line on a lake, immediately drop your rod tip to the water, *and keep it there*. Now, as you retrieve the fly, your tippet, leader, and line all run straight to your rod tip and then straight up the rod's guides to your hand—you'll feel even a touch at your fly.

When you need to feel the take on a floating line, same story. Smallmouths, large-mouths, panfish, same story.

A consistently wet tip guide results in strong communication from fly to hand.

Tip 86 With Sinking Lines in Lakes, Keep Your Rod at an Effective Angle to Your Line Tr-L Lg-L Sm-L Pf-L

In the previous tip I described how experienced lake fly fishers hold their rod tips down to the water when they're fishing full-sinking lines, and why they do it. What I haven't yet told you is that the angle of their rods to their lines is also important.

Imagine you're one of those fly fishers, out in your anchored boat with your fly down near the lake bed, your rod tip down, your tippet and leader and line running straight from fly to rod tip—all set, right? Well, maybe . . .

You also need your rod, from a top view, in line with your fly line. If your rod is off to one side or the other, and there's an angle created between line and rod (still from a top view), then the rod's flex may cushion a take of your fly and you'll feel nothing, then do nothing in response.

Just line up rod and fly line. Looking down on them, you should see no angle.

But what if you can't line up rod and line? (It happens: boat has shifted in the wind, a second angler in the boat somehow makes it impossible, whatever . . .) Then go 90 degrees. I call this the lever retrieve, since the rod becomes a long sensitive lever at this right angle, transmitting every nuance to your rod hand as you work in the deep fly.

Lining up fly line and rod is the best approach, but the lever retrieve works, and is sometimes required.

What I call the "lever retrieve," rod and line forming a 90-degree angle

Rod and fly line aligned—the best way to feel a take of the fly. I used a yellow floating line for this photo, rather than the usual dark full-sinking line this technique usually applies to, so you could easily see the line. If you need to feel a fish take with a floating line, again, aligning your rod and line pays off.

Tip 87 Try Indicator Nymphing the Hatch When Floating Flies Fail

Picture this: A fair hatch of tiny mayflies spreads across a broad, smooth river. But here, where two currents meet, the insects collect—the length of a foamy current line bustles with waving wings, with struggles to extract bodies from shucks. But why are trout rising only here and there, now and then, and ignoring dries and emergers? They must know what happens here—they should be crowded in along the line of current, gorging. Fact is, they probably are.

Spotty rising, lots of bugs, no takers on floating flies—perhaps the trout are taking the nymphs below the river's surface and showing only when they chase a nymph up or grab an emerging dun on impulse. This, I'm now certain, is exactly what was happening. Oh yeah, it's real—I was there.

I could've tried a dry-and-dropper rig, but that current seam was choppy and a size 14 dry fly might've sunk. A big dry fly might've alarmed the fish. So I slipped a green pea–size strike indicator up my tippet, tied on a tiny nymph, fixed the indicator about a foot and a half up my tippet from the nymph, and, well, caught some fine trout—a rainbow and a couple of browns of around 14 to 17 inches.

After that, the hatch slowed—I'd probably caught it near the end. I went off then to fish other water in other ways.

Point is, the tiny mayfly-imitating nymph not far below a midget indicator (a white one, to blend in with the foam, easy for me to spot with its perfect-circle shape) did the job after plausible dry flies and floating emerger flies didn't. And did it better than a dry-and-dropper rig would have done it. Keep this strategy, and rig, in mind.

Tiny indicator, tiny nymph. Could be the right combo during a hatch of tiny mayflies.

Even in a pool this thin and window-clear, a large trout may hold close to the bank—and in such clear, thin water that trout will be in a state beyond skittish. That's why I'm squatting a few feet from the water and casting upstream with a low rod, along the pool's edge. I did hook and land a 17-inch rainbow here within a minute of Carol's taking this photo.

Tip 88 Respect the Edges

Tr-S, Tr-L   Lg-L   Sm-L, Sm-S   Pf-L

Here's the fly fisher you *don't* want to be: When you reach the water, you just trudge mindlessly out until you're knee deep. Then you start casting. The fish, however, were holding calf deep. But they're all off somewhere else now, of course, in shock.

Here's the fly fisher you do want to be: Back from the edge of the water, you stop and watch. Maybe you see a fish move in close, take a mayfly, churn the shallows after fry. But even if you don't see fish, any fish—largemouth, trout, green sunfish, whatever—or any sign of them, you do this: stay back and quietly work the close-in shallow water before you even think of walking up to the water's edge, much less stepping in.

Because you always do this, you hook many of your fish, sometimes big fish, where the water is thin.

Trout, largemouth and smallmouth bass, and some panfish will hold and feed right next to shore, even if the water barely covers their dorsal fins. I've seen it in both rivers and lakes.

I once caught a 12-inch rainbow that was sipping mayfly duns in the nearly dead water of a bitsy side channel way off the main river. I couldn't believe the fish was happily feeding in that ankle-deep puddle. I've caught good largemouths and smallmouths in standing water under a foot deep. In my relatively long life I've caught so many fish in still, swift, cloudy, and clear water along the edges of lakes and rivers that I always approach the edges with care and try fishing them before I fish farther out.

Tip 89 Here Are Some Two-in-a-Boat Strategies  Tr-S, Tr-L   Lg-L   Sm-L, Sm-S   Pf-L

There are good reasons to fish two in a boat—in a low johnboat or even a tricked-out bass boat on a lake, in a slender Au Sable river boat or bowed McKenzie drift boat on a river. Two in a boat allows one to fish while the other rows (when rowing's required), offers the testing of two flies or lines or techniques at once to determine which is best, allows two minds to work closely in figuring out the strategy of the moment or day, and turns fishing from a solitary into a sociable sport.

But it has drawbacks. Two waving rods so near one another is an invitation for tangles, or worse, hooks in anglers. A hooked big fish can tangle with the other angler's line. A clumsy move by one can throw the other off-balance—in firm-bottomed boats it's common for anglers to stand as they fish.

All these potential problems can be avoided. To keep from tangling lines when you and another fish from a boat, cast one at a time and talk. When you cast, say "Up," and when you're finished, say "Down." When you hook a good fish, the kind that goes wherever it wants, tell your partner; your partner should then quickly pull in line and fly. To keep from chucking each other out of the boat, move slowly, smoothly, with care, and warn your partner before you do anything that will tip the boat.

Tip 90 Save That Nymph or Streamer

Tr-S, Tr-L   Lg-L   Sm-L, Sm-S   Pf-L

I *hate* losing a nymph or streamer. But I do realize that losing these flies is often part of fishing them effectively, which consoles me, some . . . On the bright side, hating to lose flies has made me good at saving them.

The first principle of fly recovery is to pull the fly out opposite the way it went in. A nymph drifts downstream and gets stuck; you walk upstream and pull. Of course, if trying to pull the fly out opposite the way it went in doesn't work, you pull from other angles.

Get your fly stuck in a limb or log, and that's grim, though there's hope. First, don't tighten if you haven't already; then try the opposite-direction pull described above. You might get lucky . . .

If the fly just won't budge, tighten until it comes loose or until you near the breaking point of your tippet. Eventually you have to just pull until the fly comes free or the tippet breaks.

Always pull with the rod mostly pointed at the fly—this kind of pressure could break a deeply bent rod, and the bending serves no purpose. And snug down the ferrules first: With no fly to stop it, a section could slide down and away forever.

When my fly is stuck on a rocky streambed, neither too deep nor in water too swift, I'll wade out, pull the leader taut so I can determine where my fly is, and then push the stones around it with a boot. Often, rocks shift or part and the fly comes loose.

Tip 91 Work a Shoreline Thoroughly and Thoughtfully Tr-L Lg-L Sm-L Pf-L

If you drop your fly *randomly* around shoreline cover and features—docks, weed beds, fallen timber, boulders, or a gravel bed a few feet underwater—you'll miss fish you shouldn't have missed. Fishing lake shorelines can be very productive, but you need to fish them well.

So *read* the shoreline and try to identify the best cover (a floating log, a dense bed of lily pads. . .) or the most fish-attractive features (a tight, deep, little notch in the lake's edge, a rocky underwater shelf . . .). Then work that shoreline *systematically*. Put your fly along a dock next to shore; then drop it a little farther out the next time, progressively covering the whole dock, both the sides and the end. Of course, if you come to a complex spot, a patchwork of tiny weed beds for example, stop and work all through it. And if you catch a fish somewhere, it only makes sense to put your fly there a few more times to see if fish are clustered there.

Now drop your fly every foot to three feet along the shoreline, working your way to the next really promising spot—skipping none of it, because the fish may not agree with your assessment of where they should be.

The point is, you're now working the shoreline progressively, in a pattern, giving every possible fish-holding spot a chance and concentrating most on the best places. How wise you are.

Tip 92 Try the Mid-Depths for Trout

Tr-S, Tr-L

It's only logical that trout feed at the surface of a stream or lake when insects are floating on it, are gathering just under it, or are stuck for a while in it during the process of hatching. It's equally logical that when nothing's going on at the top of the water, trout will hold near the bed of a stream or lake where most of their predators can't reach them and where most of their feed lives.

But . . . fishing and *logic*? You can never rely on those two to get along.

So, for reasons mostly understood only by trout (if, in fact, there *are* reasons; logic and trout make another unstable pairing), you may find them feeding somewhere in the middle depths. It could be about comfort: oxygen levels, temperature, current. But when trout feed in the middle, it often seems they do so only to give logic a slap in the face.

I've found trout 25 feet down both along steep shorelines and out in open water where the bottom was at 50 or 60 feet. I've found trout feeding on caddis pupae halfway between the bottom and surface in a river matted, in some spots, with floating caddis adults.

So, if you're not catching trout at the perfectly logical top or bottom of a lake or stream, try the mid-depths.

Tip 93 Fish Where the Guides Don't Take Their Clients

 Tr-S, Tr-L   Lg-L   Sm-L, Sm-S   Pf-L

Fishing guides and their clients have the same right to the water you and I have. But we needn't all share the same parts of it.

Example: Two weeks ago Carol and I hiked upstream from a public boat launch on a large Montana river to fish some braided water. A drift boat would occasionally come through, but always through the largest braid, where there was room for a boat. None of the guides parked their boats and walked their clients up to fish the creek-size braids we fished. But those little braids were good. In one I landed an 18-inch rainbow and a bunch of cutthroats of various lengths while Carol happily took photos.

Guides often ignore braids because (1) guides have to hit their takeout points on time and can't afford to dally, (2) braids can be tricky to fish, and (3) a little braid isn't going to satisfy a client who came to fish a large river.

We also found a small, tight, deep eddy with trout rising among patches of white foam. An awkward spot to fish and a tough one to figure out. We finally realized we had to just keep putting the fly in the foam until a trout happened onto it. But would a guide set a client on that water and expect that client to make cast after cast to the same small area until something happened, while complex currents tried constantly to put drag on the fly? A smart guide wouldn't—most clients would fumble the spot, or grow bored with it.

Rivers, lakes, trout, bass—there are typically all sorts of awkward or difficult or challenging places holding plenty of fish that guides and their clients don't bother. So go to those places and bother some fish.

Tip 94 Find a Favorite Piece of Water and *Learn* It   Tr-S, Tr-L   Lg-L   Sm-L, Sm-S   Pf-L

Trout stream, bluegill pond, largemouth lake, whatever—you can learn a lot by turning a little lake, a reservoir bay, or a stretch of stream into your home turf. There are two main advantages of adopting a piece of fishing water of manageable size: (1) the more you understand it, the more fish you catch from it, and (2) you eventually see the patterns.

Number 1 just makes sense: If you fish the same water often, you'll learn what flies and techniques catch fish there and where the fish hold. So, more hookups—who doesn't want that?

Number 2 has much wider meaning. Let's say you've found a mile of trout stream you love. Keep going back to it. Try it in the morning, in the evening, in June when it's brimming, in September when it's small and clear. In time, the patterns of the fish—where they lie in high water, where they lie after the water drops, when they rise and when they won't, and a thousand other insights—reveal themselves. Patterns of fish, of feed, of method, and more all emerge when you keep returning to a trout stream, a smallmouth stream, a green sunfish pond, or *any* fishing water.

I had to stay low and cast quietly in order to present my fly to the nervous trout that were holding in this soft, shallow side channel. (Note the river to the left.)

But it worked! It'd be a rare client a guide would put on this water and on these trout. Guides want steady action for their clients, and some fine fishing places like this offer only action that's slow, demanding, and uncertain. Awfully fun, though.

What you learn on any water is universal to fishing (even if every water is also unique—a conundrum, eh?). You'll use that knowledge to guide you often for as long as you fish.

Tip 95 Fish Around

 Tr-S,Tr-L Lg-L Sm-L, Sm-S Pf-L

Advising you to try ever-new waters may seem to contradict the previous tip about finding some water you like and making it your second home. But it doesn't—you need familiar and unfamiliar water both to really grow as a fly fisher. The familiar water shows you those patterns I mentioned in the previous tip; the *un*familiar waters show you how wildly those patterns can vary, and how they are sometimes absent altogether. New waters open your mind.

Example: On nearly every trout stream I fish, I spend the bulk of my time wading the edges and casting out to deeper water or upstream along the bank. But years ago on a Pennsylvania stream new to me, I was told to wade quietly up the center of a pool and cast to the edges because that's where all the trout were. Why? I still have no idea. The center of the stream was good holding water; the edges seemed too slow and thin to hold trout. But there they were: trout rising in that slow, thin water. And there, I was also told, they always were.

I've seen lots of fishes break their patterns in certain waters. I've seen insects hatch when they shouldn't and hatch longer than they should. I've seen largemouth bass insist day after day on hair bugs fished far too quickly.

New water, new lessons. Besides, exploring a stream or lake you've never fished is fascinating, and fun.

Tip 96 Change Something

 Tr-S,Tr-L Lg-L Sm-L, Sm-S Pf-L

After the four years I spent fishing with, and calling, emailing, and plain hounding trout-lake guru Brian Chan with questions during my writing of the first edition of our book *Morris & Chan on Fly Fishing Trout Lakes*, I felt I'd earned my trout-lake bachelor's degree (still working on my master's; Brian holds a doctorate).

One day on a lake, when Brian said it was time to move, already our third move that morning, I asked why. He said something like, "Because we're not catching fish." I followed that up with a string of new questions. Here's essentially what Brian told me, way back in the mid-'90s: "If you're not getting fish after a while, change something." I'd already been doing that, for a long, long time, but I'd never thought about it until he put it neatly into words.

So what is "a while"? Brian recently clarified that by laying out a formula that gets a smidge complicated. But the bottom line I get from it is this: change location, fly pattern, water depth, fly depth, technique—change *something* if you don't get a take after 10 or 20 minutes.

The real point here is that you shouldn't just rig up a fly, find a spot, and, despite failing to move even one trout, stick with both all day. Instead, give a fly, a spot, a presentation a little time, and if it turns up nothing, try another fly or spot or presentation. *Change* something.

Same with largemouth, smallmouth, panfish—if they're not biting, change something.

Tip 97 Fish the Right Sinking Line for the Right Retrieve

 Tr-S, Tr-L   Lg-L   Sm-L, Sm-S   Pf-L

In lakes, to keep a fly down just off the bottom while retrieving it at a proper speed, you'll need the *right* full-sinking line. Unfortunately, all the different retrieves for various imitations and all that range of depth make it impossible to fit everything into a complete, simple formula. (Though you could fit it all into a very complicated one . . .)

A formula for identifying when you're using the *wrong* line? *That* I can do: If you use the countdown method and keep snagging bottom near the end of your retrieve, your line sinks too quickly; if you use the countdown method and the boredom is painful from counting so high, and your fly still never touches the lake bed, your line sinks too slowly.

A formula of sorts can work, provided it's really broad. Here's one for lakes: fast retrieve, fast-sinking line; slow retrieve, slow-sinking line; deep water, fast-sinking line; water shallow to middling deep, slow-sinking line. As you can see, this stuff requires some experimentation, and experience. Just go spend time fishing lakes with sinking lines; you'll work it out.

It's really the same with sink-tip lines in streams: faster-sinking lines for fast retrieves, deep water, or both; the reverse for slow-sinking lines. But you have to consider current speed too, so: fast currents, fast-sinking line; slow current, slow-sinking line. Any formula for streams will be an especially sloppy formula because streams often change so much from stretch to stretch. So you just coax whatever line you chose into doing more than it wants to do.

Tip 98 Keep Crimping

 Tr-S

Why do so many fly fishers resist adding more than one split shot to their indicator nymph rigs? Yes, even one split shot may be unnecessary with one or more heavy nymphs, especially if the water's neither fast nor deep. But currents quick, deep, or both may require two, perhaps three big shots to a get a nymph down to the fish. Your nymph (or at least the lowest one in a multiple-fly dropper or trailer rig) typically needs to bump the streambed now and then to ensure it's down where the trout are. If it doesn't, keep adding shot until it does.

I can't even hope to recall how many times, while fishing some river or creek, I added one more shot and suddenly slow fishing started to sizzle.

Yes, every added shot makes casting a tad clumsier. But if you're fishing a nymph rig with one or more weighted flies, and perhaps a strike indicator—already a caster's plague—why not?

CHAPTER 3

TECHNIQUES THAT CATCH FISH

Tip 99 Learn the Hand-Twist Retrieve

 Tr-S,Tr-L   Lg-L   Sm-L, Sm-S   Pf-L

The most natural way to work in fly line and make a fly swim is the strip retrieve. But there's a weak step in the strip retrieve that tends to lose fish.

There's no weak step in the hand-twist retrieve.

The hand-twist also slows the newbie to a real creeping of the fly—new fly fishers nearly always whip their flies in way too quickly with a strip retrieve. The hand-twist is used mainly for fishing lakes and sometimes for streams. On *trout* lakes it's standard practice. Some of us, however, use it often in lakes for the basses and panfish. I use it on trout and smallmouth streams regularly.

The hand-twist starts with the rod's grip and the fly line both held in one hand, then:

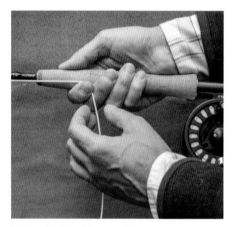

The hand-twist retrieve, step 1 SKIP MORRIS

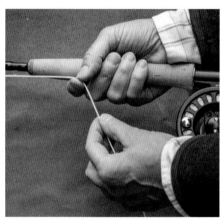

The hand-twist retrieve, step 2 SKIP MORRIS

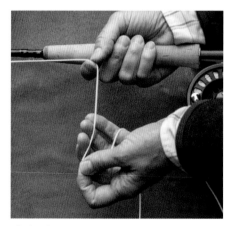

The hand-twist retrieve, step 3 SKIP MORRIS

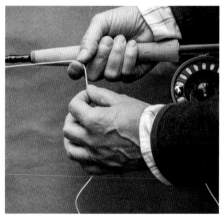

Just keep going, beginning again with step 1.
SKIP MORRIS

The free hand grasps the line and then rotates, lowering the thumb and first finger and raising the little finger, while pulling a few inches of line down from the rod hand.

The raised little finger reaches up and catches the line.

The hand rotates back to raise thumb and first finger as the lowering little finger draws a few more inches of line from the rod hand.

With the little finger holding the line, thumb and first finger again grasp the line, and then go down again pulling in another few inches of line, and so on.

The retrieving hand is constantly releasing the line it captures so the line hangs and does not kink or tangle.

Tip 100 Get the Most Out of the Strip Retrieve Tr-S, Tr-L Lg-L Sm-L, Sm-S Pf-L

New fly fishers, even if they're not shown the strip retrieve, usually figure it out because it's just so logical. But that doesn't mean they do it well.

When you hold the fly line lightly between your thumb-tip and the first, and perhaps second, fingertip of your rod hand, then reach up and grasp the line just below that hand with your free hand and pull down to draw some in—*that's* stripping line. You can strip quickly, slowly, an inch or two up to over a foot of line in each strip.

First: Remember to always grasp the line *below* the hand holding rod and line—never reach for the line *above* the rod-line hand.

Second: Be sharp—there's a weak moment in stripping line, and fish seem to know exactly when it comes. That's the moment when you grasp the line for a strip, the moment when you naturally loosen your grip on the line to help it start sliding through— the same moment the fish grabs your fly. You swing the rod tip back for a hook set, but all that happens is the line just slips through your wimpy grip and out the guides. The fish, of course, smug, a big grin on its slippery lips, glides off with a hearty laugh. But if you're really on your toes, you can clamp onto the line in time to tug the hook home.

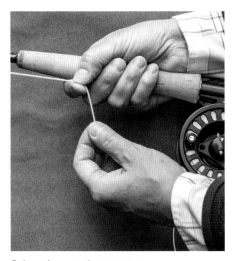

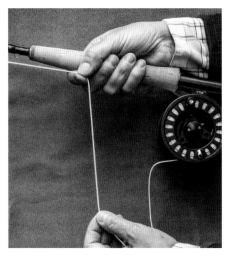

Strip retrieve, step 1 SKIP MORRIS

Strip retrieve, step 2. Easy, eh? Has its advantages, disadvantages. SKIP MORRIS

Tip 101 Get Indicator Nymph Fishing Down Tr-S

The standard and most versatile method for fishing a nymph in a trout stream is still to hang it from a strike indicator. It's not complicated. You (1) cast everything upstream; (2) watch the indicator and set the hook if it tells; (3) raise your rod tip high as the indicator drifts near, then lower the rod as it continues downstream; (4) let the indicator pause at the end of the drift; and finally, (5) pick it all up and cast it all upstream again.

Indicator nymphing may be simple in theory, but it's easy to get wrong. That's why even though some of what follows appears elsewhere in these pages, I put the key elements and some extra guidelines here, in one place, so you can see how they function together.

Let's flesh this out. The numbered comments below correspond to the numbered steps above: (1) cast smoothly, with long strokes, wide loops; (2) set the hook at even the *slightest* tell of the indicator; (3) raise the rod tip to allow indicator and nymph a long drift—the longer the drift, the more water it covers; (4) pause once the indicator stops at the end of the drift to swing the nymph upward—that can trigger a strike; and (5) make each drift, or each second drift, of the nymph out just past the previous one, to run the fly through all the good water.

Additionally, the nymph needs to ride inches off the streambed, which means you'll snag the bottom now and then; it also means you'll never really know if you got a take or your fly tapped a rock, so don't guess—just *set* that hook. Getting your nymph down may require weight up the tippet; use as much as it takes. Finally, set the hook *immediately* when the indicator tells. And, of course, rig right. (See tip 276.)

Tip 102 Find a Reason to Set with a Strike Indicator Tr-S,Tr-L

A friend of mine who likes to snorkel in rivers (friend A) once settled into a clear pool until the trout took him for granted. Then another friend (friend B)—a first-rate indicator nymph fisher—fished a nymph. Friend A watched through his diving mask as, in his words, "Trout kept taking that nymph without B setting the hook—on one drift, *four* different fish." A asked B why he never set the hook. B said, "Because the *indicator* didn't move."

Jason Randall, from his book *Nymph Masters: Fly-Fishing Secrets from Expert Anglers*: "Countless hours of underwater filming have convinced me that we're missing far more fish than we're catching simply because we're not detecting strikes."

The point: When you fish a strike indicator and a nymph, set the hook at any possible tell—a dip, a twitch, even a touch of increased drag. You can't count on trout to jerk that indicator down.

Rick Hafele (entomologist, author of *Nymph-Fishing Rivers & Streams*) suggests you watch your indicator closely and find a reason to set the hook on *every* drift. Searching for any irregularity—for the slightest *excuse* to set the hook—will put you and your indicator tightly in tune. Goes for indicator fishing in trout lakes too.

Tip 103 If You're Not Losing Nymphs, You're Nymph Fishing Wrong Tr-S

I have a nymph fisher's malady—I hate losing flies. This makes me a smidge timid when I nymph-fish streams, whether indicator style, Czech-nymph style, hopper-dropper . . . So I press myself to do the right thing: to get that nymph down among the streambed cobble and boulders and occasionally lose a fly. And then I catch more trout. I'm a good person. I want to do the right thing.

You can overdo the right thing, though—if you're losing a nymph, say, every 10 minutes, even every half hour, that's too much. Lower your indicator, remove a spit shot, do whatever you have to do to raise that nymph so it's only ticking a streambed boulder now and then rather than snagging constantly.

It's reasonable to lose one or two, perhaps even four nymphs in a day's indicator or Czech-nymph fishing on a stream. But beyond that? Probably too many.

Some streambeds are loaded with rough, fly-snatching volcanic stone or submerged logs or tree limbs that grab a fly and hold on to it—in such waters you just have to fish the nymph higher than you'd like. It'll still find trout.

It's true that a nymph in a trout stream is normally most effective when it's drifting just off the bottom where the trout hold. But there are exceptions and sensible limits.

Tip 104 Raise Your Rod When Indicator Nymphing Tr-S

When you toss a strike-indicator rig upstream, the nymph, perhaps along with split shot or other weight up the tippet, sinks quickly. But as it's sinking, it's getting swept downstream. Soon, it reaches The Zone, down where the trout normally hold, only inches off the streambed; by that point, however, your indicator is probably across from you. Until then, until the nymph is deep, your odds of a take are low.

Therefore, you want the indicator and nymph to keep drifting past you as far as reasonably possible, right? The more water the nymph covers down in The Zone, the better its chances of meeting a fish.

This is exactly why good indicator nymph fishers raise their rod tips ever higher as their indicators drift downstream ever closer, to take in line without pulling it in through the rod's guides: The line's then easy to feed back out, by just slowly lowering the rod tip.

Still, there are reasonable limits. With the tip of a rod pushed to maximum height, the arm stretched up to its limit, how do you tug the hook home? You really can't. It's okay to pull in some line if you need to as the indicator comes close, and to waggle that line back out to feed the rig's drift.

An upstream cast, rod tip at a comfortable height.
SKIP MORRIS

Indicator nears, rod tip keeps rising. (The arm can be raised if needed.) SKIP MORRIS

Indicator drifts past, rod tip descends. SKIP MORRIS

Tip 105 Give Czech Nymphing a Whirl

 Tr-S

Czech nymphing (also referred to as "Euro nymphing" and other names) has been all the rage for some years now. And I'm finally just good enough at this method to competently introduce you to it.

There are two standard approaches. The first is under-or-nearly-under-the-rod-tip Czech nymphing, which George Daniel says in his book *Dynamic Nymphing* is "not practical for low, clear, or placid water." He says it's for "heavily riffled water" and "high and dirty water"—stream types and stream conditions that allow you to get close to trout without spooking them.

Second is the reaching-out kind of Czech nymphing, where you cast your flies up to 40 feet out into the current. This reaching-out approach works with about any kind of stream because you're far enough away to go unnoticed by the trout (if you're stealthy, that is).

In *Nymph Masters: Fly-Fishing Secrets from Expert Anglers*, Jason Randall, the author, says the key difference between close-in and reaching-out Czech nymphing rigs is that "lighter flies and longer leaders" go with reaching out. The result: With either approach very little line is out the rod tip.

George presents a standard rig for Czech nymphing, and a slightly simplified version is all laid out in the illustration below. Note the "sighter," usually some stout, colored monofilament (for close-in Czech nymphing only).

CLOSE-IN CZECH NYMPHING

Creep into position slowly, quietly. Lob the flies upstream and not far out. Let the sighter lie on the water as the nymphs sink. The moment the leader or sighter jerks, as the nymphs touch bottom, raise the rod tip and lift the sighter off the water. Swing the elevated rod tip downstream *slightly faster* than the flies to keep tension on them. If you feel a stop of the flies or the sighter twitches—set the hook.

REACHING-OUT CZECH NYMPHING

Pretty much the same as close-in Czech nymphing, but you cast the flies well out before you let them sink and then lead them with your rod tip. And no sighter.

This all sounds pretty easy, but in fact requires practice.

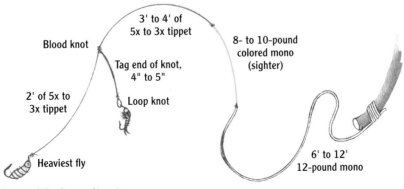

An all-around Czech-nymphing rig

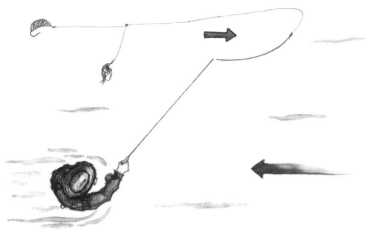

Step 1. Work quietly into position. Lob the nymphs (or nymph) upstream.

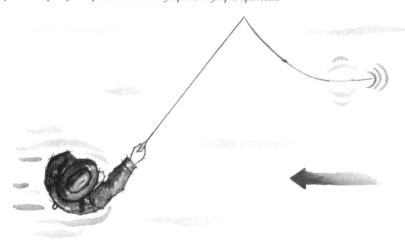

Step 2. Let the nymphs (or nymph) sink freely.

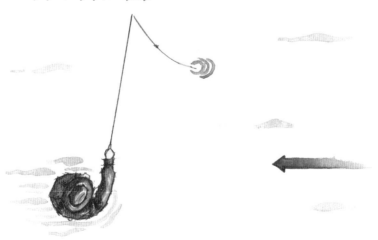

Step 3. Raise the rod tip, in turn lifting the sighter above the water. Swing the tip downstream only slightly faster than the leader.

Tip 106 There's More Than One Good Way to Pop a Popper (Two, Actually, at Least That I Know)

 Lg-L Sm-L, Sm-S Pf-L

Usually, the best way to fish a hair bug or popper for largemouth bass, smallmouth bass, or panfish is to start by giving it a pop. Actually, more a chug or gurgle—tell some people to pop a popper, and they'll mimic the jarring backfire of an '84 Plymouth.

One problem with making a popper or bug fuss is that you may move the fly away from that ideal spot where you put it. Here are the two ways I get a little commotion out of a hair bug or popper without moving it much, or at all.

The first way: With the popper on the water, and a little bit of loose line hanging beneath the rod's tip (held low, just above the water), I snap the tip to the side, usually not very far, then snap it right back to where it started. The effect: The slack line runs quickly out and the momentum of the rod tip suddenly hits the line to jerk the popper; but before the line can drag the popper, the rod tip is back in its starting position and the line hangs limp from it once again.

The second way: The fly *smacks* down to alert the fish, and stays right where it landed. I make a low forward cast with a tight loop, a little extra force, and even a little pulling back on the rod at the final moment to speed up the fly. It hits the water, *wham!* This way is best with buoyant but somewhat heavy flies: poppers, foam flies, sodden hair bugs . . . (I especially like to smack down my Predator, a stout fly composed mostly of fleshy foam.)

Tip 107 Learn the Countdown Method for Lakes Tr-L Lg-L Sm-L Pf-L

Picture this: The trout or bass or panfish are feeding within a foot or two of the lake bed. You're sitting in your anchored rowboat. You need to get your sinking line (and consequently, your fly) within a foot or two of the lake bed.

How can you be sure the fly is down with the fish, not 4 feet above them or dragging across the lake bed? Use the countdown method.

1. Make a long cast (the longer the cast, the more water your fly covers) with a full-sinking line (not a sink-tip).
2. Count as you let the line and fly sink. (I go, "One one thousand, two one thousand . . .") Just hold the line and do *not* pull any in whatsoever.
3. When you figure the fly and line are near the bottom, retrieve the fly at a pace neither so slow it lets the line and fly keep sinking nor so quick it drags them upward.
4. When the line's in, check the fly. If it's clean and you never felt the tug of the lake bed during your retrieve, add another count or two before starting your retrieve after your next cast. Keep adding counts until you find the lake bed, then back up one count. But if you check your fly and find a bit of aquatic plant or such on it or you did feel the pull of the lake bed during your retrieve, shorten up your count

before retrieving after the next cast. Keep subtracting counts until you stop touching the lake bed with your fly.

Now you can count your fly down into that zone just above the lake bottom where the fish are holding, on every cast. Perfect.

Tip 108 Avoid the Standard Trolling Mistakes Tr-L Lg-L Sm-L Pf-L

Dragging a fly behind a boat or other watercraft on a lake—that is, "trolling"—may seem unworthy of our refined, elegant, venerable sport, but I do it all the time. I also sling weighted nymphs that whizz past my ears and engage big largemouth bass in something like hand-to-hand combat. Refined and elegant don't worry me—I just want to have fun . . . and catch fish.

Trolling catches fish. I use the method mostly for trout, but I've caught smallmouths, including some big boys, while trolling in lakes and reservoirs and occasionally caught largemouths by trolling, and I fall back on the method during the summer fishing slump for such panfish as bluegills and yellow perch.

Guess what? Trolling is actually tricky.

The first big mistake many new trollers make is failing to get their flies deep enough—only a *full-sinking* line with a type III sink rate, or higher, will normally do it, and on average at least *two-thirds* of that entire line must be out the rod tip if it's going to *stay* near the bottom in water a dozen to 16 feet deep, the typical trolling range. Yes, trolling the mid-depths can be effective, *very* effective. But typically, it's not.

The second big mistake new trollers make is to troll far too fast. Fast trolling hauls the line and fly back up. Row or fin lazily to troll.

The third mistake: putting all the line out right away. To avoid snagging the bottom, make a long cast, row or fin a ways, let out maybe five feet of line, row or fin . . .

The fourth mistake: not stripping in the fly (don't reel up all that line—*strip* it in) to check it for debris every 10 or 15 minutes.

Tip 109 Troll So That Your Fly Swims Naturally Tr-L Lg-L Sm-L Pf-L

You can troll for trout, the basses, and panfish at a constant speed and direction, never touching or, if you're holding it, never moving your rod, but I advise against it. Few of the critters down in a lake swim in straight paths at a robotic pace.

So turn your boat now and then, do a little zigzagging. Slow down and then row or pump your fins a little faster, varying your speed. Make your fly lurch occasionally, either by jerking on your rod or, if your rod's set in a rod holder or lying on your boat seat, giving the line a quick pull just above the reel. Give that trolled fly some personality.

Tip 110 Use Your Trolling Time Wisely

 Tr-L   Lg-L   Sm-L   Pf-L

It's a shame if you troll but troll carelessly. Trolling a nymph or streamer in a trout, smallmouth, largemouth, or panfish lake shouldn't be a careless affair—you need to gauge your depth, check your fly regularly for debris, stay alert for a strike, experiment with different flies and areas of the lake if your action is slow. But eventually you can do all that and still use part of your attention in highly profitable ways.

I especially like to troll when I first meet a new lake. Of course, if a big chironomid hatch is on or I find bluegills bunched together back in the shade of a big leafy tree, I'll focus on that. But if nothing special is happening, I'll likely troll.

I troll, in part, because trolling a fly can be a deadly method. But also because it allows me to explore. As I troll, I can watch the shoreline for weed beds and fallen timber and other things that attract fish. I can find the bays and my deep fly can tell me when I've found a shoal or a drop-off (even though my fish-finder will tell me what's down there far better). I can watch the water's surface for the shucks of hatched insects, watch other anglers to see where they're finding fish and how they're catching them.

Trolling can be highly profitable, both for fish catching and for learning. You just have to take all of it seriously.

Tip 111 Beware the Trolling Tap

 Tr-L

Trout are pranksters. One of their favorite tricks is to jerk on my trolled fly to make me leap for my rod, set the hook, and then expect to feel one of them going wild on the other end. But they're just down there, laughing it up.

When you get a tug on your deep, trolled fly and your rod tip does a short, quick dip and then immediately straightens back up, wait a moment before doing anything. Odds are you got a useless tap (I have no idea how trout do that without getting hooked). Now, watch that rod tip closely and be ready to set the hook—a tap is usually followed soon by a solid take.

Yeah, trout . . . Real funny.

Tip 112 Try Topwater Trolling

 Tr-L

Here's one you never hear about: trolling a *floating* (or barely sunken) fly on a *floating* line. To nearly all fly fishers, trolling is a deep-fly method, and that's that.

Sometimes I feel as though I'm the only one who trolls with a floating line. I even had to name the technique myself.

I topwater troll when trout are showing casually but steadily on the surface, usually when the floating feed is a mix: perhaps flying ants and a few mayfly spinners, along with some hatching caddisflies. The trout have enough to make rising pay off, but only if they take it all. They're up, but scattered, hard to target.

On the left is the Tom Thumb, a Canadian pattern, and in the center is my Morris Emerger. Each has a wing of fanned hair that tilts forward—that wing allows the fly to skim the water, even pop back up onto it after a dunking. On the right is another Morris Emerger with its half-circle wing shown from the front.

You can use any reasonable fly out there in the mix, but you have to really cover the water. Trolling in any form covers lots of water because the fly is always moving and it's always out with the fish.

There are two approaches to topwater trolling: a floating fly and a barely sunken nymph. Any reasonable nymph will usually do, something in a 14 or 12 perhaps, with some weight, imitating something that might be up there such as a mayfly nymph or caddis pupa intent on hatching. (No scud with an ounce of dignity, for example, would swim up near the surface.)

A floating fly must stay afloat. I like a fanned-wing fly such as the Tom Thumb or my own Morris Emerger—their tipped-forward wings skim the water as does the angled bow of a boat.

Dry fly or nymph, topwater trolling should be a slow affair, with pauses, the fly out there on plenty of line with plenty of leader and tippet. (I use a 9-foot leader and 3 feet of tippet.)

Tip 113 Try a Floating Nymph on a Sinking Line   Tr-L   Lg-L   Sm-L   Pf-L

Sounds weird, doesn't it, dragging a buoyant fly around in a lake on a sinking line? Well, it's effective: The line rides down near the bottom with all its snaggy weeds and water-logged wood, while the fly swims safely along just above all that trouble.

Do I see the glow of enlightenment rising in your eyes?

Flies made largely of foam rubber—and there are many such flies these days—are the most stubborn floaters of all and therefore the best for this business. The trick lies in finding the ones that are designed for fishing deep. For trout, a popular buoyant fly for sinking-line fishing is the Boobie Fly. I fish my pudgy, foam Predator fly on a sinking line often for largemouths, smallmouths, panfish, and trout. Both flies tend to gill-hook, and therefore injure or kill fish if not fished properly. The trick is to keep these flies moving so a fish doesn't have time to swallow them.

Keeping a buoyant fly fished on a sinking line in motion is a good strategy for large-mouth and smallmouth bass and panfish too, but in their case because they'll bite it and spit it out in a blink—but a blink is all you need if that fly keeps moving. You'll feel the take right away.

Sometimes I anchor and use the countdown method with this setup; sometimes I troll. Goes for trout, bass, panfish.

Tip 114 Consider Tenkara

 Tr-S

Tenkara fishing is practiced with a very long and limber rod entirely free of guides, with no reel, and the line fixed to the rod's tip—so what happens if, on this setup, you hook a hot 18-inch rainbow trout that wants shoot off 80 feet? Well, at least you can relax for the first 20 feet. . . . But, really, here's your best strategy: Don't hook an 18-inch rainbow.

Tenkara is a traditional Japanese style of fly fishing designed for small trout in creeks and mountain streams. Mostly, I suspect, to test the limits of tenkara tackle and technique, some fly fishers will use both to hook big trout in rivers. I don't recommend it.

Tenkara's not for streams hemmed by trees either—imagine waving an 11-foot rod in the sort of tunnel their trunks and branches form over the water. Pains me to envision it: a steady succession of fly snaggings.

So, you need a creek or stream that's fairly open along its banks, one offering little chance of hooking a hot trout over, say, 13 inches. Find that and you're set. But, set to do what?

To do this: flick a casting loop down the surprisingly wispy line, and then, once the fly lands, to discover that you can throw curls and waves down that line to make the fly flip from side to side on the water, even do somersaults. The fly looks so real, so alive, so . . . unlike an artificial fly. I've seen these tricks make trout go mad, charge a fly with a wild carelessness.

Tenkara is for fishing dry flies, but I've done well tenkara fishing with tiny indicators and small nymphs. And it's (just my opinion) a hoot!

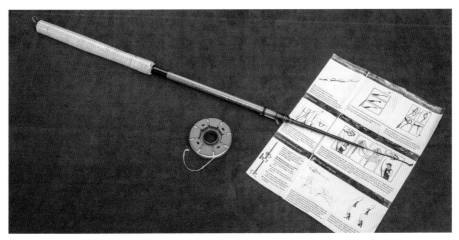

Modern tenkara rods like this one pack small, each short section slipping down inside the one below it.

A tenkara rod (and my wife Carol) in action—long rod, eh? (The wife is of average height.) Tenkara rods tend to be long. (I recently saw one that was 14 ½ feet.) SKIP MORRIS

Tip 115 Here's How to Fish Tenkara Style without a Tenkara Rod  Tr-S

With a reel seat, guides, and finish-coated thread windings to secure those guides, no conventional fly rod is ever going to feel like a long, limber, ultra-lightweight tenkara rod. And that length and willowy action of a tenkara rod are part of what makes fishing one a delight. If I can fish a real tenkara rod when I fish tenkara style, I do.

Sometimes, though, I can't, or at least it's not practical. Then I cheat.

I bring a longish standard fly rod for a light line—say, a 9-foot 4-weight—to a stream or creek, and in a pocket in my fishing vest I carry a typically short and crazy light tenkara line. Maybe there's brush at first, so I fish in the usual Western way. Then things open up: a meadow stretch. I cut off my tippet, store it, and tie the tenkara line to the point of my leader. Then I reel the connection between the two up to my tip guide, and start tenkara fishing with my conventional fly rod.

A few things must be in order. The tippet on the end of the tenkara line must be lighter than the point of my tapered leader so that if I lose the fly, I won't lose the tenkara line with it. I'll set the drag on my reel just tight enough so that the spool doesn't slip as I fish—if I hook a fish that runs, I lighten the drag setting immediately.

Tenkara cheating may lack that airy freedom of real tenkara fishing, but it works.

Tip 116 Animating Dry Flies Can Pay Off

Tr-S, Tr-L   Lg-L   Sm-L, Sm-S   Pf-L

For trout or smallmouth bass rising in streams, you normally want to make your dry fly drift freely on the currents ("dead drift"). On lakes, among rising trout, or largemouth bass, or panfish (and probably rising smallmouths too, though I haven't yet seen that on lakes), you often give your fly twitches between pauses, or even skim the fly across the water. But there are times when you'll catch more fish in streams if, as is common on lakes, you animate your dry fly.

A twitched or skimmed dry fly on a stream serves one, or both, of two main purposes: (1) to imitate a twitching or scurrying or buzzing insect, and (2) to just wake up the fish.

Because stream currents like to draw down tippets, you'll probably need to smear fly floatant along yours if you want to tug on your fly without sinking it. (Obviously, work floatant into your fly too.) A fairly bushy, buoyant fly is best for twitching or skimming, especially one with plenty of hard, bright hackle fibers sticking out of it. But on slow, clear water with cagey trout, you may need to use one that's sparsely dressed.

Tip 117 Try the Old Spider/Skater Trick on Trout Tr-S

I've been skating dry flies on trout streams since I was a kid, but not often, and I've never put much effort into honing the technique—I practice it only when nothing else is working or I just want to see a trout blitz a dry fly. Normally, I go with more conventional approaches.

For spider skating, the old Badger Spider is as good a fly as any.

Ed Engle *has* worked at figuring this business out; that's obvious if you read his book *Trout Lessons*. In it, he tells about the history of a fly called the Neversink Skater, about how Edward Hewitt came up with the design clear back in the 1920s.

Ed Engle, the first Ed, advises you to cast a skated fly across or downstream, and keep the rod high to "hold as much fly line off the water as possible." Then, he says, work the fly by "lifting the rod or drawing it across your body" to "hop, skip, or skate the fly upstream or across the current." He also advises you to pause long, after a trout slams the fly, before you set the hook.

A Neversink Skater or similar fly (such as the Cream Variant or Badger Spider), with very long hackles and a light-wire, short-shank, dry-fly hook that's way too small to suit those hackles, is easy enough to tie but a problem if you don't tie: The catalogs I checked don't carry them. If you're not a tier, ask at your local fly shop if someone there will tie you up a few.

Yes, you may miss a lot of strikes while skating skaters, but those strikes will be doozies. And some strikes will take.

Tip 118 Try Dancing a Dry-and-Dropper Rig 🐟 Tr-S 🐟 Sm-S

What's more natural than a nymph darting upward or a caddisfly adult flitting up and then dropping back onto the water? *Nothing*—that's what mayfly nymphs and caddis adults often do. You can create that effect with your flies when fishing a dry fly with a nymph dropper.

In *Dynamic Nymphing*, author George Daniels goes all through this technique. He's clearly spent more time with it than I have, so I relied on him for much of what follows.

Use a long leader (and ideally, a long rod).

Stick with short casts, working the flies in fairly close with little if any line out of the rod tip.

Use a nymph of at least fair weight. (George sometimes dances two nymphs, one as a point fly and one as a dropper.)

Hold your rod high and well out at the end of your raised, extended arm.

After the flies have drifted far enough for the nymph to have fully sunk, raise and lower the dry fly, up off the water and then back down to it, in turn raising and lowering the nymph.

The trick, of course, lies in getting close enough to pull this off without scaring off the trout. Some water depth, quick currents, brush to blend in with, and crouching can all help you.

I've tried this trick only occasionally for smallmouth bass in streams, and it worked. Dancing a dry-and-dropper rig for smallies makes sense to me. I've long noticed that smallmouths typically prefer a lively nymph over one fished dead drift. And why wouldn't they like a lively dry fly, suggesting a lively insect? (My point: They would.)

Tip 119 If Your Line Isn't Moving, Neither Is Your Fly

Tr-S, Tr-L   Lg-L   Sm-L, Sm-S   Pf-L

There are rare situations in which your fly is animated while your line remains in place—chironomid fishing for one, where the waves on a lake raise and drop a strike indicator and the fly hanging below it—but normally, your line must move for your fly to swim.

Watch your line. Whether it's a sinking line or a floating line, if it's moving through or across the water, your fly is active (unless there's slack somewhere between it and your fly). If it's not moving, neither is your fly.

Often, because of the peculiarities of a stream's currents or because of wind pushing a boat around on a lake, the fly fisher may be drawing in line with strips or the hand-twist while the line and fly remain stationary. To prevent this problem, watch the line and draw it in a little faster, then a little faster yet, until you can see it moving.

When fishing sinking lines, just watch the section of the line you can see in the water and note if it's moving *through* the water or not. Floating lines are easy: Since they're up on top and usually of pale or even bright colors, just watch the line's tip.

Don't get get caught retrieving line while not retrieving the fly. Just watch the line.

Tip 120 Smack Down *Some* Flies

 Tr-S,Tr-L   Lg-L   Sm-L, Sm-S   Pf-L

A hair bug or popper smacked down hard onto the water can be just right for large-mouths, smallmouths, and panfish. The smack catches the attention of the fish, and does it *without* your having to tug the fly away from where you wanted it in the first place. A grasshopper fly can stay close to a cutbank, a hair bug can stay inches from a lily pad. Get a fly too far from fish cover—"too far" sometimes determined by mere inches—and the fish may lose all interest.

So you aim your forward cast low, overpower it, send a tight loop down the line, perhaps even pull back on the line slightly just before the fly hits the water, and *smack*, it hits hard. It gets noticed. And stays home.

Tip 121 Learn Underappreciated Dapping, and Here's a Trick to Make It Go Smoothly Tr-S

It's almost a sure bet: The method that first put an artificial fly in front of a fish was casting-free, dirt-primitive dapping. Here's how dapping worked then and works now: (1) with the fly hanging straight below the rod tip on some tippet (or woven animal hair or gut or whatever the earliest fly fishers used for leader or tippet), hold the fly over the fish and then (2) lower the fly to the water. No caveats required here—that's it.

Most fly fishers reserve dapping for creeks, where, indeed, it's a lifesaver. Brush, tree limbs, tiny pools under fallen timber—dapping lets you reach slowly in through all the trouble, perhaps with just a foot or two of tippet between fly and rod tip, and set the fly where the trout are. But dapping can serve on larger waters. I've dapped from the one open spot on a high bank or through the brush of a side channel on streams and even plain-big rivers to catch trout I couldn't have reached any other way.

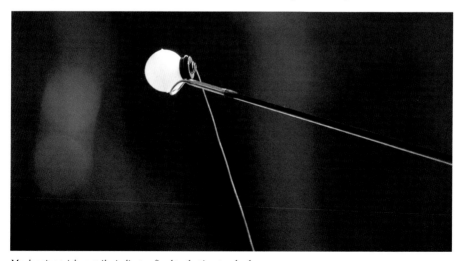

My dapping trick: a strike indicator fixed to the tippet or leader

Why struggle to cast into that dinky pocket under the complication of those outstretched branches when you could just set the fly on the water? SKIP MORRIS

Though dapping is always presented as a dry-fly method, I use dapping sometimes with nymphs, with or without a strike indicator. And, though rarely, I've dapped to catch smallmouths, largemouths, and bluegills.

The problem with dapping is that the line is heavier than the tippet and fly, so it drops and consequently pulls the fly up to the rod's tip guide. My solution: Attach a tiny strike indicator to your tippet or leader—the line can't pull in the indicator, of course, but if the fish runs, the indicator goes out with it. An indicator that attaches and comes off easily, without being threaded up the tippet and leader (such as a screw-cap indicator), is the handiest for this business.

CHAPTER 4

CASTING—DELIVERING FLY TO FISH

Tip 122 Casting Is Key

 Tr-S, Tr-L   Lg-L   Sm-L, Sm-S   Pf-L

There are a lot of tasks that must be accomplished at least adequately in order for you to hook and land a fish: identifying fish lies, selecting a suitable fly, hook setting . . . But I'll call it: Casting is typically the most important of them all.

With the exception of trolling, it's casting alone that gets your fly out to a fish. If you don't get your fly out far enough to reach a fish or accurately enough for the fish to see it, you don't catch the fish. It's that simple.

So develop your casting. Make it smooth, to avoid tangles. Work up, *patiently*, *gradually*, to some distance, so you have it when you need it. Develop accuracy. Practice. Casting practice is always time spent wisely, especially in the beginning.

Tip 123 Pick a Grip

 Tr-S, Tr-L   Lg-L   Sm-L, Sm-S   Pf-L

Most newbie fly casters naturally hold a fly-rod handle, its "grip," as they'd hold the handle of a hammer: fingers curled around, thumb on top. That is, in fact, the standard grip (way of holding the handle, the grip) for fly casting. It's the one I always use, *always*—for dinky pumpkinseed sunfish at 10 feet or 12-pound silver salmon at 70.

But there's another grip: the index-finger-on-top grip. Or, as George Daniels refers to it in his book *Dynamic Nymphing*, the "three-point grip." George says that this grip is good for beginners to start out with because it "makes it difficult to break [bend] the wrist." Right—bending the casting wrist is disastrous for newbies.

The standard way to hold a fly-rod grip is like this, thumb on top. This way has advantages, and disadvantages. SKIP MORRIS

Some hold a fly-rod grip with their first finger on top—again, advantages, disadvantages. SKIP MORRIS

He takes everything a step further by holding "the grip a little higher up on the handle to allow the tip of the index finger to touch the rod blank, as this increases sensitivity and allows me to feel more fish takes." (He's speaking here about Czech and similar nymph-fishing styles in which a take isn't so much seen, as with a dry fly, as felt.) Makes sense.

George adds that he casts with his thumb atop the grip "for additional power for longer distances." Longer *casts*, that is.

So give the three-point grip a whirl for your Czech nymphing and general shorter-line casting if you like. But keep the hammer grip on tap. I watched a three-point-gripping friend, who normally fishes middling-size trout streams with dry flies, struggle to shoot out a big streamer fly into a stiff wind from the shore of a vast trout lake a couple of years ago. Once I got his thumb on top, he did fine, hooked a big one.

The thumb-on-top grip is always your fallback.

Tip 124 Fly Casting Is about the Wrist, and Mostly about Not Bending It

 Tr-S, Tr-L   Lg-L   Sm-L, Sm-S   Pf-L

If you're new to fly casting, you're almost certainly messing it up by bending your wrist. Bending the wrist is instinctive—and a fly caster's plague.

Your instincts want you to work your wrist, as you do when you throw a rock or a stick. But a fly rod is unnatural, an entirely artificial construct that requires unnatural movements in order to make it function properly—and requires a *locked wrist*.

I teach people at sportsmen's and fly-fishing shows to make a fishable fly cast in 10 minutes, and mostly what I concentrate on is keeping my subjects from bending their

Help train your wrist by tying the butt of your rod to it with some string, or just slip the rod's butt into your shirt cuff as shown here. SKIP MORRIS

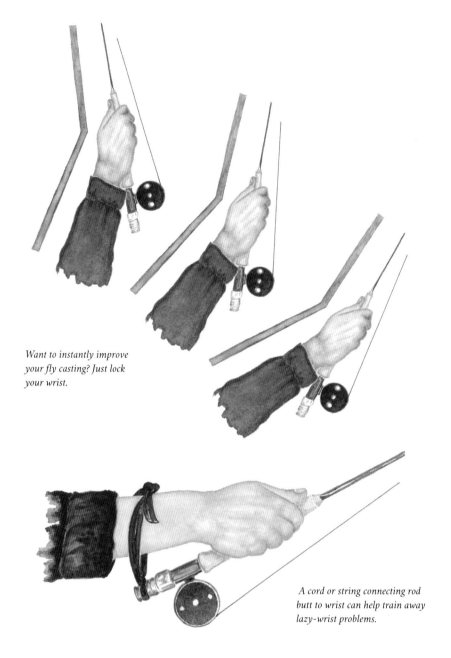

Want to instantly improve your fly casting? Just lock your wrist.

A cord or string connecting rod butt to wrist can help train away lazy-wrist problems.

wrists. Sometimes I watch seasoned fly fishers letting their wrists go and, if I know them well enough, I tell them. Then their casting really sharpens up. At least, as long as they remember to keep their wrists locked.

It's easy to slip back to bending the wrist. It's *natural* to slip back. But it's perilous.

How to fix the problem? Have a friend tie a string around the butt of your rod and then around your wrist, so it keeps your wrist straight (or use one of the gadgets made for this or just catch the rod butt in your shirt cuff). Or, turn your head to watch your wrist on every stroke. Best: Do both—inhibit the wrist mechanically *and* keep an eye on it.

Yes, in certain aspects of fly casting, very brief wrist bending has its place. But it must be performed with precise timing to help rather than harm. So learn to lock your wrist, enjoy the blessings it bestows on your casting, and then learn about how to use a *little* wrist—properly—if you like.

Tip 125 Keep Your Casting Strokes on One Plane Tr-S,Tr-L   Lg-L   Sm-L, Sm-S   Pf-L

It's a big deal: Your backcasts and forward casts need to aim straight at one another, line up, follow a single plane.

What happens if, say, your backcast angles down but your forward cast is dead horizontal? You win yourself a "tailing loop," the line crossing itself as it glides out. With a tailing loop, odds are high the fly will catch on the line and you'll have to stop, drag it all in, and straighten it all out. If your backcast is higher or lower than your forward cast—either way—they're on different planes, an invitation for a tailing loop and a snag. Backcast and forward cast: *one* plane.

So how do you avoid a tailing loop if you aim your forward cast high? Just aim your backcast low. Want your forward cast *low*? Well, it's obvious, but I'll say it anyway: Aim your backcast high.

Add to this single-plane business the following (covered in other tips)—(1) not bending your wrist, (2) using technique and timing instead of force, and (3) halting the rod

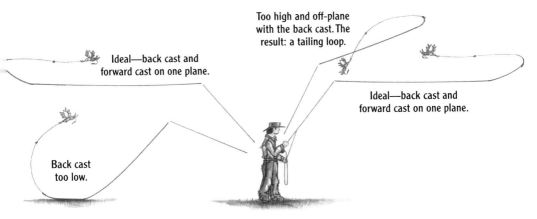

Too high and off-plane with the back cast. The result: a tailing loop.

Ideal—back cast and forward cast on one plane.

Ideal—back cast and forward cast on one plane.

Back cast too low.

Keep your casting strokes on one plane.

at the end of a casting stroke—and you've got what I'd call the Four Golden Rules of Casting. Follow those rules and your casting is bound to look good, feel good, and do its job honorably.

Tip 126 Remember: Where Your Rod Tip Goes, So Goes Your Line (Except on a Drift)

If at the end of a casting stroke your rod tip goes too far—that is, it swings out and then down—your fly line will also go out . . . and down. If your line goes down, of course, it will slap the water or catch on grass or brush behind you. Bottom line: Your casting won't work.

But if your rod tip swings, and *stops* where it should, your fly line will sail out comfortably high, just as you want it to.

It can really help your casting to remember that where your rod tip goes, so goes your line. Keep that in mind while making a mend, a curve cast—*any* kind of cast or manipulation of the line—or just a long cast with a narrow line loop, and things are bound to go well.

Exceptions? The only one I know is rod drift, which is the rod tip continuing to swing *slowly* a little—only *after* the required sharp halt of the stroke—to drop the tip away from the line and fly as they sail past. It helps avoid the fly snagging the rod or the bottom of the casting loop. The key to proper rod drift really is to make it slow, slow enough that it doesn't influence the line's path. Rod drift is always optional.

Tip 127 Halt! (and then, Maybe, Drift)

Tr-S, Tr-L   Lg-L   Sm-L, Sm-S   Pf-L

Next to bending the wrist—the absolute topper—failing to stop the rod firmly at the end of a casting stroke probably comes in at no. 2 on the list of fly-casting errors. If you just follow merrily on through, or only start *decelerating* the stroke after it should have stopped, the energy that was supposed to carry the line forward instead dissipates in an arc: The energy travels forward, yes, but also down a little, and a little more, and more, and more . . . It's diluted to death.

But if you make the proper smooth acceleration of the rod tip and line, and then, at that proper point, *halt* the stroke—stomp on the brake pedal of your casting—the energy will all flow in one direction, carrying the line out efficiently in a neat loop.

There may be some disagreement as to where, against that big, imaginary clock often used to describe casting strokes, the rod starts and stops, but wherever it stops, it should *stop*. Some say stop the backcast at 10 o'clock and the forward cast at 2 o'clock; others say 11 and 1:30; yet others, 11 and 1—to me, it's all the same general range: When the rod tip's a little past vertical, stop it.

Then, there's the "drift," which after learning about the stop can get confusing. I won't let it, though. The drift is a *slow* swing of the rod—slow!—after the stroke completely stops. *After.* So you make the stroke, stop it cold, and then lazily swing the rod tip forward a little farther. The drift (1) lowers the rod tip to keep it away from the sailing fly and (2) provides some extra length on the next stroke, which is handy.

The drift is optional.

Tip 128 Casting Is about Timing, Control, Grace, and Some Other Things—*Not* Really about Strength

 Tr-S, Tr-L   Lg-L   Sm-L, Sm-S   Pf-L

If you want to teach someone to fly cast, and you want the teaching to go smoothly, efficiently, teach a woman. Typically a woman will listen, then begin slowly, apply force gradually and thoughtfully, stop and consider when there's a problem—every instructor's dream student.

No offense, guys. I run on the same angry hormones as you do, which are handy for swimming across rapids to reach productive hunting grounds and for defending the tribe from charging woolly mammoths. But those same hormones really mess up the learning of how to cast a fly rod. A man will often rush ahead of instruction and consequently miss half of it, and try to muscle through the job. Both are problems. It's the muscling we'll address here. I'll leave it to you and your hormones to work out the rest.

Applying more force than a rod can handle ruins casting. Jerking the line in a hard, rushed stroke ruins casting. Failing to halt the stroke because anxious muscles are running off on their own ruins casting. Yes, some force is required for casting, a bit more for long casts, but rarely very much.

Men, learn from women. (And aggressive women, learn from calm women.) Learn to drop your expectations, quiet your ego, take your time, apply force in proper amounts rather than maximize it, work toward smooth acceleration in your strokes, and pay attention to the details: timing, wrist . . .

And if your hormones get surly, swat 'em!

Tip 129 Tick, Tock, Tick, Tock . . .

 Tr-S, Tr-L   Lg-L   Sm-L, Sm-S   Pf-L

My friend Jeff, a fly fisher of only a few years' experience, told me recently that he started out in fly casting with the classic newbie problem of wanting to keep the rod constantly in motion. That . . . doesn't . . . work. The rod must pause to let the loop in the line roll out.

Then he told me how he cured that problem: He thought, *Tick, tock, tick, tock* . . . In other words, whenever he stopped his rod at the end of a stroke, he thought, *Tick*, and when he stopped it on the next stroke, *Tock*. Thinking, and even saying aloud, these words in the rhythm of a windup clock forced him to include his pauses.

If you're a musician or ever had music lessons, you've probably worked with a metronome, a gadget that ticks (typically, no tocks) precisely at set intervals. Thinking of a metronome (and perhaps speaking its ticks) is another way to get in your casting pauses—and because the tempo of a metronome is adjustable, you can easily imagine the pauses between ticks running anywhere from short to long, just as the pauses between casting strokes should be long for long casts and short for short ones.

Tip 130 Cast with Both Hands

Tr-S, Tr-L   Lg-L   Sm-L, Sm-S   Pf-L

Moving *both* hands with each stroke is important in making a standard fly cast, and in making most kinds of fly cast.

Example 1: You make a comfortable standard backcast, swinging the rod back with your rod hand and holding the line secure in your other hand, your line hand. But you do *not* move your line hand. So what happens? As the rod moves away from that stationary line hand, line is pulled through the guides—it has to be. The result: The line picks up extra speed, as though you gave it a little haul.

Now you make the forward cast, with your line hand still in its fixed position—the hands come back closer together, and line *slips out* the rod's tip. The result: The push of the line you want, in order to send it sailing out in a loop, is drained. Slipping line is energy lost. You get a gutless, pathetic forward cast that may collapse in a useless, embarrassing heap.

Let's fix that.

Example 2: You make your backcast while keeping both hands, your rod hand and your line hand, a *constant distance* apart. That is, you move both hands during the stroke and stop them together at the end. Then you move them together and stop them together on the forward cast.

Just keep on doing this and your casts will roll out with fine spirit, in just the way you intended.

Tip 131 Turn Your Head, Watch Your Line

Tr-S, Tr-L   Lg-L   Sm-L, Sm-S   Pf-L

Want to improve your casting with almost no effort? Watch the line—specifically, turn your head to watch your backcasts. It's amazing what you'll see back there: line too low, loop too wide, forward stroke started too soon or too late . . .

It's much easier to make a good forward cast if it follows a good backcast. A good backcast, especially in the early years of fly casting, usually comes from routinely turning the head and watching.

Tip 132 Follow the Line Down

Tr-S, Tr-L   Lg-L   Sm-L, Sm-S   Pf-L

You make a couple of false-casts to work out line and reach for your target, you complete the final forward cast and stop the rod—now what? This is what, and it's important: Lower your rod tip slowly to follow the line down to the water. Your rod tip needn't reach the water, just drop to within a foot or two of it.

What if you *don't* follow the line down? Gravity drags the near part of the line back in. You intended to put your fly out 45 feet to cover that rise alongside a current tongue, but held your rod tip high and, consequently, got only 40 feet. So not only did you miss your target, but your line kept slipping back after it landed on the water until it was pulled straight, that slack you carefully put into it, gone—which spoiled your dead-drift presentation.

All that trouble could have been so easily avoided, just by lowering your rod tip at the end of your cast. Lake or stream, hair bug or streamer, nymph and indicator—doesn't matter: Holding your rod high after a casting stroke causes problems. So . . . don't do that.

Tip 133 Here's How to Work Line Out *and* How to Shoot It

 Tr-S, Tr-L   Lg-L   Sm-L, Sm-S   Pf-L

The key to working line out while false-casting is also the key to effectively shooting line: Release the line *only after* stopping the rod. You *halt* the casting stroke at the end, and *then* you release the line. If you release the line *before* the stop, the line slips out the guides as all the energy that was supposed to power the cast just dies.

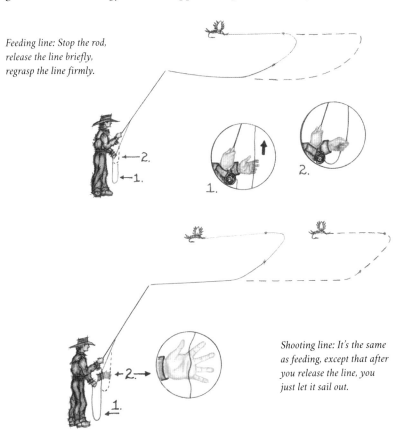

Feeding line: Stop the rod, release the line briefly, regrasp the line firmly.

Shooting line: It's the same as feeding, except that after you release the line, you just let it sail out.

To lengthen your false-casts, stop the stroke at the end; let a couple of feet, or more, of line slip out of the rod's tip; and then clamp quickly onto the line again and continue false-casting. You can feed out line on either backcasts or forward casts or both.

To shoot line is just to release the line altogether so that it sails on out. Shooting done well adds real length to your longest casts. It also makes long casts easier in general. I'll say it again: Hold the line firmly until you stop the stroke, and only *then* let it go.

Any good fly line will shoot, but weight-forward tapers shoot better than double tapers. Some lines are designed for long shooting, with fine, pebbly textures that make the line ride only on its high points through the rod guides.

A haul on the line at the end of the forward stroke will really blast out the shoot.

Slack-line casts are difficult to make when shooting line, but long tippets will partly compensate by dropping on the water in curls and waves.

Tip 134 If You Fish Streams, Learn the Standard Slack-Line Casts

 Tr-S   Sm-S

Fish much with a floating fly for trout in streams, and if you know the three casts below, you'll wind up using them all. That's because different casts work best in different situations. You really need not just one favorite but all the common slack-line casts.

So, I present to you the casts you'll use with floating flies for as long as you fly fish: The lazy S, or S, cast; the reach cast; and the pile cast.

(Note: Not everyone agrees on the names of casts or just how they're executed, but what follows is pretty standard.)

S Cast

Lazy S, or S, cast

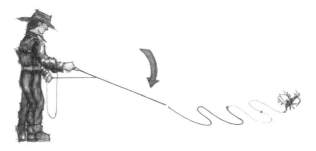

2. *Just follow the line down to the water with your rod tip, as if you were completing a standard cast.*

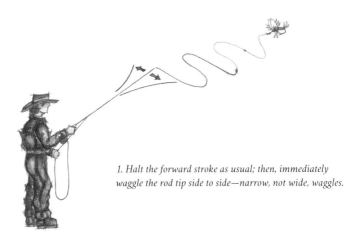

1. *Halt the forward stroke as usual; then, immediately waggle the rod tip side to side—narrow, not wide, waggles.*

Reach Cast

Reach cast

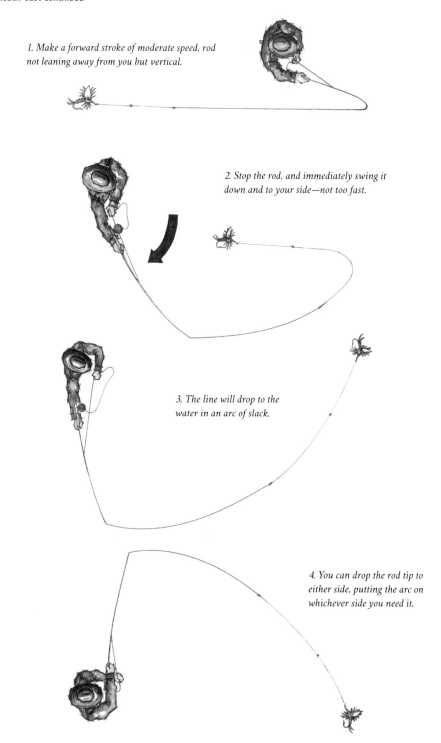

1. Make a forward stroke of moderate speed, rod not leaning away from you but vertical.

2. Stop the rod, and immediately swing it down and to your side—not too fast.

3. The line will drop to the water in an arc of slack.

4. You can drop the rod tip to either side, putting the arc on whichever side you need it.

Pile cast

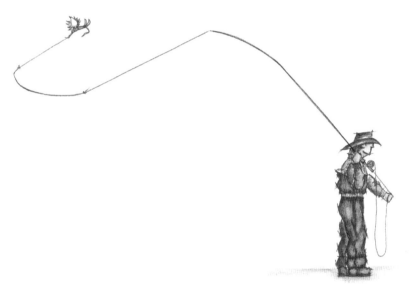

1. Start with a low backcast.

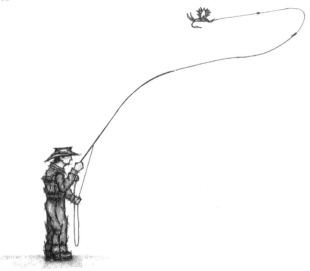

2. Make a high forward cast.

3. Immediately after you stop the rod, lower the tip to the water—quickly, but don't rush.

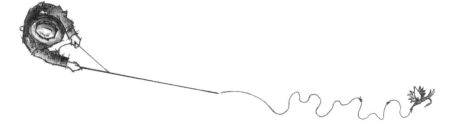

4. The line will drop on the water in waves of slack.

Tip 135 The Tuck Cast Gets Nymphs Deep Fast

Tr-S   Sm-S

It's easier for a nymph to sink under a loose pile of leader and tippet than for it to pull down tippet and leader lying straightened on the water: That straight filament, held back by the line, must slice down through the water; loose tippet and leader just follow the path of a weighted fly down. Your standard fly cast drops everything—line, leader, and tippet—straight. That's where the tuck cast comes in: It doesn't. The tuck cast piles tippet and leader over the nymph.

In a stream, getting a nymph down to the streambed before the current's swept it off to the end of its drift is truly that clichéd half the battle. The tuck sends nymphs down fast.

Tuck Cast

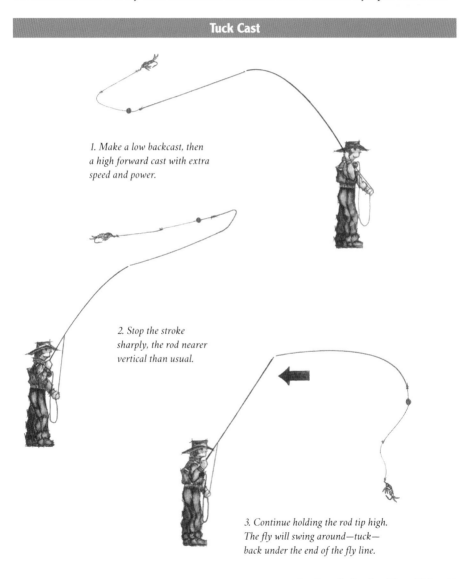

1. Make a low backcast, then a high forward cast with extra speed and power.

2. Stop the stroke sharply, the rod nearer vertical than usual.

3. Continue holding the rod tip high. The fly will swing around—tuck— back under the end of the fly line.

Note how this tuck cast positions the end of the fly line over the indicator and fly.

Lefty Kreh, a famous caster, says in his book *Fly-Casting Fundamentals* that, in making the tuck, "many anglers, besides not stopping the rod sharply enough, cast too low on the forward cast."

Here's how to tuck:

Make a *high, overpowered* forward casting stroke, sending the heavy fly (must be heavy) out beyond where you want it to drop.

Stop the rod *sharply* at the end of the stroke and do not let it drift forward.

Hold the rod high in its halted position as the weighted nymph swings down and back under the tip of the line.

Once the nymph is done swinging and the line begins to drop, only *then* follow the line down with the rod tip.

Tip 136 Learn My Crash Cast

 Tr-S Sm-S

Big dry flies are heavy, heavy enough to sail out on slack-line casts and pull out all tippet slack. Through a slow evolution I came up with a cast that holds its slack against the momentum of a soggy size 6 Stimulator: my crash cast.

Apparently this is my own original cast. I checked with a casting fanatic friend and researched books and the internet and couldn't turn up another like it. If someone really has developed and named it before me, my apologies. Even if I'm the first to name it, I'm certain I'm not the first to use it.

The crash cast is not really for smooth water—but how often do you cast a hulking dry imitation of a hulking stonefly or caddis or grasshopper onto smooth water? Not often.

A big dry fly and at least a little current chop make my crash cast shine. Before it can sail off to straighten tippet and leader, the fly stalls out. As it drops, that blessed and needed slack falls in waves and coils of tippet onto the water.

Here's how to make the crash cast. After a high backcast, aim your final forward cast low with a narrow line loop and a little extra punch. The loop's *crash* onto the water kills

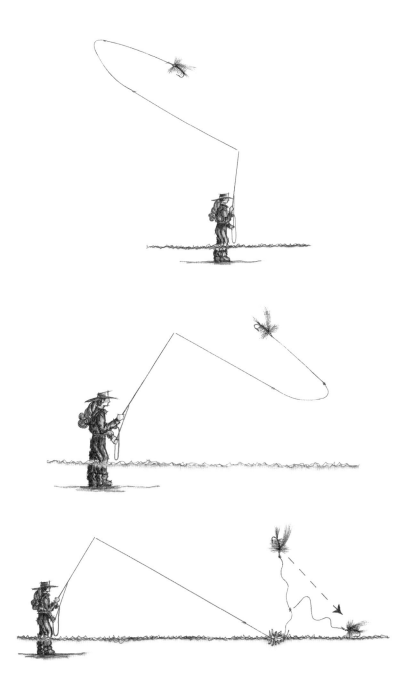

its momentum, and the fly continues out a little farther under its own momentum and weight, but not far. The leader and tippet drop and the result: slack, and a long, natural fly drift.

That line-loop crash is a bit . . . harsh . . . on smooth water, but lost to the fish in even a fairly quick and rough current.

Learn this unsightly brute of a cast, and use it. (Try using it with smaller dries too. That's been working for me lately.)

Tip 137 Learn the Shepherd's Crook Cast Tr-S Sm-S

"Shepherd's crook" . . . so poetic. I learned the cast by its *original* name long ago, before the Information Age or Technology Age or whatever Age we're currently in. The shepherd's crook is now the "negative curve cast." Ick.

Whatever you call it, it's miraculous for getting crazy long drag-free drifts of floating flies on streams. It's also tricky to make well and trickier yet to make accurately. Still, it's worth learning. I use it often, especially on really fussy trout.

The *shepherd's crook* (I refuse to call it anything else) also presents the fly to the trout ahead of the tippet. This cuts down the odds of the trout noticing the tippet.

Because, under any name, it gets considerably less press and chatter than the standard slack-line casts (lazy S, reach, etc.)—and because I've found it the most challenging of all slack-line casts—I gave the shepherd's crook its very own tip. Here's how it goes:

Cast upstream (this is a cast for standard upstream fly presentation), but with your rod leaning to the side.

Use less punch in your stroke than normal, so that the line loop runs out of momentum and drops to the water unstraightened. Result: The upstream line lies on the water in the shape of (wait for it . . .) a *shepherd's crook*, the fly, tippet, leader, and end of the line curving back downstream, riding one thread of current.

If you put too much power into the cast, you can compensate by pushing the rod tip forward at the end. Too little power, draw the rod tip back at the end.

A completed shepherd's crook cast. The fly, tippet, leader, and even the tip of the line set to ride one seam of current to a trout holding just downstream of this caster.

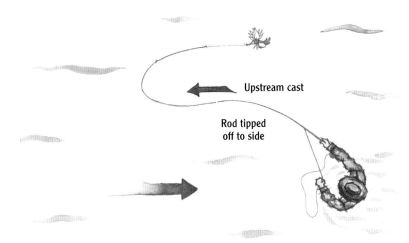

Shepherd's crook cast, step 1.

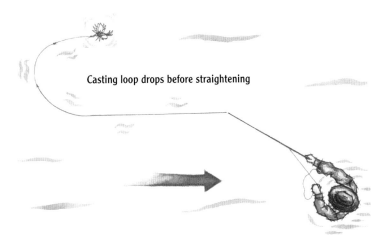

Shepherd's crook cast, step 2.

Tip 138 Learn the Parachute Cast for Downstream Fish Tr-S Sm-S

The parachute cast is sort of a pile cast that quit trying halfway through. Sure, there's more to the parachute cast than that, but overall it's a pretty good description.

You start the parachute cast as you start the pile: a backcast aimed low followed by a forward cast aimed high. You stop the stroke, and the rod tip, as always, but with the plane of the cast tilted, the stop will come slightly earlier than usual.

Then you just . . . hold the rod (and rod tip) up right where you stopped it. The line drops and, because the rod remains high, the line is pulled partway back in—good! Now you have a bunch of spare line next to you, from your high rod tip to the water.

This is mainly a cast for *downstream* presentations of a floating fly or a sunken nymph (typically, below a strike indicator). As the line and fly drift off downstream below you, just lower the rod tip to feed line and keep the fly (or indicator) drifting naturally.

Forward cast angled up, rod tip kept high as the line drops—that's pretty much the parachute cast.

1. Make a low back cast followed by a high forward cast.

2. Stop the forward casting stroke early, with the rod closer to vertical than usual. Continue to hold the rod up.

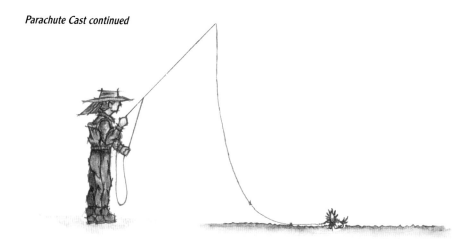

3. Just let the line drop to the water, still holding the rod up where you stopped the stroke.

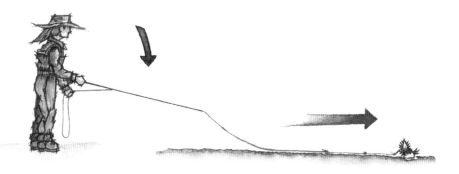

4. As the fly drifts downstream to the fish, lower the rod to feed out line and lengthen the drift.

Tip 139 Learn the Roll Cast. Just . . . Learn It

 Tr-S, Tr-L   Lg-L   Sm-L, Sm-S   Pf-L

I seldom use the roll cast—but when I do use it, I'm grateful for it. The roll cast does what no other cast can do: It throws the line and fly forward without any need of a backcast.

No backcast: Situations where that's a blessing are common on creeks and far from uncommon on streams and rivers—on a creek with a fine pool before you and out-stretched tree limbs behind, on a river with trout rising out along a thread of current but with a high rock face at your back, etc., etc.

Begin a roll cast with the line out on the water in front of you. (Important: you can't make a roll cast without the resistance on the line from water.) Swing the rod *slowly* up,

1. Swing the rod slowly back.
Let the line slide back.

2. Make the same acceleration-
and-stop forward stroke you'd
make for a standard cast.

3. Make sure you tip the rod out
to your side for a roll cast.

A wall of tall trees behind? Time for the roll cast.

tipped off a bit to your side. Continue swinging the rod, still slowly, back about as far as you normally would for a backcast. Stop the rod. Give the line a moment to slide back just behind you and stop. Now make a spirited forward stroke, the standard acceleration building to a firm halt of the stroke.

In *Fly-Casting Fundamentals*, author and casting ace Lefty Kreh says, "Most fly fishermen perform this useful cast poorly," and then explains that this is because "they tend to aim the rod tip downward, rather than straight ahead." So don't swing the rod tip down for the forward stroke in a roll cast—push that line out ahead just as you would with any cast.

Tip 140 Learn to Mend Line—It's Important

 Tr-S Sm-S

On a trout stream, and during those infrequent times (infrequent in my fishing anyway) on a smallmouth stream when insect hatches draw the bass up to rise like trout, it's tough to get along without mending line. No matter how much slack in line, leader, and tippet you drop on the water, a confusion of stream currents will typically draw it all out and start dragging your fly or strike indicator before you want it to.

So, you mend the line.

If you want a soft-hackle or wet fly to swing in only gradually, to stay out with the feeding trout while a quick current works to rush your fly across, what do you do?

Again, you mend.

A "mend," the throwing of a belly into floating fly line, can be made upstream or down—whichever direction kills drag. Mending, like casting, improves with practice. Do practice mending (and practice it on water, not dry land). It's a good investment of your time and attention.

Mending line

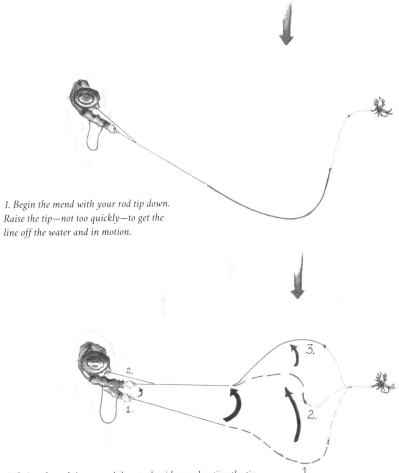

1. Begin the mend with your rod tip down. Raise the tip—not too quickly—to get the line off the water and in motion.

2. Swing the rod tip up, and then to the side, accelerating the tip smoothly and gradually and then stopping it sharply. The belly in the line should now lie opposite the side it started on.

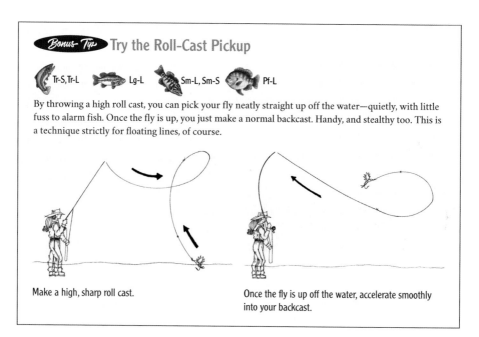

Bonus Tip · Try the Roll-Cast Pickup

Tr-S, Tr-L   Lg-L   Sm-L, Sm-S   Pf-L

By throwing a high roll cast, you can pick your fly neatly straight up off the water—quietly, with little fuss to alarm fish. Once the fly is up, you just make a normal backcast. Handy, and stealthy too. This is a technique strictly for floating lines, of course.

Make a high, sharp roll cast.

Once the fly is up off the water, accelerate smoothly into your backcast.

Tip 141 Learn the Double Haul

Tr-S, Tr-L   Lg-L   Sm-L, Sm-S   Pf-L

The double-haul cast is about pulling on the line to make long casts easier, and longer. Some casters prefer to start the pull—the *haul*—as the stroke begins, pulling ever faster as the stroke increases speed. Others like to make the haul a short snap at the very last moment of the stroke. My haul is a blend of both approaches. Not because of some principle or theory but just because, well, because it is; over the years it just settled out that way. I suggest you try both approaches and see which best fits you (or whether somewhere in the middle, neither a long nor short stroke, suits you as it does me).

However you haul, your haul's speed should peak just as the speed of the line and rod tip peaks. The haul should end in a sharp halt right when the casting stroke ends, in an equally sharp halt.

Wind makes the double haul a real gift. That pull on the line narrows the casting loop, offering less for the wind to push against, and the increased line speed from the haul drives the loop straight on through.

Just remember that with a haul it's easy to overdo. Make it too long or too quick or both, and the rod gives out and the cast falls apart. For a cast of only modest length, the haul might be only an unhurried few inches. When hauling, a little is a lot.

Tip 142 Try a Single Haul

 Tr-S, Tr-L   Lg-L   Sm-L, Sm-S   Pf-L

I often make a haul on my backcast but no haul on my forward cast: a *single*-haul cast. This really loads the rod for my forward stroke so that tossing a fly out a fair distance feels like only a thought. I'm not sure why I usually haul on the backcast rather than on the forward. I guess it just feels right. But sometimes, hauling on the forward cast *is* right.

If there's wind, it makes the decision for me—with wind coming from behind, I haul on the backcast to snap a quick narrow line loop into it. With wind hitting me in the face, I haul on the forward cast to punch the line through the resistance.

Big flies can cast best with a single haul. Take a hair bug for bass: It *is* big, and its broad face catches air, but a haul on the forward cast fires the bug out. If you want to overpower a casting stroke to smack a fly down on the water, perhaps a floating bass fly or a grasshopper for trout, a little haul can really help.

To learn a proper haul, see the previous tip on making the double haul. But remember that the single haul, at least as I practice it, isn't so much for dazzlingly long casts as much as for making day-to-day casting a little easier, a little more efficient.

Tip 143 Learn to Deliver Your Fly on Your Backcast  Tr-S, Tr-L   Lg-L   Sm-L, Sm-S   Pf-L

The normal way to cast a fly is usually the best way: a backcast to load the rod, a forward cast to deliver the fly to the target. But sometimes it's more practical to put the fly out with the fish on the backcast.

Example: You're at one end of your anchored boat and your friend is at the other end, and you decide to try the water behind you. You don't want to fuss with the two of you switching ends of the boat or pulling up the anchors for this little experiment. If you turn around, you'll then be tipping your rod toward your friend (nearly all casters tip their rods out a little)—your odds of hooking that friend will go up. But if you just keep facing the same direction and deliver your fly on your backcast, problem solved.

It's not just about boats. When there are trees, brush, whatever behind you, turn to face these fly-snaggers. Aim your forward cast at the openings and make your *back*cast send the fly to the fish. There's also plain laziness—you think, Do I really need to turn around to try that one little, only mildly promising pocket? If you can make a good backcast delivery, then probably not.

Tip 144 Practice Casting with Your Rod Down Sometimes

Tr-S, Tr-L   Lg-L   Sm-L, Sm-S   Pf-L

There's a lot involved in making a good fly cast. Stopping the rod properly and making a smooth stroke are key, but neither means much without just the right amount of speed

Keeping your rod low lets you watch your line the entire time you're casting it.

and good timing. Then there's lining up the forward cast and backcast. There's the wrist. It's enough to make you dizzy.

Long ago I decided to push my casting up a level or two. I got a couple of books on the topic and went at it. Somehow, I stumbled onto a trick that really served me: I tipped the rod way down so my casting loops were nearly, if not truly, parallel with the ground.

Casting with a low rod changes things, mainly gravity—now it's pulling the loops you form in your line down from their *side*. That relieves the pressure on you to keep your line and its loops up. And, of course, when you go back to casting with an upright rod, gravity will go back to pulling down your loops. But in the meantime . . .

In the meantime you can easily watch your forward casts and backcasts throughout their length—it's all down there in plain sight. Casting practice with a lowered rod just seems to make it easy to sort things out. Try bending your wrist and see what happens, now lock it. Shorten your strokes to see how narrow you can make your loops. Experiment with timing, speed, acceleration, with *everything*. Even a dozen feet of line out is enough to teach you the mechanics of fly casting in short order.

One more benefit of practicing this way: You'll get good at making casts that shoot a fly back under low-hanging tree branches, since a low sidearm cast is exactly how that's done.

Tip 145 Look Back Before You Cast

 Tr-S, Tr-L   Lg-L   Sm-L, Sm-S   Pf-L

Here's what often happens when you don't glance back before you start casting: You waste a fair chunk of fishing time. That's the bottom line. Of course, you also suffer the frustration of trying to find your snapped-off fly among a dozen or more tree branches, or if it's still on your tippet, struggling to break it off or free it where it's pinned, a dozen feet up, in the trunk of a birch tree. But, at least to me, it's the lost minutes that should have been spent presenting the fly to and perhaps hooking fish that matter most.

Look, I've been fly fishing for decades and I still snag trees and telephone poles and brush on hillocks on my backcasts. Everybody does that once in a while—on creeks,

Lake fly fishers are usually safe from snags because they're fishing well out from shore in boats, but if you're fishing a lake on foot, well, not so safe. Not so safe fishing from a boat in brush- or tree-lined lake channels either. A high snag like this is especially troublesome.

Oops. Now comes the lost fishing time spent trying to recover the fly.

rivers, ponds, and even when fishing from boats near the shorelines of lakes. But if you just turn your head, take a look behind you before you make your backcasts, you'll cut your snags to a minimum by directing your backcasts wisely (and spend more of your fishing time actually fishing).

Tip 146 Learn to Cast Across Your Chest

Tr-S, Tr-L   Lg-L   Sm-L, Sm-S   Pf-L

Let's say you're right-handed (a good bet, but if you aren't, pretend you are). The wind is pushing at you from your right. You try casting normally. Problem: The wind keeps throwing your fly line at you or perilously over your head. Frustrating.

The cure is simple: Angle the rod across your chest to your left, and cast away. Now the wind can push the line around all it likes; it won't hurt your casting and you'll start catching fish instead of your hat.

Rod-across-the-chest is a cure for when you end up on the wrong side of the river too. So you're still a right-hander. You're fishing upstream, to your right, from the river's right bank. Your backcasts send your line over high brush and close to all those fly-grabbing trees. The solution: Again, tip your rod over your left shoulder, putting your line farther from trouble and closer to the water and its fish.

Cross-body casting takes a little adjusting, but not a lot. Your alternative is to learn to cast with your rod in your other, nondominant hand. That takes *scads* of adjusting, though it's an option with advantages. Tipping your rod is a much easier solution, and a good one.

Above: A wall of leafy limbs at my back—here there is need. Often, in fishing streams and sometimes in fishing lakes, there is the need to cast across the chest.

Left: No need for across-chest casting here, but the light is perfect for a photo showing the technique.

Tip 147 Learn to Cast in Wind

 Tr-S, Tr-L   Lg-L   Sm-L, Sm-S   Pf-L

Have you found a fishing spot where there's never any wind? After several decades of doing lots of fishing, I haven't. And you won't. Every stream and lake gets windy days.

Wind in fishing can be good, is inevitable anyway. So you need to learn to cast in it.

Start by casting narrow loops in your line—a narrow loop cuts through air more efficiently than does a wide one. Add extra speed (but don't overdo it) to your casting strokes that go into the wind, regardless of whether they're backcasts or forward casts. The small amount of additional power necessary for creating that speed can come from a more aggressive stroke or from a tug on the line at the peak of the stroke (a "haul").

If the wind wants to push your line sideways into you (as when the wind is coming at the right side of a right-handed caster), tip your rod off away from the incoming wind, leaning the rod across your far shoulder. Now that surly wind can push the line all it wants!

Use the wind. If it's coming at your back, make your forward cast high, shoot line, and watch your fly sail out forever. . . . If the wind is in your face, let it help you lengthen your backcast.

Tip 148 Slow Down, Smooth Out, Stretch Out, and Open Up Casts for Troublesome Flies and Rigs

 Tr-S, Tr-L Lg-L  Sm-L, Sm-S Pf-L

Some flies are heavy due to a metal bead or cone built into them or wire windings hidden at their core, or both; others are heavy simply because they're big. Some rigs include dropper flies (usually nymphs, but sometimes dry flies or even wet flies) dangling off the tippet on tippet sections of their own, perhaps below a bulky strike indicator or crimped-on split shot. *All* of these things make casting awkward.

But you sometimes need these troublesome flies and rigs, so you also need to tame them. And taming them is about casting.

Slow down. Relax the tempo of your casting, and let go of impatience—it will only bring you grief here.

Smooth out. Most casters are happy as long as they can get their fly where they want it, but with heavy flies or problem rigs you need to go a step further and make your

The smooth, wide casting loop avoids tangles in wobbly nymph rigs or tangles of fly and tippet, leader, with large heavy flies such as streamers.

Open up your casting loops by swinging the rod a bit farther forward and back than usual.

casting smooth—as graceful as possible. Accelerate your strokes not as hurried flicks but gradually, evenly; this will minimize the sort of fly or rig bouncing that invites tangles.

Stretch out. Avoid short, jarring line accelerations, and instead work line speed gradually into each stroke, a stroke stretched long.

Widen. Narrow loops in a cast line are dandy for distance—but with heavy flies or upstart rigs? Disastrous. So when you're trying to get a two-nymph rig and a strike indicator out there, cast wide loops in your line. A relatively wide loop keeps flies and other snaggy stuff up away from the line or leader.

Concentrate. A moment's distraction, and that three-wet-fly rig is suddenly an intricate snarl. Give the casting of heavy flies and messy rigs your full and unwavering attention.

Tip 149 Start with Warm-Up Casts When the Pressure's On

 Tr-S, Tr-L   Lg-L   Sm-L, Sm-S   Pf-L

You're standing in a wide, slow-moving stretch of a rich trout river, with a moose of a rainbow rising out and just upstream—do you just go ahead and cast, see what happens? No, because if you do, nothing good is likely to happen. When you have to present a fly just so, and you really want to get it right, make one or more warm-up casts.

Warm-up casts are necessarily short—you don't want to drop the fly close to the fish until you're ready. So you cast the fly out toward the fish but with only perhaps half to two-thirds the distance you'll ultimately need (or the full distance, if you cast in a different direction). The line comes down, the fly comes down, and then you judge whether or not they came down correctly. Perhaps you realize you need to use a different slack-line cast, or that the light breeze you hadn't noticed is pushing your line and fly too far left, or you just need a couple of practice casts to wake up the precision in your technique.

Short warm-up casts really do help. I use them before trying to get a hair bug back into the shade under hanging tree limbs on a largemouth lake, or a popper into a little open spot in a big weed bed on a smallmouth stream. I use warm-up casts in all sorts of situations for trout, bass, whatever.

Tip 150 Prefer Short to Medium-Length Casts on Streams (Tr-S   Sm-S

Any creek, stream, or river, from slow to fast, is a tangle of currents—currents shifting, rushing and slowing, sliding against one another. So, the farther you cast line, leader, tippet, and fly out across those currents, the more they'll mess with your line, leader, etc.

So if you make a long cast, your first problem is all the mischief, described above, caused by all those currents. Your second problem is trying to find your dry fly or strike indicator way out there on dark, broken water. Third problem, setting the hook on a take way out there while already coping with problems #1 and #2. The solution (to all three problems): Take a little time to work quietly up to the water you want to fish, within, say, 40 feet, and you'll see your fly or indicator plainly; have good line control and consequently good fly or indicator drifts; and with perhaps only 25 feet of line out (plus rod length and leader/tippet length = 40 feet), you can set the hook as soon (if soon is appropriate, as with a nymph) as your skills allow.

With stealth, you can get close to most stream trout and smallmouth bass—fishing quick and broken water, Czech nymph aficionados often get their rod tips right over the trout they catch. So, you're going to hook more and land more stream trout and bass if you keep your casts down to about 12 to 45 feet in length. Of course, sometimes, that's not an option . . .

Tip 151 Don't Make Long Casts a Habit on Streams, but Don't Avoid Them Either (Tr-S   Sm-S

I'm recalling a day on a spring creek in Oregon called the Metolius River. It's as pure and cold as a spring creek ought to be, but it's mostly fast, which spring creeks really shouldn't be, and, down where I was fishing it, big—the pool before me was at least two long casts across. Which was pretty easy to figure since I had to make one long cast to reach the middle. And I did have to reach the middle, or close to it.

It was the river's Green Drake mayflies I'd come for, a hatch of giants in comparison to normal Green Drakes. And conditions were dandy: late May, late afternoon, with overcast. The Drake duns were so big I could see them clear out in the swirling mid-river. Didn't see many in closer, though, so naturally, the trout were out with the Drakes. My shorter casts ran around 50 feet.

That's one of many times and places the long cast has caught me fish that lesser casts wouldn't have. If you can cast long, you can sometimes reach fish few bother, trout and smallmouth both. Sure, all that line and all those currents cause problems, but if it gets me action, I'll deal.

I'll fish an indicator nymph rig far off—"long-distance nymphing" some call it—and, again, reach fish few others tempt.

Prefer the short to medium-length cast on streams, but if a long cast is the solution, cast long.

Tip 152 If You Want to Fish Trout Lakes, Learn to Cast Long

We are warned from the time we begin fishing streams that short to medium-length casts catch fish best, and I fully believe that's true (despite that I do fish long casts on streams fairly regularly). But lakes? Uh-uh.

In lake fishing, especially when fishing a sinking line deep, long casts are fish-catching casts. The key to most effectively fishing near the bottom of a lake is to cover as much of it as possible on a cast. Long casts cover more water than do shorter casts. And all that current business that causes mischief on streams? It just doesn't exist on lakes. Lakes are still, standing water. What little current they present is close in at the mouths of feeder streams and during sluggish seasonal turnover. Really, there's near-zero chance that lakes are going to give you problems on long casts.

So you make that 55-foot, perhaps 65-foot cast, let your sinking line sink, and then work your fly in, usually close to the bottom, as it covers all that trout, bass, and panfish turf down there.

When a lake is flat, and bluegills cruise in pods just under the water's surface or when trout rise to pick floating or hatching insects off it, the long cast is, again, invaluable—it keeps you far enough from the fish to avoid spooking them with your waving rod (though for this fishing, casts may need be only mildly long, just long enough the fish don't notice you).

So practice. Gradually work more distance into your casts. And if you already can cast long, do so on lakes.

Tip 153 Learn the Art of Casting Short

I've seen casters who can punch a fly out 65 feet struggle with a short cast. A short cast: that's 15 feet or under from rod hand to fly, at least by my reckoning. Adding together the lengths of rod and leader and tippet may exceed that 15 feet—short casts are often about tapered leader and little, perhaps even no line.

So how do you make such a cast smoothly, efficiently? The simple answer: the same way you make a smooth medium or long cast, but with the motions compressed. All the elements of *any* cast belong in a short cast: the locked wrist, the smooth acceleration to a crisp stop of the rod tip, the optional little drift of the rod, the pause as the loop sails down the line (or leader), then the smooth acceleration in the opposite direction . . . It's just that the stroke, the drift, the pause, and the rest are all scaled down.

I just conducted tests, with the help of my wife. With an 8½-foot rod and 12 feet of tippet and leader combined, my hand traveled 20 inches from backcast to forward cast to put a fly out 45 feet. To make an efficient 14-foot cast with that same rod, leader, and tippet: 6 inches. Just a 6-inch stroke from backcast through forward cast.

I use short casts often on creeks, often enough on streams and rivers, sometimes even on lakes. Develop a good short cast and, when it's appropriate, use it.

Tip 154 A Sort of Roll Cast Can Free a Snagged Fly Tr-S, Tr-L   Lg-L   Sm-L, Sm-S   Pf-L

In a smallmouth lake or a trout stream you try to get your fly in close to that dock or alongside that log lying in the current, but you cast a little too far—you're snagged. Here's how to get your fly *unsnagged* without moving either boat or foot.

Do *not* tighten on the fly. If you pull on it, it'll dig in and you'll have to go over and unhook it (if you can).

Pull some line off your reel until you're sure you have enough slack line out so that you can make a proper roll cast.

Get the rod tip behind you and your rod tipped off to your side a bit (standard roll-cast prep)—and then make a sharp forward stroke and a halt of the rod to send a tight loop down your line.

When the loop passes your snagged fly, your fly will—with a little luck—pop free.

Swing your rod up and back in a smooth backcast as soon as your fly comes free—this will lift fly and line upward, and bring them back to you.

Sometimes you might have to throw two or three of these pseudo roll casts to free your fly. After that, you're beaten—go ahead and row or wade over and unhook your fly.

Tip 155 Here's How You Determine Where the Slack Goes Tr-S   Sm-S

Mending line is an excellent way to keep a floating fly or strike indicator on a dead drift, but, of course, only if you mend in the right direction. Same goes for the reach cast: You can send that curve of slack upstream or downstream.

How do you know where to send the slack?

The formula is simple: If the current between you and the fly (or indicator) is *faster* than the current the fly (or indicator) is riding, you want the slack line upstream; if the current between is *slower* than the current carrying the fly, the slack goes downstream.

Stop fishing, then take a good look at what's before you—compare the currents, see which is hurrying ahead of the other—and only *then* decide which way to throw the slack line of a mend or reach cast.

Also, experiment occasionally. Throw slack both up- and downstream on a section of stream to see what happens, how it affects the fly's drift. And learn.

CHAPTER 5
FIGURING OUT WHERE THE FISH ARE

Tip 156 Know Your Standard Trout-Stream Lies  Tr-S

Long ago, fly fishers identified the features in a stream that attract trout; then they named them. They're the classic lies, and they're the ones we'll consider here. But, as tip 162 explains, the best thing about understanding classic lies is that it helps you recognize all that fine fish-holding water that isn't classic.

RIFFLE
A medium-quick flow over a relatively flat streambed, the depth fairly consistent from end to end and bank to bank, perhaps one and a half to four feet deep. Riffles are bug factories, which attracts trout. Riffles hold trout in depressions and behind boulders small to large, where the relentless current slows.

Riffle

POOL
A deep spot in a stream (or river or creek) where the current dies, or barely moves. The "current tongue," that long triangle of chop where the flow comes in at the "head" of a pool, attracts trout. The "tail" of a pool, where the current picks up again to leave, can be good. The deep center of the pool usually holds few trout.

Pool

Fed and drained by small waterfalls—can this really qualify as a pool? Probably, but regardless, when I fished it, it held trout. Classic fish lies are almost rare and lots of not-classic water holds lots of fish.

RUN

A sort of half riffle/half pool, a run is normally waist-deep or deeper with lazy currents and usually some large boulders. Riffles may feed into runs, which may deepen into pools, or each may stand alone.

Run

POCKETWATER

Basically, a riffle studded with exposed boulders. Behind each boulder is a depression, a *pocket*, in which trout can hold next to the current.

BANK

A deep edge of a stream, usually the outside of a turn in the stream's course. An "undercut" bank is concave under the water.

Bank

Undercut bank SKIP MORRIS

EDDY

A pocket off the main flow where the water slowly rotates, usually deep. Trout love eddies.

Eddy. Note how the white foam forms a circle, riding the eddy's circular currents.

Pocketwater

Side channel. The main river, broad and deep, runs on the right. On the left is the side channel that narrows just upstream; it was shallow too, but deep enough to hold a few 12- to 15-inch cutthroat trout. SKIP MORRIS

SIDE CHANNEL AND BRAIDS

A side channel is exactly what it sounds like: a smaller flow branching off the main stream, eventually returning to it. Braids are where a stream diverges into three or more channels.

Braids. How many do you see here? I count four. (The farthest one is hard to see.) SKIP MORRIS

Tip 157 Know Your Standard Trout-Lake Lies Tr-L

Other than also containing trout (and water), trout lakes couldn't be more different from trout streams—different hatching bugs and other feed, no currents, and entirely different lie where trout hold and feed. The word *lies*, whose meaning applies so neatly to streams, is a stretch here, since trout in lakes move around a lot.

Anyway, below are the standard places where trout gather in lakes. (Read tip 162 to help you find nonstandard places.)

SHOAL
This is the major attraction for trout in lakes, usually the best and most reliable one. Where the bed of a lake is fairly flat, gradually deepening as it goes out, that's a shoal. Lots of trout food there.

Shoal. That broad pale area is a shoal.

DROP-OFF
Where a shoal turns abruptly down into deep water: drop-off. When trout aren't up feeding on the shoal, they're often hanging at the drop-off or just below its rim.

STREAM MOUTH
Where a river, stream, or creek empties into a lake, trout may gather to find oxygen, colder water, or feed.

Drop-off. See that dark water along the outer edge of this weedy shoal? That's the drop-off.

Stream mouth. Always try fishing around the mouth of a stream feeding a trout lake.

SPRING

A pale patch on a lake bed, perhaps with a stream of bubbles, indicates a spring. Trout often hang around springs.

Spring. These springs are too shallow to attract trout regularly, but springs in deeper water? Trout will visit them year-round.

SHALLOWS

Spring, fall, morning, evening, under cloudy skies—there's food in that skinny water, so when oxygen and water temperature are acceptable, trout may forage in shallows.

Shallows—surprisingly large trout will feed in them on occasion.

Tip 158 Know Your Standard Smallmouth-Stream Lies  Sm-S

These are the features in a river, stream, or creek where smallmouths like to settle in. They are the *standard* features. There are many nonstandard ones that can be just as good or better; read tip 162 about using standard lies to identify nonstandard lies.

ROCKS

Boulders and stones along banks, stone ledges underwater—if it's rock, smallmouths like it.

Rocks

WATER PLANTS

The creatures smallmouths feed on in streams—insects, little fishes, and such—love beds of all kinds of water plants. Consequently, so do smallmouths. Bass will hunt all around these beds, in channels running through them, and right inside them. Sometimes just a few spare stick-ups can attract more smallmouths than seem to make sense.

OBSTRUCTION

Whatever breaks the flow of a stream is, to me, an obstruction: a boulder, a log slanting into the water, a finger of stone jutting out into the flow . . . Smallmouths find cover and a break from the push of the current under, behind, or in front of such objects and structures.

EDDY

Just like trout, smallmouths love those swirling side-pools in rivers. In fact . . .

Water plants

Obstruction

Eddy

OTHER LIES

The standard trout-stream lies in tip 156 on trout lies in streams (pool, riffle, run, bank . . .) can all hold smallmouth bass—both fishes are looking for a comfy, safe place with food, so it just makes sense. But why go through all the trout lies twice?

Tip 159 Know Your Standard Largemouth-Lake Lies 🐟 Lg-L

Largemouths, like smallmouths and trout and most panfish, love shade; they also love reeds and lily pads, floating or sunken branches and logs—whatever sort of tangle they can find to squeeze into.

Following are the standard largemouth-bass lies in lakes. Tip 162 will help you figure out other, less obvious lies in largemouth lakes.

WATER PLANTS

Largemouths will hold around and in clumps to fields of lily pads, primrose, or whatever sort of aquatic vegetation a lake, pond, or reservoir offers. Fish all around water plants and in the open pockets and channels in beds of them, and, using weedless flies, right in the heart of the greenery.

DOWNED TIMBER

Fallen trees and brush offer largemouths excellent overhead protection from predators, along with shade. Bass know all about this and love such cover.

Water plants SKIP MORRIS

A dock and a moored boat SKIP MORRIS

DOCKS, MOORED AND ANCHORED BOATS
Thanks to the protection from predators and shade such artificial cover provides, large-mouths are all in.

Downed timber SKIP MORRIS

STRUCTURE
Largemouths will gather around nearly any irregularity of a lake bed out in open water: the original creek channel in a reservoir, deep weed beds, ridges, drop-offs. These can be tricky to find (almost impossible without a fish-finder), but if you can find them, and get a fly down there on a full-sinking line . . . wonderful things can happen.

Tip 160 Know Your Standard Panfish-Lake Lies Pf-L

How do you nail down the standard lies for all the panfish when their habits vary so widely? Easy: Address the troublemakers first.

The rock bass likes rocky lake beds and points; it also likes weed beds and brush. Both the black and the white crappies like to spread over weedy flats or hunt along drop-offs. The yellow perch, white bass, goldeneye . . . If I do them all, this one tip will turn into a chapter of its own, and that makes no sense. So, to all the panfish I've named thus far, and some I haven't, from this point on, sorry, you're out.

That leaves the sunfishes, a pretty conformist group overall. Widespread and popular too. The bluegill, pumpkinseed, warmouth, and the green, redbreast, longear, and redear sunfishes, together probably the most popular members of the sunfish clan—here are the standard places where they like to hold. (But read tip 162 to figure out other, less obvious panfish lies in lakes.)

LARGEMOUTH BASS LIES
The subhead tells it all: Sunfishes like to hang around the same places—weed beds, docks, timber, moored boats, etc.—largemouths like. The difference occurs when these fishes go deep: Largemouths head for structure when sunfish may only move to the outer edges of weed lines. Though in clear water (or, really, any water) sunfish may go deeper, even beyond 20 feet.

It's common to fish for sunfish and catch largemouths too, or vice versa—*that's* how much they both like the same lies.

Tree branches that extend out over a lake's shallows can really group bluegills and other sunfishes in their shade.
SKIP MORRIS

Figuring Out Where the Fish Are **145**

Point

Tip 161 Know Your Standard Smallmouth-Lake Lies  Sm-L

When it comes to where they'll hold and feed in lakes, smallmouth and largemouth bass overlap. So if you've already read the tip about largemouth lies, expect to see some of them covered here. The differences count, though—especially the smallmouth's affection for boulders, cobble, anything made of stone. Largemouths and stone? Eh . . .

Following, then, are the standard places smallmouth bass like to lie in lakes, ponds, and reservoirs. If you want to find other odd or hard-to-define places where smallies may gather in a lake, read tip 162.

ROCKY SHORELINE
These are stone-loving smallies after all. Where you find a shallow, rocky lake bed extending out from shore, you may find smallmouths either shallow or farther out where it's deeper. They especially like shallow water next to deep. (See tip 177.)

POINT
Where a rocky finger of land continues out and down into the depths, there may be smallmouths. Just fish the ridge on top and along the sides, working out ever deeper.

DOWNED TREES, DOCKS, AND BOATHOUSES
I lumped these together because they're all solid overhead cover and they all provide shade. And, of course, because smallies like them. (See tip 159 for photos.)

 Largemouths Like Corners

 Lg-L   Pf-L

After picking off one here, one there along a shoreline, I've often found several largemouth bass crowded into a corner of a lake or pond. It's as though the bass worked down the shoreline until they hit a right angle, and just stopped. Panfish will sometimes do the same. So fish corners with extra patience and care. Same goes for anything resembling a corner: an indentation, the inside of a point . . .

WATER PLANTS
As in streams, smallies in standing water find cover and food in all sorts of water plants, ones that thrive around a lake's edges or grow shaggy down on a lake's bed. In lakes jammed with vegetation, try the open spots, free of it, too.

FEEDER STREAMS
Always worth a try. At a stream mouth smallies sometimes really crowd in. (See tip 157 on trout-lake lies for a photo.)

Tip 162 Learn Standard Fish Lies First, Then Use What You've Learned to Find More Fish

 Tr-S, Tr-L   Lg-L   Sm-L, Sm-S   Pf-L

There are the established places, "lies," where trout, the basses, and panfish hold in streams and lakes, and recognizing these is where you start. The next step is to understand why these lies attract fish.

Fish, regardless of species, seek cover, food, and comfort.

Cover can be almost anything that protects fish or hides them from predators or even just makes them hard for predators to spot. A half-sunken log, lily pads, a tree's shadow, wind roughing up the surface of a lake, currents making chop on the surface of a stream, and so on, and so on . . .

Food is . . . food—mayflies, crayfish, minnows, whatever.

Comfort is oxygen, current, water temperature.

Once you understand what fish seek in a lie and come to see how that plays out in the classic lies, use what you've learned to ferret out those odd spots most anglers miss and that can be so productive: an isolated depression in a streambed where smallmouths crowd in; a channel with more depth than you'd expected, running far back into what you judged as only swampy shallows, that holds largemouth bass all down its length; a midstream slot carved deep into basalt by currents over unimaginable time and where a big brown trout holds in shadow; a bay only three or four feet deep where rainbows come to leap for flitting and floundering damselfly adults.

Learn to identify standard fish lies, then just keep learning from there. The payoff can be big.

It'd be a stretch to call any part of this water a classic trout lie. But there were trout all through it.

Tip 163 Fish Where Fish Are

 Tr-S,Tr-L   Lg-L   Sm-L, Sm-S   Pf-L

Standing on the bank of a trout stream, seeing it wind past you through riffles and pools, pocketwater and runs, you're looking at a lot of water. But only certain parts of it hold fish. That's right: Even in a red-hot trout or smallmouth stream, a lot of water is fish-empty. The fish go to the good places, where there's cover, for survival, and food, and ignore the poor ones.

Some largemouth bass, smallmouth bass, and panfish lakes are good all around their edges; others are good for a stretch, poor to useless for the next, good again for the stretch after that. But when these fishes go deep in that standing water, they can *really* cluster. Same with trout in lakes—much of your typical trout lake is fishless most of the time, perhaps all the time.

 **Break Large Rivers Down**   Tr-S   Sm-S

A river that's several long fly casts across is bound to make a fly fisher who's used to dropping a fly along the far bank with ease uneasy. Solution: Break that big water into small water. First, in most large rivers, the fish hold near the banks—that makes your target water relatively small, and close. Second, in that band of shore water you can just look for the places you seek out in streams: riffles, side channels, and current tongues in pool-like pockets. Use your small-water experience to catch fish when you're on big water.

There are tips in this book on how to "read water," how to recognize the places that attract particular species of fish (tips 156 through 161). Read those tips, use them. But also remember: Most of the water you see is just . . . water, not fish lies.

Tip 164 Fish Lies Can Change

 Tr-S, Tr-L   Lg-L   Sm-L, Sm-S   Pf-L

It makes sense that fish in both lakes and rivers will move to different places as the water level rises or drops. A trout or smallmouth stream at middling height can become a whole new stream in late summer when it's crazy low—some of the former hot fishing spots are now just dry, sun-whitened streambed stone, and some of the previously too-fast sections have smoothed out to where the fish like them.

Rivers, streams, and creeks especially change as annual flooding scours and reshapes them, and the fish move accordingly. But lake lies can change too. Season can also be important: Trout or bass or panfish may move to suit changing water temperatures and other factors.

Year to year, fish lies can change. I used to hook several largemouth bass nearly every time I worked the corner of a little local lake. This went on all through every summer for a decade. Then the bass lost interest the spot.

Now *why* in the name of Izaak Walton (look him up) would they do *that*?

I don't know why, but it makes a point: Fish will often change holding water as conditions change, but sometimes for reasons we'll never understand. So accept, adjust, and keep an open mind about where fish lie.

Tip 165 Think Like a Fish

 Tr-S, Tr-L   Lg-L   Sm-L, Sm-S   Pf-L

Neither you nor I will ever see a beautifully proportioned rainbow trout across a crowded riffle and break into the chorus of "The Indian Love Call"—in other words, we'll never truly *experience* what it's like to have a fish brain. That's definitely good, overall. Still the old advice to anglers to "think like a fish" makes a worthy point: If you understand what's important to a fish, you improve your odds of both finding it and convincing it to take your fly. The three things most important to a fish are (1) survival, (2) food, and (3) making more fish.

SURVIVAL

Give a fish a reason for concern—and it's gone. It's *watching* for moving shadows, for anything flying overhead or dropping on the water. It's *listening* for a splash, for the crunch of gravel. You need to get your fly to that fish without alarming it. Become a ninja.

To survive, a fish must also go where water temperature and oxygen are acceptable, and, often, where there's some form of cover for protection.

FOOD

Fish go where the food is. If there's a hatch of midges, *there's* the food. Minnows, food. Crayfish, food. Find the food, imitate the food with your fly, and you're probably on the path to catching fish.

MAKING MORE FISH

Fish preparing to spawn or having just spawned act in strange ways, may go places they won't normally go, and may feed aggressively or not at all. You need to understand how spawning makes your target fish behave. Whether or not you should target pre- or post-spawn fish depends on the particular fish, and sometimes on your ethics. (See tip 47.)

Tip 166 Don't Be Quick to Write Off Water

Tr-S, Tr-L   Lg-L   Sm-L, Sm-S   Pf-L

So your fly-fishing friends tell you that if you work a certain river upstream from a certain bridge, the fishing will be great. You go, and it isn't. In fact, it's lousy. What happened?

Did your friends all lie? Probably not. More likely you failed to do your homework. That is, you didn't check around online, didn't ask at your local fly shop, didn't even ask your friends when and under what conditions their bridge water was good. Two months later or one month earlier it might have been spectacular.

If I tried to make a list of all the waters I know—lakes, streams, reservoirs, beaver ponds, etc.—that are good only under the right conditions and at the right time of year, it'd be a very long list. Imagine how many others I *don't* know that are just as dependent on timing and weather as these. I know streams that freeze solid every winter and whose trout are slow to return once the ice goes, largemouth lakes that provide very consistent action until after Labor Day weekend and then, as far as the fishing along the shoreline goes, simply shut down, and so on, and so on . . .

So do your due research. And don't be quick to declare any water as poor for fishing unless you really know it is.

Tip 167 Crowded Fish Offer Fast Fishing

Tr-S, Tr-L   Lg-L   Sm-L, Sm-S   Pf-L

I've noticed that on streams packed with smallmouth bass, the fishing often sizzles and . . . the bass are small. It's about competition—all those bass are struggling to get their share of the food. Change the balance and you change the behavior: Take a bass-filled stream and cut the fish population by, say, two-thirds, and you're going to catch fewer, larger bass—and they probably won't be particularly aggressive. Why should they be? No one's crowded up around them grabbing the food before they can reach it; crayfish and stonefly nymphs are everywhere for the taking.

Here's the whole point tightened up: Lots of bass = easy, reliable fishing for small-ish fish. Not too many bass = sometimes challenging fishing that requires timing for bigger fish.

Though I've observed this principle at work in smallmouth bass streams in particular, I've seen it with largemouth bass nearly as often. Sometimes with smallmouths in lakes. Too many trout in a stream or lake also makes for fast, consistent fishing. Trout creeks, generous in spawning opportunities and often stingy in feed, usually qualify. Panfish? Well, I fished a lake hours away last spring that was crammed with bluegills and I could hardly make a cast without hooking one, but on a local lake of few but large bluegills I have noticed that they often take a crazy long time to rise to a popper or floating bug . . .

Tip 168 Whatever Holding Water You Get, Work With It (That's What the Fish Do) Tr-S, Tr-L Lg-L Sm-L, Sm-S Pf-L

If you find neatly defined riffles and runs and pools in a trout stream or classic lily pad fields in a largemouth lake, fine, fish those. But if you encounter such oddities as car bodies packed into the bank of a trout river for erosion control, concrete bridge supports in a smallmouth stream, or a waterweed-chopping machine docked in a

In the current breaks among these old car bodies set into a stream bank up in British Columbia, trout were there, waiting for a dry fly.

Close against this bridge pier in Montana, a 16-inch brown trout grabbed my soft-hackled fly—then charged off downstream.

Man-made structures like this . . . whatever-it-is in an Arizona reservoir can attract bluegills, smallmouths, and other warmwater fishes, especially where they create shade.

largemouth-and-bluegill lake, and they seem to offer a good lie for fish, fish those too. I have, in fact, fished each of those three peculiar features and caught fish at all of them.

Fish want cover, overhead or side, and shade, and they're fine with whatever provides them. Humans see a weed-chopper and never give it a thought—it's nothing like the bluegill lies they've read about and fished before. But the bluegills don't care about any of that; they're happy there in the shade of that predator-proof cover.

Fish long enough and you'll see all sorts of odd or uncommon spots that can attract the fish you seek to catch, some as natural as a waterfall, others as unnatural as a giant yellow inflatable duck beached half out over a couple of feet of lake water. Even your own boat, if it, and you, sit quietly long enough, may attract trout or bluegills to hold in its comfortable shade.

Tip 169 Fish Often Move In and Out of and Around in Streams

 Tr-S   Sm-S

Trout and smallmouth bass have no qualms about running up a stream they vacated back when it was too high or too low, too cold or too warm, or about to freeze. Makes sense: Fish are pragmatists, and there's food in there to be got. This means that, depending on your timing, you may find a stream (or river or creek) loaded with trout or smallmouths or free of either of them.

There's seasonal migration, which tends to be fairly reliable. Also a lot of trout and smallmouth relocate as a stream drops or rises. But smallmouths are . . . weird. They sometimes just move up and down a stream, for no clear reason, in swarms. You go back to some stretch that two weeks earlier was loaded with smallies, and now? Nary a fish. But a week later they'll jam back in.

My point in all this: Don't be quick to write off a trout or smallmouth stream. Your poor fishing today may just be a matter of poor timing. Do a little research by inquiring at the nearest fly shop or going online. Or just drive up- or downstream a few miles and try again.

Tip 170 In Lakes, Trout Move

 Tr-L

In streams, trout let the current do much of their work: pass oxygenated water through their gills, slide them over to meet food or take cover with just a tilt of their fins or arch of their bodies, and present them constantly (though in varying abundance) with feed of all kinds. In streams, a trout can take up a lie and just stay there. But in lakes? Whole different story. There's no current (except at a stream mouth), so trout get none of the benefits current provides. In lakes, trout must compensate for the lack of current by spending most of their time on the move.

By swimming, trout in lakes find food, get their flow of oxygenated water, find comfy oxygen levels and temperatures.

All very interesting, you say, but how does this affect my fishing?

Bonus Tip Seeing Fish Is Good

Tr-S,Tr-L   Lg-L   Sm-L, Sm-S   Pf-L

Twenty years ago, as lake-fishing virtuoso Brian Chan and I were dropping anchors over a shoal, a couple of trout shot up out of the water nearby. Brian then said something like this: "At least we know they're here." He doubted those fish were feeding, had theories about why they leaped like that. But his point was plain and applies to nearly all fishing: However you spot fish, any fish, at least you know they're around to be caught.

Here's how: Effective stream fishing usually requires a constant covering of new water, but in lakes, because the trout are moving, you can often plant yourself and let them come to you.

Sure, trolling in a lake is a way of covering ever-new water. Sometimes it's the best way to work a lake, perhaps because the trout are spread out, and the fly that gets around eventually connects with them, or because the trout are gathered off somewhere and a trolled fly may find them so that you can stop and then work them with another method, or just . . . because.

But sharp, seasoned trout-lake fly fishers often fish with anchors down, working one patch of water to catch one trout after another for an hour, or for two or three. And they fish that way because they know trout keep moving in lakes and that if they just keep working an area of heavy trout traffic, odds are high they'll find trout. That should settle the matter for anybody.

Tip 171 Expect Odd Flows from Tailwaters   Tr-S   Sm-S

However you feel about the practice of damming rivers, streams, or creeks, the flows that emerge from one or more dams can be exceptional trout or smallmouth bass water. In *Fly Fishing Tailwaters* (a book about trout fishing), author Pat Dorsey says that sometimes "mediocre fisheries have become great because of the cold, nutrient-rich releases flowing from below the dams." Note that he says "because."

So tailwaters, the streams below dams, can be good fishing waters. But they can also behave weirdly.

Washington's Yakima River typically swells onto its banks and storms through its bed, high and angry, in August, when it should be low, sedate. Sure, any river can do that after heavy thunderstorms, but the Yakima does it because someone upstream pulls a lever or turns a dial or does something to let all that water out of one dam or another.

There are tailwaters like the Yakima everywhere. Rivers are more likely to be tailwaters than are creeks—the larger the flow, the more likely it's got a dam, perhaps several dams, somewhere upstream.

In the Deep South, stream levels of tailwaters can fluctuate wildly. During the hours of low demand for electricity, only one turbine may run and a river can look like a little canal way down at the bottom of a small, stony, steep-sided valley. When demands are high, only hours later, all turbines running, that same valley is brimming with river.

An Oregon tailwater river. Don't expect it to behave naturally—natural it is not.

A sudden rise or drop in volume every few weeks can put trout off feeding for a day or more in most streams. But in streams where such changes happen daily, as in the South, the trout just keep feeding.

With tailwater fishing, the rules get complicated, unnatural. So you need to figure out how all this affects any streams you plan to fish. Call or visit an area fly shop, go online. Plan accordingly.

Tip 172 The Best Cover Often Holds the Lunkers Tr-S, Tr-L   Lg-L   Sm-L, Sm-S   Pf-L

Big trout, smallmouths, largemouths, and panfish usually take up residence in the best cover. A big fish *needs* the best cover—such cover provides the space and concealment and protection from predators its bulky self requires. A log angling out over the black water along a cutbank: a fine place for a big brown trout. A large boulder down in a deep run: a fine place for a big smallmouth. A tree-shaded notch in the shoreline for bluegills. The one dock on a largemouth pond . . .

You get a sense about this business with time. You look around and a particular spot lights up your brain—before you can even think, you know the odds of a big fish there are good. Keep fishing and you'll grow ever better at recognizing big-fish lies.

What fine depth and flow and cover for a big brown trout—care to toss a nymph or streamer in there and see if you find one?

Tip 173 In Summer, Fish Deep, Early, or Late for Panfish, Largemouths, and Smallmouths in Lakes Lg-L Sm-L Pf-L

Not all panfish species go deep during the midday hours under hard sunshine in summer but invade the shallows and edge cover in the dim light of morning, evening, and cloud cover (the yellow perch, for example, is nearly always down at least 4 and sometimes 20 or 30 feet deep, sunshine or clouds regardless), but most do. As do largemouth and, in lakes, smallmouth bass. So if you can't get out at dawn and have to be home in time for dinner with your visiting aunt on a hot, glaring August afternoon, put on a sinking line, or at least a well-weighted fly on a long leader and tippet with a floating line, and reach into those invisible depths to find some bluegills.

Panfish and largemouths may hang close to the bottom just outside of weed lines at such times. Or they may hold where points of land continue off under the water. (Or they may go really deep, which gets tricky.) Smallmouths in lakes often hold in relatively shallow water next to deep, and head right off into that deeper water when the sun is bright and high overhead. Bottom line: They all go deeper, typically, under bright light.

Mind, this whole bright-day/deepwater thing is mainly about summer; the warmth of the sun may have other effects on these fishes in spring and fall when water temperatures are still warming toward comfy or cooling away from it. And even in summer it may not actually happen—all gamefish are rebels, basses and panfish included—but usually, it does.

Tip 174 Fallen Timber Appeals to Fish

 Tr-S,Tr-L Lg-L Sm-L, Sm-S Pf-L

A downed log is often a fine target for your fly—every year I catch largemouth bass holding under logs floating in the shallows, trout holding in the shade under one lying just over or only partly under the water, bluegills, smallmouths . . . Logs provide fish with serious cover, a barrier impenetrable to predators. Logs can even form new cover— in streams, big trunks anchored in the water by their sheer weight may tighten and angle currents to eventually carve good lies out of the streambed above and below them and along their sides.

Since trout, both basses, and panfish will often hold close to or under a log—for protection, shade, or both—you'd be wise get your fly under or within inches of that fallen cottonwood tree.

In a stream, for trout or smallmouth bass, your fly or popper should drift back, if possible, into the shade beneath a tree lying just over the water. In a lake, try to shoot it back there. A tree *in* a lake requires you to drop your fly or popper either right up tight to the wood or, in a stream rather than a lake, in an upstream spot where the current will carry it there. In streams with logs only *half* submerged, I've sometimes had to get my dry fly so close, in order to move a fish, that it occasionally touched bark on its drift.

Trees down in fishing water: a fine thing. Now you know what to do about it.

Care to bet there are no trout holding near and under all that wood in this trout stream? Don't bet. Keep your money.

Largemouths and panfish, possibly trout and smallmouths, will hang around such downed trees as the ones along this lake shoreline.

Tip 175 **Try the Stream Mouths**

 Tr-S, Tr-L   Sm-L, Sm-S

It's getting late in the season, into the hot, oppressive days that warm a lake beyond the comfort of trout. A lake just sits there under the sun, holding pretty much the same water, rising steadily in temperature. But a creek, a river? They flush themselves out all the time, new cool water coming down from high shaded valleys upstream. So in summer lakes, trout are likely to gather around river, stream, and creek mouths for all that cool, oxygenated water.

But trout will gather there any time of the season. Perhaps the lake is quiet but a hatch of mayflies is coming off a feeder stream, pouring the insects out into the lake. Happens all the time. The trout would be crazy not to cash in.

In some lakes with few trout per acre, feeder streams are where most of the fishing goes on all season because they're the one place enough trout congregate to make fishing worthwhile. Why all season? Trout in lakes just seem to like hanging around feeders.

So do smallmouth bass, and I'm not sure why. But, who cares why? They do it, and we should make that work for us.

Actually, it's not just about lakes. The mouths of tributary creeks and streams feeding rivers can attract both trout and smallmouths too. In *Fly Fishing for Western Smallmouth*, David Paul Williams, the author, says that "feeder creeks or tributaries" are a smallmouth "magnet." And David knows smallmouth bass . . .

Tip 176 Foam Is Home/Food

 Tr-S Sm-S

Fly-fishing guides have long said that "foam is home," which is a tad misleading. While trout certainly feed often and well on the insects that are drawn, along with white foam, into lines of current, likely few if any spend most of the time, day or night, there. "Home" is more likely a deepish, comfy lie fairly safe from predators. Perhaps this is why, more and more, I hear the guides saying, "Foam is food." And it is. Well, I mean, the foam itself isn't food, but it accompanies food.

In this odd sort of side pool/pocket, all the surface-feeding trout stayed within the borders of the foam.

This trout (showing only a dorsal fin) and a dozen others worked this foam line for hours.

Trout will often gather and feed in even a slim, spare line of foam like this one.

Foam is also cover. Patches of foam drifting regularly over trout or smallmouth bass may not *hide* these fishes from the predatory eyes of osprey and eagle, but they certainly make drawing a bead on them a challenge.

Foam comes in different forms, usually in a loose line of misshapen polka dots not far from a stream bank and sometimes in a line well out from the bank. But the broadest collections and the biggest rafts of foam I've seen were circling atop eddies.

Food and cover. No wonder trout and smallmouths love to pick at the water's surface where foam collects.

Tip 177 Lake Smallmouths Like Deep Water Nearby Sm-L

While I do find that when smallmouths hold in the shallows of lakes it's usually near deep water, I recently was fishing a big lake where I caught my largest smallie of the day near shore on a cobbled flat only around three feet deep—where there was no deep water anywhere nearby. Still, it's a (nearly) certain fact: Smallmouth bass in lakes would rather hold in relatively shallow water with the safety of depth close by than shallow water bordered by more shallow water. A lake bed sloping down from its shoreline or a shallow shelf that drops off a dozen feet out, for example—primo.

David Paul Williams, in his book *Fly Fishing for Western Smallmouth*, backs me up: "The best smallmouth flats will have deep water nearby. The fish can move onto the flats to feed, then scurry to safety in the deep water if necessary to avoid a predator."

Rock, shadows, and a sloping lake bottom provide a quick deepwater getaway—marvelous digs, from a smallmouth's perspective.

I haven't found this deepwater-getaway principle applying as much to streams—smallies, at least the small to middling-size ones, often seem happy to run way off the main flow into clear, still backwaters only two feet deep. The standing water of a lake and the standing water of a long backwater—what's the difference? Fish . . . go figure.

Tip 178 Cash In on the Crappie Season of Love Pf-L

Crappies, especially black crappies, can be hard to find most of the season, but they really bunch up for spawning—and when they're bunched the fishing can be *fast*. All this can start as early as January way down South (Alabama, Florida . . .) to as late as June way up North (Michigan, Washington State . . .). The fish typically hold somewhere between the bottom and the surface of water about 3 to 10 feet deep.

Crappies haven't much brainpower, but spook easily—employ stealth.

Try working your fly (something that'll sink down to them, a nymph perhaps, or you can cheat and cast a small crappie jig) at various depths among sparse waterweeds, around and in pockets in beds of thick weeds, and around flooded stumps and brush.

Lakes that hold largemouths and other warmwater fishes often hold crappies. but some don't. Find one that does, during their crappie lovefest, and amazing things can happen. . . .

Keep moving, fellow fly fishers, nothing to see here, just some fish-heavy pocketwater you wouldn't like. Please, go on up and fish the next pool.

Tip 179 Pocketwater Has Advantages

 Tr-S Sm-S

The best thing about pocketwater, a section of creek, stream, or river where largish to plain big boulders split quick currents, is that it's largely ignored. Your average angler looks at that riot of currents banging off each other like billiard balls on the break, and just passes quickly on in search of water that seems more promising.

Oh well . . . Their loss.

And those poor, untrained and eager, abundant (well, sometimes abundant) fish just go on waiting for you and me to come along and hook them, one after another.

No, pocketwater in a trout or smallmouth stream isn't always dynamite. But wherever a boulder shelters a depression, and strong flows hug that boulder to provide cover and a steady supply of nymphs and larvae to eat, there may be several fish holding in its wake. And if there's a pad of stalled water in front of that boulder, perhaps one or more fish holding there too.

Work pocketwater with a nymph for trout (though a dry fly or streamer can sometimes be good), dropping it upstream and letting the current carry it along the edge of the pad in front and then down a side. I usually work smallmouth pocketwater with a streamer or crayfish fly.

Always give pocketwater a try, if for no other reason than because few others do.

Tip 180 Don't Be a Pool Junkie on Creeks Tr-S 　 Sm-S

It's logical to assume that in a trickle, the only place a fish of even passable size can live is in a pool, where there's the most room, the most depth. But even on some creeks I've reckoned too small to hold *any* fish, I nonetheless found fish in all kinds of places.

I fish pretty much the same lies in creeks that I fish in rivers: pocketwater, riffles, banks, runs, pools (of course), and so on. There's usually good holding water of every variety for trout and smallmouth bass all through a creek—and, often, the best of it is ignored by most, even all, other anglers.

Don't pass up pools in creeks: I'm not suggesting that at all—creek pools can be excellent. My point: Don't concentrate on them to the exclusion of all those other fine lies.

Tip 181 Look for the Mud Line

Tr-L

It's tempting to get off a lake when the wind really comes up—the rocking boat, the slipping anchors, the frustrating casts, the slow torture of ceaseless pressure against the neck and ears. Frankly: yuck.

Trout don't mind it a bit, though, especially if the breaking waves beat a shoreline raising a band of muddy water along it—those waves will pound a lot of underwater bugs out of their hiding places. Trout learn to recognize the pattern of wind, mud, and feed along a downwind shoreline of slapping waves, and they appreciate the cover of cloudy water. Your job: Be there to offer those trout your fly among the displaced nymphs and scuds and larvae.

Whitecaps, a wave-battered shoreline, a murky band along that shoreline—the band holds a lot of kicked-up insects and other feed, which means it likely holds trout.

But being out in a boat is dangerous if the winds are seriously strong and the waves are big—don't fish or stay out on a lake in a threateningly heavy wind. But if it's a manageable, only annoying one, *fish*.

On a lake with a clear shoreline you may be able to fish from the bank, since the trout are in close. But most trout lakes lack clear banks. That means that in a boat you need to anchor upwind of the shoreline, a comfortable casting distance. It also means you need good wind-casting skills and sufficiently heavy anchors on long enough lines to hold you in place.

But if you have all that, just toss a reasonable nymph or streamer into the mud line and work it. Then brace yourself . . .

Tip 182 Smallmouths Love Weeds, Up to a Point . . .  Sm-L, Sm-S

Smallmouth bass have long been associated with rocky streams, at least partly, I suspect, as a way of setting smallmouth apart from largemouth bass in the minds of anglers. But that's flawed thinking. Indeed, smallmouths love boulders, cobble, and stone, but they also love weeds. Mostly . . .

They love weeds for exactly the same reason largemouth bass love weeds: Weeds grow food. Insects live among them, and delectable little fishes hide and feed among them. Weeds also provide cover for mature bass, hiding or obscuring them from predators.

If your smallmouth lake or stream is short on aquatic weeds—lily pads, primrose, whatever—always give beds of these plants a good working over with your fly. The

Weedy, weedy, and a good smallie on

fewer weeds a stream supports, the more smallies seem to like them. Fish open slots and pockets among the weeds, and fish the edges of weed beds. If the bass will come up for a hair bug, use that. If they're down and staying down, try a deep streamer or perhaps a crayfish pattern.

But if your smallmouth stream or lake is crammed full of weeds—and some *really* are—look for clear spots *without* weeds. Sounds odd, but it's worked for me. Maybe smallmouths get fed up with squirming through dense weeds. Those open spots next to rock walls, behind boulders, or just appearing over cobble seem to give smallmouths a chance to breathe, at least figuratively, and smallmouths seem to like that.

Tip 183 Look for the *Shady* Rocks in Smallmouth Lakes

 Sm-L, Sm-S

In lakes, smallmouth bass tend to hang around boulders, small to large, high enough to cast shadows—shadows that hide or obscure the bass from predators, and from the prey they seek to ambush. Must be a boon to a smallie, being able to pop out of nowhere and grab a baby bass or shiner before it can even try to dart off.

Author David Paul Williams comes close to backing me up in *Fly Fishing for Western Smallmouth* when he says, in his section on smallmouth lakes, "The greater the disparity in the size of the rocks making up the reef—from baseball size to Smart Car size—the more fish will be found." Variety in rock size may be his point, but he clearly includes big rocks, with *shadows*.

Lake beds, of course, can be composed of all sorts of rock—cobble, fist-size stones, flat rocks, etc.—that will attract smallmouths at times. But none of them provide enough shade to be worthwhile. Boulders and large rocks with real height provide lots of sneeze-worthy shadows.

Streams? Sure, the shade of boulders offers the same advantages to smallies there as in lakes. And they do take advantage of that—I've found smallmouths crammed in along the length of a slim shadow against a rock ledge in a stream. But, at least in my experience, rock shade is a bigger deal in lakes than in streams.

Tip 184 Try the Shallows for Trout

 Tr-S, Tr-L

It's a given that largemouth bass and panfish spend a lot of time hanging around the edges of lakes, often in surprisingly shallow water (though less surprising after you've chased these fishes long enough). I've certainly caught smallmouth bass in thin water edging lakes and streams. But trout, even large ones, in a lake's or stream's shallows? Yup, it happens, which makes sense—there's food in there.

I've caught 20-inch browns and rainbows that were cruising open channels among a lake's shallow weed beds, water just a couple of feet deep—on dry flies. Seeing a dark elongated form swaying in the clear water, dropping the fly a safe distance ahead, seeing the fish tip its body up to glide toward the fly, a nose emerging quietly to drop over it. Just . . . heavenly. And I've found large trout holding in the thin water of streams many times.

Shallow trout in streams and lakes will take dry flies, nymphs hung from dry flies, nymphs swung or swum, streamers—all the standard stuff. But remember: They're nervous in there. Use stealth.

In lakes, trout go to the shallows when the shallows are cool and well oxygenated— spring and fall possibly all day, midseason in the morning and evening. Streams? There, it can happen about any time.

In shallows, a stream trout, especially a large one, is more likely to hold next to a boulder or a grassy cutbank— somewhere with at least some cover and depth—than out in the thin, open, flat water you see along this stream bank. Still, could be a 20-incher there. It happens . . .

Dropping a fly in a lake's shallows: There's food in there, trout food, so there could be trout in there too.
SKIP MORRIS

CHAPTER 6
HOOKING, PLAYING, LANDING, HANDLING, AND RELEASING FISH

Tip 185 Try to Adjust Your Hook Set by Fish Size  Tr-S, Tr-L

Fly fishers often talk about the big fish they've broken off when setting the hook: "Three X just snapped like . . . *nothing*." They're still looking, it seems, for an explanation.

I think I know what happened.

Consider this: When you set the hook hard on a 10-inch trout, weighing only about 6 ounces, you'll drag it perhaps an inch or even two before it bolts. Set the hook hard in a *20*-inch trout, of perhaps 3 pounds . . . *and*? You won't budge it. The fish that relents, or more accurately, gets drawn by the hook set, cushions the tippet. The fish that doesn't, like a concrete fly shop, strains the tippet to the max.

Or beyond it.

So the exact same hook set that's fine for a 10-incher snaps off the fly on a 20-incher.

What do you do with this information? First, if you *see* your trout and it's big, back off a little on your hook set (unless your big streamer fly or cluttered nymph rig or such requires a hard set). Second, if you *can't* see your trout, have no idea how big it is, *assume* it's big and set firmly, sure, but not *too* hard—this way you'll probably get the hook well into a smaller fish, but if it's a big one, you'll avoid a hook-set break-off.

I haven't noticed any of this affecting my largemouth or smallmouth fishing, probably because with largemouths, and to a lesser degree smallmouths, thick, tough tippets and hard, even violent hook sets are standard practice. I nearly always use heavy tippets for panfish because bass, both basses, live with them and will take panfish flies, so, here again, tippets snapping, not an issue.

Tip 186 Embrace the Dry-Fly Pause

Tr-S, Tr-L   Lg-L   Sm-L, Sm-S   Pf-L

I learned to fly fish on creeks not far from Seattle, Washington—pure, quick water holding small, quick coastal cutthroat trout. Feed is scarce in those creeks, and the trout must be quick so they catch every little bite possible. Because they're quick, so you must be quick too when you hook-set your dry fly.

Most trout live in streams, and lakes, of at least sufficient productivity that they can take their time in feeding, and do. That makes the quick hook set a problem with a floating fly. Of course, if you're nymph fishing, none of this applies—a deep nymph must be set immediately at the slightest sign of a take.

The United States has picked up all sorts of interesting things from the British: our primary language, crumpets (to a degree), the Beatles, and the dry-fly fisher's phrase, "God save the queen." Here's how that phrase works: You see the trout's rise, immediately say "God save the queen," and then just as you finish the last word, you set the hook. This gives the trout time to drift its calculated way up, open its mouth, take in the fly, and close its mouth.

Shorten the pause to as brief as "God save" if the trout are aggressive; lengthen it to "God save the queen, king, and prince" if your trout are sluggish to the extreme.

A little pausing can pay off when largemouth and smallmouth bass and panfish take floating hair bugs and poppers too.

Tip 187 As Soon as You Even Suspect You've Hooked a Good Fish, Get Sharp

 Tr-S, Tr-L   Lg-L    Sm-L, Sm-S   Pf-L

The wording of this tip is vague—what, exactly, is a "good" fish? Let me clarify. In this case, it's any fish that's big enough, strong enough, or both to take advantage of your mistakes.

Loose line in the bottom of a boat is a potential tippet snapper. The moment that big fish hits, make sure you're not standing on the line—and then do not move your feet.

There's that moment when the first pull of a hooked fish suggests you're in for a scramble. *That's* when you need to get things in order and set your mind for battle.

Actually, you'd be wise to always have things in order—line untangled and not underfoot, reel drag properly adjusted, and such—*before* you hook that maniac, Olympic-athlete trout or smallmouth, or even gargantuan bluegill. But when you do hook a powerhouse fish, you need to ready your tackle as quickly as possible.

You need to ready your mind too. First, get calm—panicking loses fish. Second, focus on the fish, where it's headed, how large and strong it feels. Third (and these steps need to whiz by—you have almost no time to get through them), identify the potential trouble waiting out there for your opponent to find: docks, weeds, fallen trees, or just lots of open water for tearing out more line and backing than you care to give, or have to give.

Tip 188 Play Fish with *Constant* Pressure, with Two Exceptions

Tr-S, Tr-L   Lg-L   Sm-L, Sm-S   Pf-L

Fish find ways to come off hooks whose barbs are fully intact, never mind hooks whose barbs are smashed down or nonexistent.

Which brings us to the matter of slack. Not slack that's about curves or waves in tippets and leaders and lines on the water for creating dead drifts of dry flies or indicators; here we're talking (or at least I am) about slack that comes with letting a rod go straight and a fly line go limp when a fish is on—*this* sort of slack is the enemy.

A fly fisher may lose a big fish, and then say, "But I kept the line tight almost the whole time!" Yeah, *almost*. That brief moment the line went soft, went *slack*, was probably the moment the fish came off.

So, once a fish is hooked—smallmouth, trout, largemouth, panfish, whatever—from that point on, you must keep the pressure *constant*. A heartbeat of slack is the heartache of losing a fish. Hope that wasn't a lunker . . .

The exceptions? A trout, in a stream or lake, is running for a tangle of submerged branches or under a log and it's too strong to stop. If you can't turn the fish, you can give it . . . slack. That's right: Drop the rod tip to let the line go limp. The trout figures it's free and *sometimes* will stop or change direction. Sometimes. The other exception is when a large fish leaps—you drop the rod tip to slacken the line. If that wildly flapping tail hits a tight tippet . . . *snap!*

Tip 189 Play a Fish with Your Rod at a Right Angle Tr-S, Tr-L Lg-L Sm-L, Sm-S Pf-L

To complete the tip title above: . . . at a right angle *to the line*. When you're playing a fish, any fish, your rod is bowed—how do you create a right angle, any angle, with something curved? Answer: You form the right angle between the taut line and the lower, nearly straight third or so of the rod, down by the grip.

Not passing this angle keeps you from bending the rod back too far and possibly breaking it against a strong fish. Actually, it's fine to pass it—a little. And that's going to happen when you've got a crazy fish on the line. Just don't pass the right angle by a lot.

If a rod is angled toward a fish, it's nearly impossible for a big fish to break even a supple rod designed for a light fly line.

Shoot for a right angle between rod and line, but don't fret when you lose that angle by a bit. Just try to keep it down to a bit.

A big trout may take your entire line and keep going, and going. . . . That's why fly-line backing is invaluable.

Tip 190 Give Line to a Fish That Insists on Taking It Tr-S, Tr-L Lg-L Sm-L, Sm-S Pf-L

Large trout, when hooked, love to charge off for the horizon. Clamping down hard on the reel when a big trout (or any big fish) is running can only end in a busted tippet or a lost fly, a lost fish, and heartache.

Your strategy for handling a big trout begins well before it's hooked, with your reel's drag. Set that drag consciously, so that it releases line with real resistance but not so much resistance that the tippet will break against it. (Fly fishers who "palm" their reels may set their drags a tad lighter than those who don't.)

Therefore, you need a fly reel with a smooth, reliable drag if you expect to ever hook a large trout. (But remember: Large trout are often unexpected.)

Here's what you need to do. When the trout runs, hold the line lightly (that is, a bit under the breaking point of the tippet), and let the trout pull out line between your thumb and finger. When the extra line is almost gone, let go of it and lower the rod tip—this gives the reel's spool a chance to get turning. Now let the fish peel off line as long as it wants (against the properly set drag . . .). When the trout stops, start to "pump" it back in (see the next tip). But if the trout starts to run again—let go of the reel handle and let it run. And don't even touch the reel handle until the trout stops running.

A largemouth or smallmouth or panfish making a real run is uncommon, but if you hook one of these fishes and it's in a mood to really charge off, treat it like a running trout.

Tip 191 Learn to Pump In a Fish

 Tr-S,Tr-L   Lg-L   Sm-L, Sm-S   Pf-L

In the previous tip you learned to let a running fish run. But what do you do when the fish stops running? You pump the fish in. Here's how:

Reel in line as you *gradually* lower the rod tip forward while maintaining *constant* pressure on the fish. This reeling and lowering probably won't move the fish much.

Once the rod tip is low, draw in the fish; in other words, raise the rod tip while holding the reel's handle, or holding the line or palming the reel. Now you're pulling the fish in.

When the rod tip's up comfortably high, stop raising it, and reel as you lower the rod tip again.

Every *moment* in the process of pumping in a fish, expect it to run again, and stay ready to let it. If the fish runs, whip your reeling hand away from the reel immediately—if you even *touch* the spinning reel handle, the tippet may break.

Pumping works for every large fish I've ever caught: trout, both largemouth and smallmouth bass, big bluegills, Pacific salmon, steelhead, black rockfish, carp . . .

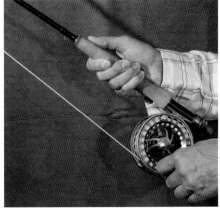

Lower the rod's tip and reel in the line. SKIP MORRIS

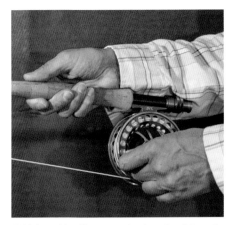

Hold the reel handle as you raise the rod and draw the fish in. SKIP MORRIS

The fish bolts—get your hand away from that reel! SKIP MORRIS

Tip 192 Chase a Fish If You Must

 Tr-S, Tr-L   Sm-L, Sm-S

A trout or smallmouth that's exceptionally big, strong, or *both* may, on the hook set, charge off for the horizon. And keep going. No one carries enough backing on their reel for that.

So you follow your fish, you *chase* it. If you can, that is.

I once hooked a wild, mighty rainbow trout of probably four pounds in a broad, swift spring creek in Oregon. The fish shot off downstream and I shot off after him along a blessedly clear bank, practically running rather than wading across a quick feeder creek. Finally the trout came to a canyon and sailed downstream into it where I couldn't possibly follow and where it would have been dangerous to try. Yeah, he broke me off.

There are two key points in this story: (1) I nearly ran across the creek, rather than wading across it carefully and safely—which was foolish and dangerous and do *not* ever do that yourself—and (2) I was wise enough to not possibly *die* for a fish—by following it down into the swift currents pressing the steep walls of that narrow canyon.

In the excitement of a big fish, you can make bad decisions. Don't make them dangerous ones.

On the other hand, if it appears your backing is running thin and your fish is still charging away, follow carefully up- or downstream in pursuit, or if you're in a boat with a friend, have your friend row or fire up the outboard and chase after the fish.

If you're in a boat by yourself, well, that's tough. Best of luck. You can let off the pressure, hope the fish stops, then runs off in a better direction when you tighten again. Here too, best of luck . . .

Tip 193 Control That Line

 Tr-S, Tr-L   Lg-L   Sm-L, Sm-S   Pf-L

If the verb *control* makes you jittery (it does sound, well, confrontational), replace it from here on in your mind with the gentler word *manage*. Frankly, though, I do think that here, the sterner word fits best.

Lose control of your line and you lose control of your hook sets and of your fish. That leaves you with lots of missed and lost fish. Typically, you lose control of your line when you have too much of it lying on the water.

Okay, with all those tips that talk about *intentionally* creating slack in fly line, I can see how this tip could confuse. Here's the point: You want *enough* slack in your floating line so that a dry fly or strike indicator can ride a current dead drift (if a dead-drift presentation is appropriate)—but not so much slack you can't set the hook right and then keep tight to the fish.

Sometimes—but rarely—the problem is slack line out near the fly; nearly always, though, the problem is too much slack line in near you. The fish takes, you try to set the hook, and all you accomplish is to pull in only part of all that loose line strewn on the water: The hook never gets tugged into the fish, the fish spits out the fly with a sneer and swims away.

Bonus Tip **In Lakes, Play Trout Hard** Tr-L

Whatever the reason, I find that in streams I land the most trout by playing them with firm and constant pressure, but in lakes, with pressure greater than firm—"heavy" might describe it best. (And, of course, also constant.) My trout-lake-icon friend Brian Chan and I have confirmed it to our satisfaction: The best way to play trout in lakes is *hard*. (When any fish needs to run, though, a trout in a lake included, do let it run.)

The solution: Keep track of the slack fly line outside your rod's tip, and just draw some in when you feel there's too much of it for you to set that hook when the need suddenly arises.

There's almost never a reason for any slack line on a lake (with the exception of the line belly wind creates in chironomid fishing).

Tip 194 Don't Reel In Line Unless You Need To Tr-S, Tr-L Lg-L Sm-L, Sm-S Pf-L

It's fine to have extra line hanging below your rod or line hand and your reel; in fact, it's usually an advantage—whenever you need some more line, there it is, waiting at your convenience.

New fly fishers tend to spend much of their time pulling off line, and reeling it back up. It's orderly, sure, and they deserve a merit badge for neatness, but it's unnecessarily distracting and a waste of perfectly good fishing time.

On the other hand, when casts are going to be of only 25 to 35 feet for a while yet 60 feet of line is off the reel, that's a lot of loose line piled at the feet or swinging downstream in the current. It gets tangled, caught up in feet, in boulders, in the branches of fallen trees . . . So wind some of it up. But leave some out too, because cast length in actual fishing is rarely constant.

This is all about line between hand and reel—none of it has anything to do with line outside the rod tip. That's different. (See tip 193.)

Tip 195 Play a Fish on Your Reel Only If the Fish Makes You

Tr-S, Tr-L Lg-L Sm-L, Sm-S Pf-L

It's logical, once you've hooked a fish big enough and strong enough to take out line, to reel up any loose line and play the fish off the reel. But logic can be false, and in this case, it is.

When new fly fishers keep losing fish and I finally stop fishing to watch them, I often see them struggling to reel in extra line. While their attention is on that, of course, it's not on maintaining pressure or managing the fish so, one way or another, the fish usually comes off.

If you have a dozen feet of line hanging between your hand and your reel and you hook a fish that wants to run, don't start reeling—instead, create the same resistance you'd want from your reel's drag by squeezing the line between thumb and finger.

Often, a running fish (usually a trout, but not always) will take some of the loose line and stop, never taking it all. If so, just work the fish in, letting it run when it wants (against the line-squeezing pressure from your hand).

What if the fish takes all the loose line? No problem, let it. *Then* play the fish off the reel. Now when it runs, the fish runs against the reel's drag; when you work the fish in, you *reel* it in. (Or more likely, you pump it in. See tip 191.)

Here's a tip-within-a-tip: As the end of the slack line hits the reel, lower your rod tip to soften the transition. A static reel spool wants a little help to beat inertia and get spinning.

Tip 196 Play a Largemouth Hard, and Expect a Dirty Fight Lg-L

Hooked, a trout becomes a sprinter, charging off into the distance (if it's big enough and strong enough and has room to sprint). A hooked largemouth? Street fighter.

The moment it's stung, a largemouth bass will head straight for a branch on a sunken tree and run circles around it, winding your tippet on tight. Chance? I doubt it. Largemouth bass know how to fight dirty and seem to like doing it. They also like to occupy places tight with lily pads, stumps, bulrushes, primrose—stuff that lends itself to dirty fighting.

What can you do about it? You can show up with the right tackle. A rod stiff enough to handle at the very least a 6-weight line, preferably a 7, perhaps an 8 (at the extremes a 9 or 10—or *11*). Heavy leaders with heavy tippets. A 1X tippet is none too stout where a 6-pound largemouth is possible.

You can also show up with the right strategies. Immediately after setting the hook, try to slide the bass away from cover before it knows what's up. After that, just keep the pressure on and try to guide the bass away from the worst of its options. If it burrows back into weeds or wood, stay calm and see if you can work it back out once it's tired. If you really have to dig the bass out and there are nasty snakes and snapping turtles and such around, dig it out with an oar or a long-handled net.

Tip 197 Play Crappies Lightly

Pf-L

Crappies aren't like other panfish. What most sets crappies apart from the rest, to my mind (other than their dead-low IQs): They're fragile.

Crappie enthusiasts sometimes call their beloved disc-of-a-fish the "paper mouth" based on the ease with which a hook tears free of their mouths.

Their fragility doesn't end with their mouths—it's easy to injure or kill a crappie by handling it roughly. So be gentle, careful. And don't try to "lip" a crappie or you'll condemn it to a broken jaw and probably a slow death by starvation.

But crappies are wonderful gamefish—great fun! Don't avoid them just because they require some extra care in playing and handling.

Tip 198 Net Right

 Tr-S, Tr-L   Lg-L   Sm-L, Sm-S   Pf-L

Look at a fisherman's net, and you'll notice that it's a sort of parachute with holes. It'll sweep through air no sweat. But through dense water? With sweat. Fish are infinitely more streamlined than nets—in an underwater race between a net and a fish, the fish wins eleven out of ten times.

So don't chase your fish with your net in a race you'll almost certainly lose. You'll more likely bang the tippet and break it than net the fish. Here's the right way to net a trout (or a bass or panfish, which is sometimes the best way to handle them too):

Head up

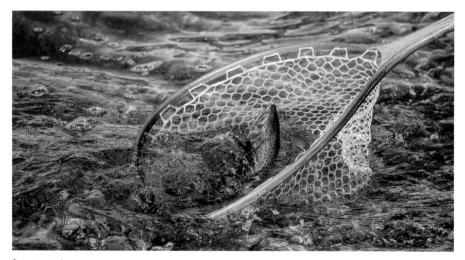

In past net rim

Net up

1. Play the fish long enough so that you can slide it in with its head up at least partly out of water. (But try not to play the fish longer than necessary.)
2. Before the fish comes near, lower the front of your net's rim well down into the water and hold it there, still.
3. Slide the fish in over the submerged rim of the net.
4. Raise the net—and there it is: netting done right.

Tip 199 Playing a Fish? Keep That Line-Leader Connection Outside the Tip Guide Tr-S, Tr-L Lg-L Sm-L, Sm-S Pf-L

There are several ways a tapered leader can be attached to a fly line—by interconnected loops, one pre-tied in the butt of the leader and the other built into the tip of the line;

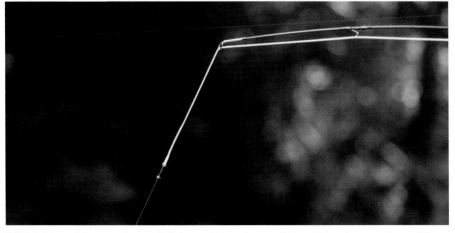

While fighting a fish, you can leave as little line as this out of your rod's tip guide—as long as you're careful not to pull or reel the line in during the skirmish.

by a nail knot; by a short, thick stretch of monofilament attached to the line with a nail knot and attached to the leader with a blood knot; and so on—and they can all cause a problem. The problem is, they catch in the rod's tip guide. Even the smoothest connection is stiff enough and lumpy enough to hang up in the tip—the fish bolts, pop goes the tippet.

The solution: When you're playing a fish, keep that connection—or any knot high up a leader—*outside* the tip guide. Wait until you're confident your fish is done running before taking that connection inside the tip guide. Or, if possible, don't take it in at all.

If you're willing to do a little stretching of the arms you can often reach back with the rod and well forward with the net and net the fish while keeping the end of the line still outside the rod, even with a fairly long leader-tippet rig. A long-handled net helps.

Tip 200 Never Squeeze a Fish

 Tr-S, Tr-L   Lg-L   Sm-L, Sm-S   Pf-L

We fly fishers forget that we're humongous in comparison to even a hefty smallmouth bass or trout. But we are . . . Human: 175 pounds. Hefty trout: 3 pounds. Ratio of human mass to trout mass: 58.3333 (etc.) to 1. So this middling-size man is a tad over 58 times the size of this fish. He must therefore be at least 30 times stronger.

So imagine if we were talking about two people, and one was fully *twice* as strong as the other—that's a *huge* difference, right? Between man and fish we're talking not about twice or 4 times or even 10 times, but *30* times the strength.

Imagine how easily you could hurt a fish.

One light squeeze from you could be fatal, injuring organs, the beginning of a slow and miserable death. Even if you plan to kill a fish, you surely don't want it to suffer. If you plan to release it, you want it to neither suffer nor die.

So if you need to hold a fish's body in your hand—do not squeeze. You can cradle the fish in stiffened fingers to control it; just (again) *don't* squeeze it, not even for a moment, even if it shimmies wildly in your hand. A net can sometimes make fish easier to manage as you unpin the fly or work a throat pump.

Tip 201 Turn Over a Trout

 Tr-L

Another lesson from my friend and coauthor (not on this book, but on another), trout-lake-master Brian Chan: Before you extract your fly from a trout (or pump its throat), turn it upside down. The trout will likely go calm, as long as you keep it—especially its head—submerged. All the better for you, and for the trout. As soon as it's unhooked (or pumped), turn the fish right side up.

Flipping a trout is a tactic for lakes, where currents don't complicate everything. Might work in the quiet parts of streams, though.

A trout turned upside down is less likely to injure itself with its thrashing than one that's right side up. That's because a flipped-over trout is unlikely to thrash at all.

Tip 202 If You're Going to Use a Throat Pump, Use It Right Tr-L

Brian Chan and I hesitated to even mention the throat pump (usually called a stomach pump) in our book *Morris & Chan on Fly Fishing Trout Lakes*, because while handy for determining what trout have been eating, and used commonly by fisheries biologists, a throat pump used wrong inflicts torture.

But, it's out there—people buy it and use it—so we figured we'd better help them use it properly. No problem: Brian is a fisheries biologist, so I ran everything below past him to make sure it was right.

Use the pump only on trout of 14 inches or over.

Keep the trout in the water, *head and gills submerged*, until it calms down. Never squeeze a trout. Cradle it in your fingers or keep it in the net. Keeping a trout flipped over, belly up, can quiet it down.

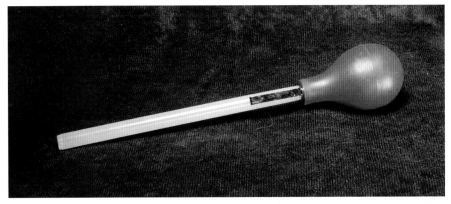

There it is: the throat pump. A harmless tool for investigatory work when used right; when used wrong, one for torture. Please, I beg of you: Use it correctly or use it never.

Fill the pump with water, then squirt the water out to clean out the pump. Depress the empty bulb.

Slid the tube gently into the trout's mouth and down into its throat. *Stop* when the tube resists even slightly—*never* apply *any* force. The end of the tube should now lie against the outer rim of the throat.

Release all pressure on the bulb. A suction seal should be formed and the bulb should remain depressed.

Back the tube out (the bulb should pop back into shape), set the pump aside, and carefully manage the trout until it swims off.

Depress the bulb again and *now* suck up some lake or river water into it. Squirt the water and contents into a clear plastic bag, a white bowl, your palm . . . If you get no samples, the trout must have swallowed before you pumped it. Just try again with another trout.

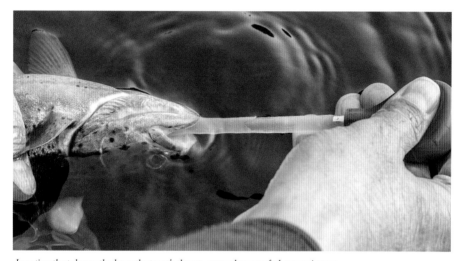

Inserting the tube gently down the trout's throat—stop when you feel any resistance.

Release pressure on the bulb. It should remain depressed. From this point, quickly finish with the trout and then free it.

Tip 203 Consider Catch-and-Release

Tr-S, Tr-L   Lg-L   Sm-L, Sm-S   Pf-L

Since at least the 1950s, anglers have realized the obvious: killing fish leaves ever fewer fish to catch. Enter: catch-and-release.

There is another option: Raise fish in hatchery tanks and then occasionally dump off a heap of these pampered innocents into a lake or stream for slaughter. The problem: Hatchery fish (at least trout) are often too easy to catch, short-lived, susceptible to disease, and poor fighters.

My all-time-favorite literary fly-fishing author, Roderick Haig-Brown, says in *Fisherman's Summer*, "Artificial hatching and rearing and planting [of fish] on a put and take basis should always be a last resort." (Reprinted from *Fisherman's Summer* by Roderick Haig-Brown, by permission of Skyhorse Publishing, Inc.)

The book was published in 1959.

There are smart hatchery programs that do make good fish. But should we use them to replace wild, native fish that have evolved over unimaginable centuries to perfectly suit their particular stream or lake?

Even with hatchery fish, you have to consider: The fewer you take, the more remain and the better the fishing will hold up.

There's a philosophy out there that says catching and releasing fish is torture and that killing every fish that's caught is kinder. I respect others' rights to their opinions. If I were a fish in a net, though, and that barbless fly hook was already backed out of my jaw, I'd just want to swim off home.

A wild cutthroat trout heads for its home in a deep corner of the stream after a skirmish and a poke in the jaw.

Tip 204 Release Your Fish Right

Tr-S, Tr-L   Lg-L   Sm-L, Sm-S   Pf-L

Broken jaws, crushed organs, torn gills, and other injuries caused by poor handling are slow death sentences for fish. The point of releasing fish is to return them to the water healthy, ready eventually to be caught (and released) again.

So if you plan to release your fish, here's how to do it well.

Fish flies with barbless hooks (that is, flies whose hook barbs you've crimped down with pliers or that you tied on hooks made without barbs). Carry forceps, or other hook-removing tools, and use them *carefully*. Back fly hooks out opposite the direction they went in. *Never . . . squeeze . . . a fish*, even a little for a moment. Keep a fish's head underwater (so the fish can breathe) and never raise it out of water beyond a few seconds. Fish are camera shy to the extreme—just take whatever photo you can quickly or give up if the fish won't cooperate. Play a fish only as long as you reasonably must so you don't exhaust it. With trout, a net may provide you the best control so you can avoid causing harm.

With both basses (and some panfish with large jaws) you can lip the fish by raising it with your thumb on top and curled first finger beneath the lower jaw, taking care not to hold the jaw open any wider than necessary (and, again, don't keep the fish's head out of water long); especially when you lip a large bass, raising it toward horizontal with your other hand under the body, back near the tail and behind the organs, adds anti-injury insurance. These days some fly fishers net or manage their bass in some other way without lipping, concerned that lipping could too easily cause injury. There's also that nasty business, in places with nasty snakes, of largemouth bass swallowing venomous snakes that bite the anglers' thumbs—a fine reason to find an alternate to lipping.

It's a fine feeling, watching a fish swim off unharmed. But that requires you don't harm it.

Tip 205 Consider Carrying Two Hook-Removing Tools

Tr-S, Tr-L   Lg-L   Sm-L, Sm-S   Pf-L

Long ago I went from carrying just forceps to also carrying the sort of hook extractor that slides down the tippet to push a fly out. Now I mostly use the sliding-down release (it still doesn't have a generic name), but when that doesn't work—thank God for forceps!

Also, having two hook removers covers me in case I lose one while fishing.

I use both sorts of tools on trout and panfish all the time. Smallmouth and largemouth bass offer a lot of working space inside their cavernous mouths, and the flies they take into them are generally big enough to provide me a good grip, so usually I can just reach in and remove the fly by hand. But these fishes can take a fly perilously deep or catch it in their gills; at such times the tools are invaluable.

Here's how to use forceps: Lightly clamp the jaws of the forceps onto the fly in the fish's jaw, and then back the fly out of the fish. Try not to tear up the fly in the process, but if it comes down to the life of a fish versus ruining a fly, sacrifice the fly.

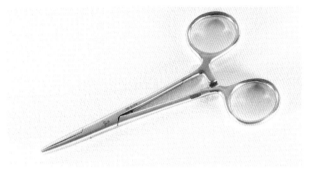

On the top is a newer sort of hook-releasing tool. On the right is the longtime standard tool for removing flies from trout and other freshwater fishes (ones that don't sting or bite): forceps.

Here's how to use the sliding kind of tool: Catch the tippet in the slotted tube at the end of the tool, slide the tube down to the fly, and push the fly out against the bend of its hook.

Tip 206 Make Sure You and Your Fish *Both* Part Ways Unharmed

 Tr-S,Tr-L Lg-L  Sm-L, Sm-S · Pf-L

Trout aren't likely to hurt anyone (though really large trout do grow teeth large enough to cut you). Both of the basses and every panfish I know have spines in their fins that will give you a good stab if you're not careful. Been there.

Really, though, this tip is about fishes other than trout, bass, and panfish—it's about those fishes you may catch that you don't know. Some of them really can hurt you.

Northern pike have long, sharp teeth set in long, strong jaws. Southern waters have bowfin, also with nasty teeth. Both can chew through even heavy standard tippet, so that fly fishers who target these fishes often use ultraheavy mono or even tippet made of wire. Imagine what such teeth could do to your hand . . .

It goes beyond pike and bowfin. Catfish, gar . . . you can get jabbed or chomped by several North American freshwater fishes that will take a fly. Africa, South America? I have no idea, but I'll bet there are *lots* of fly-fisher-chomping-and-stabbing fish species in those and in other exotic places.

Saltwater? Too many biters and stabbers—and stingers—to count.

At this point, consider yourself warned.

So what do you do when you hook a freshwater fish you don't recognize? If it seems in the least dangerous, keep your distance, cut the leader. Lose a leader, a fly, keep a finger. Excellent bargain.

CHAPTER 7

ALL ABOUT ARTIFICIAL FLIES

Tip 207 Carry a Foundation Set of Flies to Trout Streams  Tr-S

There are easily tens of thousands of established trout flies out there, but you really only need a small number of them to catch trout in rivers, streams, and creeks most of the time. After all, as I so love to say: How you fish a fly is at least as important as which fly you fish. (I love to say it partly because it's *my* saying, but mostly because it's true.) So, fished well and in the right place, the set of flies to come will typically do the job.

I selected the 14 flies—nymphs, floating emerger flies, dry flies, and a streamer—with care and thought, relying on my long experience with trout flies. (I've written nine books about tying them along with too many magazine articles to recall.) I also chose them based on their effectiveness and availability for purchase. These flies make up a team, each fly playing its critical position. If your fly shop or fly-fishing mail-order house lacks some of these patterns, ask for substitutes. You'll need two or three of each fly in each size—it's very discouraging to figure out the killing fly pattern in the killing size only to break off the only one you brought.

NYMPHS

- Beadhead Pheasant Tail
- Sizes 16, 14, 12

- Fox's Beaded Poopah, Olive
- Size 14

- Bitch Creek
- Size 8

- Copper John
- Size 14

FLOATING EMERGERS

- Brooks' Sprout, *Callibaetis*
- Sizes 18, 16, 14

- Griffith's Gnat
- Size 20

DRY FLIES

- Parachute Adams
- Sizes 18, 16, 14, 12

- Parachute Light Cahill
- Sizes 18, 16, 14, 12

- Elk Hair Caddis
- Sizes 16, 14, 12

- Stimulator, Orange (or Green)
- Size 8

- Dave's Hopper
- Size 10

- Royal Wulff
- Sizes 14, 12

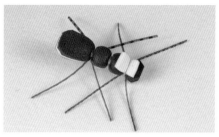

- Chernobyl Ant (lots of variations, nearly all are good)
- Size 8

- Clouser Minnow, Olive and White
- Size 6

Tip 208 Carry a Foundation Set of Flies to Trout Lakes Tr-L

As on trout streams (see the previous tip), you can cover most situations on trout lakes with only a small number of fly patterns.

Gathering up a sound group of flies for trout lakes, flies that cover all the important bases and work together as a team, is a daunting task even to the seasoned fly fisher who takes up the lake habit. Overwhelming for the beginning fly fisher. My purpose here is to de-daunt and underwhelm that task.

So here are nine trout-lake flies that will normally cover whatever's going on. They're all popular flies you can find online and in fly shops. But if your fly source lacks one or more of them, just ask for a sound substitute. You'll need at least two, preferably three, of each fly in each size. Carrying only one of a fly pattern is to tempt disaster . . .

Again relevant, my rule I so love to state: How you fish a fly is at least as important as which fly you fish. So, fish these nine flies well and they'll normally produce on lakes.

NYMPHS

- Chan's Chironomid Pupa
- Sizes 14, 12

- Gold-Ribbed Hare's Ear
- Size 14

- Damselfly Nymph (whatever green or olive damselfly nymph is currently popular; none seem to stick around long)
- Size 10 (if the fly's abdomen, not its tail, extends off the hook, get size 12)

- Sparkle Furry Dragon
- Size 6

- Scud, Olive
- Size 12

- Morris Boatman (also called the Morris Water Boatman)
- Size 14

DRY FLIES

- Morris Emerger, *Callibaetis*
- Size 14

- Elk Hair Caddis
- Size 12

STREAMER

- Woolly Bugger, Black
- Size 8

Tip 209 Carry a Foundation Set of Flies to Smallmouth Bass Streams and Lakes Sm-L, Sm-S

Trout fishing, in both lakes and streams, is often about fishing flies that imitate hatching insects—the trout make sure of that—but must the smallmouth bass fly fisher carry a bunch of hatch-matching flies? Not really.

Smallmouths are no fools—they can make you work to convince even a few of them among plenty. But when this happens, success is usually more about getting a reasonable fly to a certain depth or giving it a certain action (or lack of action) or some other matter of presentation rather than, as is common in trout fishing, about matching a particular hatching bug. (Though it *can* be about matching a particular bug, or a particular size and color of crayfish or such.)

So, you'll typically need fewer flies for smallmouth fishing than you would for trout fishing. Here are the five essential smallmouth flies I recommend.

Can't find these specific fly patterns (even if a couple aren't very specific)? Ask at your fly shop or fly-fishing mail-order house for substitutes. Get at least two, preferably three, of each fly so you don't have to fear losing that one fly that's raking in smallies.

STREAMERS

- Clouser Minnow, Olive (with a white belly)
- Size 8

- Woolly Bugger, Brown (with a metal bead or cone for a head)
- Size 6

- Whitlock's NearNuff Crayfish, Golden Brown
- Size 8

HAIR BUG AND POPPER

- Hair Bug, Brown (or tan or green or whatever, with a white or bright-colored face, so you can spot the bug)
- Body (not including tail) about ½ inch long (for some reason, bass-fly hook sizing varies wildly from one manufacturer to another)

- Popper (cork or foam, white or some pale color)
- Body (not including tail) ½ to ⅝ inch long (again, bass-fly hook sizing gets weird)

Tip 210 Carry a Foundation Set of Flies to Largemouth Bass Lakes 🐟 Lg-L

Everything I just said in the previous tip about smallmouth bass flies applies to flies for largemouths: Bug hatches are seldom important, fly presentation is the key, and you don't (normally) need a bunch of different imitative flies.

Here are the mere four fly patterns I mostly fish for largemouth bass, and they nearly always produce as well as any others. Can't find these specific fly patterns? (Though, actually, a couple aren't very specific.) Ask at your fly shop or fly-fishing mail-order house for substitutes. Get at least two, preferably three, of each fly so you don't have to quit fishing when you lose that one fly the largemouths are liking.

STREAMERS

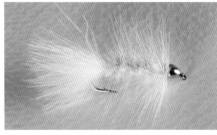

- Zonker, Olive or Natural
- Size 4

- Woolly Bugger, White (with a metal bead or cone for a head)
- Size 6

- Dahlberg Diver, White, Yellow, or Purple (a snag guard is optional, probably wise)
- Body (not including tail) about ⅝ inch long (bass-fly hook sizing is often perplexing, inconsistent)

- Hair Bug, Brown, Yellow, Tan, or Green (with a white face so you can spot the bug—a snag guard is optional, perhaps invaluable)
- Body (not including tail) about ⅝ inch long (again, bass-fly hook sizing, weird)

Tip 211 Carry a Foundation Set of Flies to Panfish Lakes Pf-L

As I keep saying (if you've been reading the past few tips in order), trout, due to their single-mindedness and bug-obsession, demand a bunch of flies. Smallmouth bass don't. Largemouth don't. And panfish don't either. Again: not because the basses and panfish are dumb, but because fooling them is more about fly presentation than about flies fished as imitations.

So, just a few flies—fished well, at the right times and in the right places—will catch bluegills, crappies, green sunfish, pumpkinseeds . . . with good consistency. (*Perfect* consistency? That's just not . . . reality, or fishing.) Here are the four flies I chose with care to make up a versatile and effective panfish team. Flies are always coming into style and then going out of style to get replaced by new flies coming into style—if due to all that coming and going you can't find one of these patterns, just ask at your local fly shop or your online fly-fishing mail-order house for a substitute. Get two, better yet three, of each fly pattern. It's the pattern that's working that, if you have only one, breaks off in a fish or on a snag.

Bonus-Tip **Snip Some Hackles, or Not**

Tr-S, Tr-L   Sm-L, Sm-S   Pf-L

Some dry flies, the Royal Wulff for example, are bristly. Wings and tails are thick brushes of hair; in front is a dense ruff of fibers, called "hackles." Those hackle fibers can protect a fish from the point of the hook, but you don't want the fish protected—you want it hooked. So you can trim out a V in the fibers that stand in front of the hook's point. It's a tradeoff: a less buoyant fly, but possibly more hookups.

NYMPHS

- Woolly Worm, Green or Olive (don't confuse it with the Woolly Bugger)
- Size 10

- Copper John (or some other shiny, weighted nymph)
- Size 10

BUG AND POPPER

- Predator, Tan
- Size 10

- Popper, Yellow, White, or Chartreuse (overall)
- Size 10

Tip 212 Let Flies Add Themselves to Your Fly Boxes Tr-S, Tr-L Lg-L Sm-L, Sm-S Pf-L

Of course, new fly patterns won't just *materialize* among the familiar ones you carry all the time in your fly boxes, but they may seem to. You stop by a fly shop near the Colorado trout river you plan to fish and ask for fishing advice. After offering suggestions on where and how to fish the river, the salesperson will eventually pick a fly out of the bins and say, "This one's been a killer lately." Presto! You've got a few in your box. Happens all the time. Or maybe you're ordering from a catalog and see a pattern that looks just right for your local smallmouths that have been so reluctant lately. Presto again! Another new fly joins your collection.

Some such experimental (or impulse) buys will be flops, others big hits. The flop flies will get some testing on or in the water until the yawns of the fish become audible, and then settle into sedentary lives alongside other flies you actually fish (unless in desperation you finally try the failed flies again and *this* time they *work*). The hit flies, however—new patterns you and your fish both like—will get used and used up and then replaced.

So, that's how a new fly pattern seems to simply *materialize* in your fly box. That's the process, always has been.

But as new patterns show up in your boxes, remember that the collections of flies for trout streams, largemouth lakes, and the rest I laid out in the previous few tips provide excellent foundations for each kind of fish and its fishing. Just add to those collections as you like.

Tip 213 Consider Tying Your Flies

Tr-S, Tr-L   Lg-L   Sm-L, Sm-S   Pf-L

Want to make a seasoned fly tier laugh? Say that you've taken up tying your own flies to save money. That'll do it.

On paper, the scheme works. In practice, it fails. Badly. That's because once you've sensibly gathered the hooks and materials required for tying all the flies necessary to comprise a sound, versatile, minimalist selection, you see some intriguing fly pattern in a fly-shop bin or online or in a magazine and your whole elegant plan crumbles. More hooks, more materials . . .

All those amazing flies out there—who can resist? So far, no one I've met.

But even if fly tying isn't cost efficient, it pays off in other ways. Scenario: You're two days away from a trip to a famous Michigan trout stream. You get word that the Hendrickson mayfly hatch has started early. Weren't expecting that. But it seems as though everybody else got the word too, and the bins of your local fly shop, the ones that should contain your favorite Hendrickson imitations, are empty. Maybe online? Nope: back-ordered.

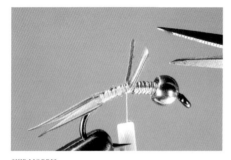

SKIP MORRIS

SKIP MORRIS

SKIP MORRIS

Alternate scenario: You hear about the early hatch, sit down, tie up a couple dozen of your favorite imitations. Done.

And you can tie each pattern exactly as you want it: thinner than the fly companies tie it, heavier, with a metal bead, with a different dubbing, in a smaller size, bigger, and so on . . .

There really are lots of benefits of learning to tie flies. Saving money just isn't among them.

Tip 214 Flies Come in Types

A perfect example of infinity—that's how new fly fishers must see the superabundance in number and variation of fly patterns. That's scary. But it needn't be.

Look, to imitate the nymph of the adult Salmonfly, a stonefly, you could select among dozens of currently hot and solidly established patterns—make that hundreds, and perhaps *thousands* if you open that to include all the obscure ones. But: You should do fine with just one good imitation. That's largely because catching fish is not usually as much about the particular fly you've chosen as about how and where you fish it. (See tip 339.)

The point: You can choose just one among the many solid imitations of a particular trout, largemouth, smallmouth, or panfish menu item and—if you fish it well—usually catch fish. Yes, sometimes a particular fly seems to work a magic no other can quite match. But that's hardly the norm.

Each of these flies imitates the gargantuan (gargantuan for a trout bug) Salmonfly nymph. They all work—I've proven that to my satisfaction.

 Bonus-Tip Long-Tailed Flies Can Be a Problem with Trout

Tr-S, Tr-L

Largemouth bass tend to get solidly hooked when they take streamer flies with long, or at least longish, tails, wings, or both. Trout are different. They seem to snap at the rear end of a fly—if the hook's too far forward and the trout lacks a big mouth (usually because it's not a big trout): missed fish. Try to fish streamers that have only modest-length tails and wings. (Unless you're strictly after trout of around 18 inches and longer, which just gobble up a whole streamer.)

Tip 215 Understand the Elements of Imitation  Tr-S,Tr-L · Lg-L · Sm-L, Sm-S · Pf-L

When I took up fly fishing and fly tying as a kid, I made a classic newbie mistake: I made sure to accurately match the colors of the insects (or other creatures) my fish were taking, figuring if I got that right, I couldn't lose. The fish disagreed.

Turns out, according to a whole lot of experienced fly fishers (me included), that successful imitation relies on several elements—a fly's color being the one that matters *least*. Here are those elements of imitation, in order of importance:

1. *Action (or the lack of it).* If adult caddisflies are scrambling and pausing on the water, your dry fly should be skimming across the water and pausing too. If mayflies drift quietly with the current, so should your imitation. If crayfish dart away in pulses (which they do), so should your crayfish fly.

2. *Size.* Your fly—nymph, dry fly, streamer, whatever—should roughly to very closely (depending on the demands of the fish) match the size of whatever it imitates. Especially true when imitating insects for trout.

3. *Shape.* To imitate a backswimmer, your fly should be plump, with two stout wide-spread legs. A skinny fly won't do at all. A fly should imitate, or at least suggest, its model's form.

4. *Shade.* Is the thing you're imitating (mayfly dun, scud, sculpin . . .) pale, dark, or somewhere in between? Match that shade. You can normally imitate a brown bug with a gray fly, for example, if the bug is *medium*-brown and the fly is *medium*-gray.

5. *Color.* With the wisest trout, color *can* matter. But it's always last on the list of imitative-fly factors.

None of the above applies to attractor flies because they imitate nothing.

Tip 216 Keep an Open Mind about What Flies Imitate (Fish Do)

Tr-S,Tr-L · Lg-L · Sm-L, Sm-S · Pf-L

An Elk Hair Caddis imitates a caddisfly, right? With a name like that, it'd better. But a floating adult stonefly has a stout body, as does a caddis adult; six legs, as does a caddis; and wings held back low, caddis. So a fly that's supposed to imitate an adult caddis can serve as an effective imitation of an adult stonefly, provided the fly is close in size (and, less important, shade and color) to the stone.

Stonefly *nymphs* are similar in form to mayfly nymphs, tiny mayfly duns are similar to adult midges, chironomid pupae resemble some caddis larvae, little fishes can resemble leeches, and the list goes on.

When your fish—trout, bass, panfish, whatever—want a specific food and you're without a proper imitation, you may have a fly on hand that, unaltered, will pass. You just have to forget labels, look at your flies, and see plainly what's in front of you. Goes for dry flies, nymphs, and streamers.

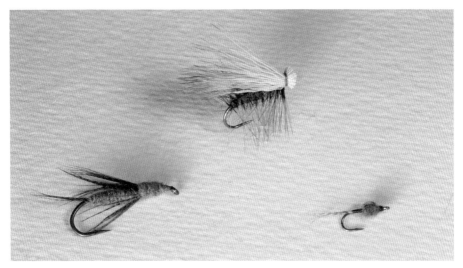

The Elk Hair Caddis at the top of the photo is a fine choice for imitating adult caddisflies, sure, but also for small to medium-size stoneflies. Way back when I was working on a magazine article about his fly, Mark Engler told me he fishes his WD-40 (the tiny nymph-looking fly on the right) awash in the surface of the water to imitate emerging midges and Blue-Winged Olive mayflies, and also below the surface as a Blue-Wing nymph for the notoriously difficult brown trout of New Mexico's San Juan River. The Bird's Nest on the left covers lots of imitative ground; a trout might take it for a stonefly or mayfly nymph, or perhaps for a caddis larva or pupa, or just for some sort of live food.

Some flies are designed to imitate a range of creatures. The Bird's Nest nymph, the WD-40 emerger, and the Stimulator dry fly are all very popular and all loose enough in form to imitate two or more insects. And what about so many fly fishers' standard go-to streamer, the plain and primitive Woolly Bugger? It's fished to imitate leeches, all sorts of little fishes, dragonfly nymphs, crayfish, and on and on.

But it's never enough just to come up with an acceptable imitation; you must imitate the natural's *movement* (or, of course, lack of movement) if you're going to convince a persnickety fish.

Tip 217 The Elements of Imitation Change with Truly Tiny Trout Flies

 Tr-S, Tr-L

When caddisflies or mayflies of fair size are hatching, you pick out an imitation by going through the list—size, shape, shade (the general paleness or darkness of a fly), and, finally, actual coloring. (The action you give a fly in or on the water—the most important

Tiny flies: emergers, dries, a soft-hackled fly, and a nymph. More important than choosing the right one is choosing one that's the right size.

Bonus Tip Big Hooks Hurt Small Fish

Tr-S,Tr-L   Lg-L   Sm-L, Sm-S   Pf-L

Big flies tied on hooks with wide gapes can injure small trout, bass (both kinds), and those panfish with mouths large enough to accept big flies. So don't offer big flies to small fish. (Or, if you tie flies, tie the big ones for small fish on hooks with long shanks and small gapes. See "Hook, parts of" in the Learn the Lingo section, page 324).

factor of all in its effectiveness—has little to do with *selecting* a fly, so I'll disregard it from here on.) That's a solid list of criteria for matching fly to insect; I rely on it all the time. But it typically changes in one critical way with flies of size 18 or 20 and smaller: Size, already the key consideration, becomes even *more* important. The other factors typically become less. (Though, like nearly everything else in fishing, none of this is consistent.)

Example: The hatch is a tan midge matching a size 24 hook. The odds are high that those fussy trout, dimpling out there on the slick tail of a big pool, will confidently sip down your emerger fly even it it's (1) an imitation not of a midge but of a mayfly and (2) not tan but black—provided it's tied on a *size 24* hook. They might take a size 22, but the odds drop.

The point: With the smallest flies imitating the smallest insects, don't fret much about shade, color, and silhouette—but *do* get the size right.

Tip 218 The Elements of Imitation Change with Truly *Big* Trout Flies #1

Tr-S,Tr-L

I just told you all about how with tiny flies the critical element for success is often size. So, in light of that, what follows should not come as a shocker: With really big trout flies, size becomes *less* important than usual.

You've heard the old adage about not seeing the forest for the trees? I think it's something like that: A huge bug, or fly, is just so big that a trout can't grasp its size. The trout goes, "*That* is *big*," and that's the end of the matter.

This can work to your advantage. Often strong, plump, beautiful trout of modest size struggle to get big bugs—and big flies—into their proportionately modest-size mouths. If you want to catch those magnificent middle-range fish (all trout: magnificent), give them something they can take in, hook point and all. Perhaps enormous Salmonfly stoneflies are today's special and only flies on long-shank size 6 hooks truly match them. But you can go with size 8, even down to size 10 long-shank flies and trout will still come to them. A size 10 offers a much better shot at a good hookup than does a 6 with a 13-inch rainbow.

Who doesn't want to catch a 13-inch rainbow?

Somewhere around size 10 or 12 hooks—of standard length or just 1X long shanks—you're back to where fly size takes on its normal, high importance in the scheme of imitation.

Tip 219 The Elements of Imitation Change with Truly *Big* Trout Flies #2

 Tr-S,Tr-L

I told you in the previous tip about how size in big flies often isn't a big deal to trout. Now I'm going to tell you about how *detail* in a big trout fly isn't either.

I'm not sure what principle's at play here. Why must a size 14 or 16 imitation of a mayfly dun or nymph have the *right* stoutness, the *right* silhouette, if it's going to fool cagey trout—when a crude and fairly inaccurate size 6 stonefly imitation hammers those same fish?

Weird . . .

The only explanation I've come up with is that big bugs and big flies overwhelm trout, so that they can't get a bead on size *or* detail. That's all I've got and, as explanations go, it's weak. Sorry.

All that said—and all that being true—flat water can change things. Example: During the hatch of the huge Golden Stonefly, the clumsy adults end up on currents from swift and wild to slow and calm, and I find that my success—on the slow, smooth currents—seems to rise when my imitation provides a good outline: an appropriately thick body, four to six thick legs to match the six of the natural.

Still, on both streams and lakes you can usually toss out some pretty rough, inaccurate dry flies and nymphs during a big-bug hatch and hook even (normally) persnickety trout.

Tip 220 Imitations vs. Attractors—Which, When? Tr-S,Tr-L   Lg-L   Sm-L, Sm-S   Pf-L

Imitative flies are usually the way to go with trout, and fairly often with the basses and panfish. But attractor flies can at times absolutely kill when imitations really can't. It's all up to the fish. And how do you know when fish want attractors? You don't. But let's back up a bit.

"Imitative" flies suggest—*imitate*—things fishes eat: stonefly nymphs, fish eggs, baby bass, crayfish . . . Some imitative patterns are loose in what they suggest; one pattern might cover stonefly nymphs, mayfly nymphs, and caddis larvae and pupae, or perhaps several different small fishes. Other imitative flies are very specific. With such features as three fringed tails, abdominal gills, a mottled back and wing case, and splayed legs, an imitation of a *Callibaetis* mayfly nymph imitates that and that alone.

"Attractor" flies don't imitate anything—in fact, they're purposely designed to look unnatural. Sure, they might have tails or legs, to identify them as part of our and the fish's reality, but along with those will be an unearthly chrome-bright body or a collar of speckled, orange-tipped tentacles—something weird or plain wrong.

Clockwise from top right: the Spruce fly, an attractor streamer from way back; my Gabriel's Trumpet, Pink, an attractor nymph; the Royal Trude attractor dry fly; Rainey's Grand Hopper, an imitation, of course; the Woven Dragonfly Nymph (self-explanatory); and my Morris Minnow, Brook, an imitation of a baby brook trout. The Carey Special in the center of the group is mainly a fly for trout lakes, generally considered such a loose sort of imitative pattern that it can imitate a lot: dragonfly nymphs, damselfly nymphs, caddis pupae.

Why do attractor flies work? There are theories, but only theories. The point: they *do* work.

So, on to that business of how to know when to fish attractors. Here's how I decide with trout: I fish imitative flies first, and if they don't work (or at least work as well as they should), I start trying attractors. With the basses and panfish it's a tossup for me: I just try whatever seems reasonable, and keep experimenting with both types of flies until I find something the fish like.

Tip 221 Here's the Skinny on Impressionistic and Realistic Flies

Tr-S, Tr-L   Lg-L   Sm-L, Sm-S   Pf-L

From the fly bins of your local fly shop you pick out a Bead Head Halfback, a generic sort of nymph. In your other hand you hold, say, my Anatomical Green Drake—a nymph pattern that makes an almost living impression with its gleaming and segmented back, gill-furred flanks, splayed tails and splayed legs, and a dark metal bead that, being tiny, actually looks like an insect head. Both nymphs are reasonable choices for imitating the nymph of the Western Green Drake mayfly—but which fly should you buy?

I'll spread my answer over the following points.

First, as I say elsewhere in this book, the most important element in how effective any fly is lies in how well you fish it.

Second, the Halfback has the advantage of suggesting a number of insects but the disadvantage of imitating none of them precisely, while the Anatomical Green Drake has the reverse: It imitates only one thing, but nails it.

Third, and here's the real answer I've been working up to: If you are confident your trout will be locked onto Green Drakes and you know those trout to be cagey, get my Anatomical, since it may provide you an edge. But if your trout might or might not be on the Drakes and they're not Einsteins with gills, the Halfback will match the Anatomical's effectiveness for imitating the Drakes and might move trout to take it for something else down there.

All this applies to flies for trout in lakes too, of course.

I've never seen the largemouths, smallmouths, or panfish so picky that they required a realistic fly, but there are some impressively realistic imitations for these fishes—flies that are nearly dead ringers for frogs, crayfish, bees, adult dragonflies . . . Maybe I just haven't met the right basses and panfish yet.

Left, my Anatomical Green Drake. Right, the Bead Head Halfback. SKIP MORRIS

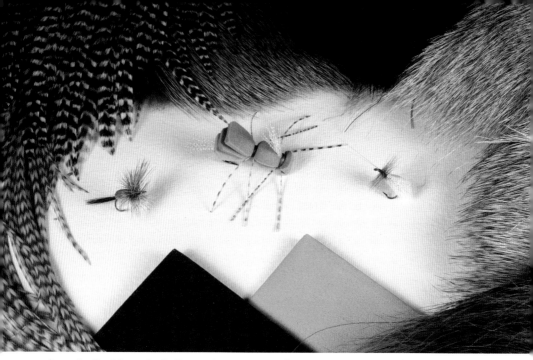

Seaworthy flies, left to right: the Humpy, the Chernobyl Ant (one among endless variations), and the Goddard Caddis

Tip 222 Seaworthy Flies Have Advantages Tr-S, Tr-L   Sm-L, Sm-S   Pf-L

Bugs that flutter, scurry, or otherwise make a fuss atop streams and lakes can be stoneflies, flying ants, grasshoppers, caddis, chironomids, and more. The solution is a similarly lively fly. The problem is, a lot of flies just sink when you try to twitch or skim them across the water. A few flies, however, are truly seaworthy.

The flies that insist on staying afloat, seaworthy flies, are, in my experience, of three sorts: (1) made primarily of buoyant foam—lots of foam; (2) bearing a fanned deer-hair wing, upright but tilted slightly forward, set close behind the hook's eye; or (3) bursting with buoyant materials. The foam flies float stubbornly because foam is permanently buoyant. The fanned-wing flies use their wings to skim the water as a boat uses its tapered bow. The bushy flies are composed of so much floaty stuff that they're, essentially, shaggy life jackets.

The ever-more-bizarre Chernobyl Ant (there are ever-new variations) floats stubbornly because it's nearly all foam and not much hook. The Goddard Caddis imitates a caddis adult's profile with buoyant deer hair bound, flared, and compressed together up the hook, then sculpted with razor blade or scissors, and includes a buoyant hackle collar. The Humpy's also got a hackle collar along with wings, a tail, and a back of buoyant elk hair. The Tom Thumb and various Morris Emergers have that fan wing that, with a tug on the tippet, can pop them back up onto the top of the water after a dunking. All these flies are tied by fly companies and easy to find for purchase (though, as throughout this book, I tied the ones shown here). There are others similarly dunk-resistant.

But it's not just when you're trying to imitate the actions of a floating insect or other creature that seaworthy flies pay off; such flies are nearly a requirement for streams that rush and bounce down their beds—no sparse, dainty dry fly is going to stay afloat long on that.

Tip 223 Here's the Skinny on Tiny Flies

 Tr-S, Tr-L

Tiny flies, the 20s and 22s and tinier, *maybe* up to the 18s, are almost entirely about trout. There are exceptions, but I've found them to be rare. Still, I have caught small-mouths, rising to bitsy mayflies, on bitsy imitations, and surely bluegills and some other panfish must occasionally concentrate on tiny bugs. Largemouths? I can't imagine even a little one aiming that cavernous maw at a minute adult midge.

Trout get onto tiny insects—mayflies, midges, caddis, even flying ants—fairly often in streams, occasionally in lakes. Tiny flies can be very simple, even rough designs, and (if fished well) still fool cagey trout.

There are realistic tiny flies—my Anatomical BWO nymph is tied by the Solitude Fly Company down to size 22, and it's got splayed-out legs and tails, a fringe of gills, a neat wing case . . . Only the sharpest trout in the pickiest mood would care about such details

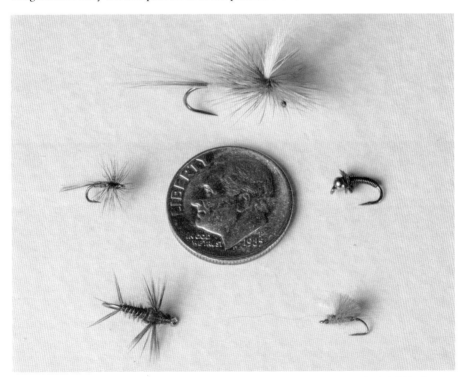

Tiny nymphs and dry flies looking dinky compared to a dime and a size 14 Parachute Light Cahill (the fly on top). Top right is the elemental Beadhead Brassie nymph, below it the equally simple RS2 emerger, then my detailed and lifelike Anatomical Baetis/PMD nymph, and on the upper left, just . . . the Midge, an old-style and still-reliable adult-midge pattern. The flies here (except for the Cahill) are on hooks size 18 down to 22.

on a size 20 or 22 nymph, but when you do come across such trout, those details can only provide an edge.

Here, then, is the all that and more on tiny flies, summed up:

1. They're nearly always about trout, in streams, occasionally about trout in lakes.
2. They can often be very simple and still (if fished well) catch fussy trout.
3. They can sometimes fool fussy trout even if tiny insects aren't hatching.
4. Most tiny flies are floaters, dries and emergers, but tiny nymphs can be deadly.
5. Tiny flies require fine tippets, 6X and 7X (I've gone to 8X and even *10*X for them).

Tip 224 Learn to Fish Streamers

 Tr-S,Tr-L   Lg-L   Sm-L, Sm-S   Pf-L

Streamer fishing is so common with largemouth and smallmouth bass, and even with some panfish (bluegills, crappies, etc.), and so straightforward when applied to these species that it's almost self-explanatory: cast out a weighted streamer on a floating line or on a full-sinking (lakes) or sink-tip (streams) line, or an *un*weighted streamer on a sinking (full or sink-tip) line, let the fly settle down with the fish, retrieve.

Streamer flies for stream trout are another matter. You can just chuck them up or across stream (on a sink-tip line, usually), let them sink deeply, then swing them slowly across the current, twitching them to add life. That works. The other standard approach is about taunting trout, challenging them—it's about putting that big fly in a big trout's face. A *big* trout? Oh yeah—big trout go for streamers.

So how do you aggravate that big trout? For starters, find a big trout. The big ones tend to grab the best lies: deep, steep banks; banks with jutting downed logs; the soft water next to the churning inflow at the head of a pool . . .

Then show that trout your streamer, up close. You can accomplish this from a position upstream of the fish, so that the fly drifts freely down to the fish and then

Big fly, big fish—been hearing that since I was a kid. While there certainly are exceptions, the old saw just keeps on proving itself. Streamers, like the one in this hefty brown trout's mug, are nearly always big flies.

begins swinging across the current (a downstream presentation). Or you can drop your streamer upstream of the trout from a position *across* the stream from it (an across-stream presentation), and then let the current form a downstream belly in your line as you twitch or even (to suggest a frightened, fleeing little fish) strip in the fly as it swims downstream. Both presentations typically include a sink-tip line to draw the fly just a foot or so underwater. With the upstream approach, the streamer faces upstream; with the across-stream approach, the streamer faces and swims downstream.

George Daniel wrote a whole book on fishing streamers in trout streams, titled *Strip-Set*. In it, he explains his preference: "Across-stream tactics are by far the most exciting." Why? He says of fishing across stream that the "takes can literally rip the rod out of your hands."

Fish streamers in rivers by working progressively not up, but downstream.

Tip 225 On Trout Streams, Carry Soft-Hackled Flies and Know How and When to Use Them—and Use Them

 Tr-S

I've had some wild fishing with soft-hackles—I mean miss-a-fish-and-then-hook-another-on-the-same-cast sort of wild. Though you shouldn't go out with soft-hackled flies expecting that (despite the fact that you might, just possibly, get it).

More likely, if conditions are right for soft-hackles, they'll provide good, steady fishing—often when other approaches fail. So, what are those conditions? They are:

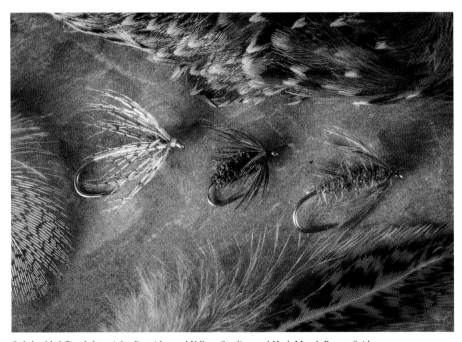

Soft-hackled flies, left to right: Partridge and Yellow, Starling and Herl, March Brown Spider

trout showing at the surface but actually feeding just *under* the surface of a stream, usually on mayfly nymphs or caddis pupae. (See tip 10.)

Here's how you fish a soft-hackled fly when trout are doing that: you *swing* it.

Cast the fly (on a floating line) across or slightly downstream.

Hold the rod tip low to the water so you can feel a take of the fly.

Mend the line as needed to keep the fly out with the fish as long as possible. (See tip 140.)

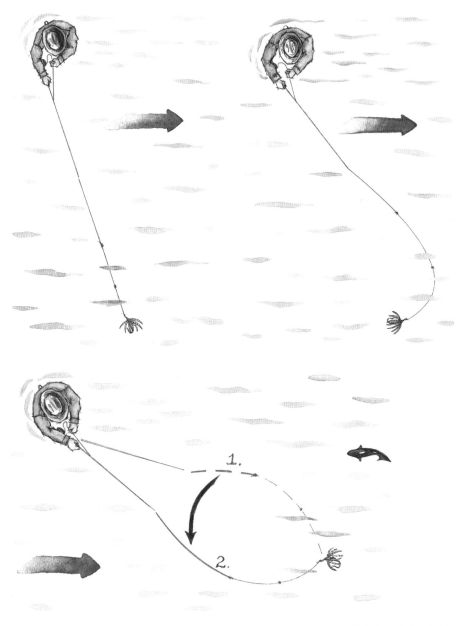

Swinging soft-hackled fly

Let the fly eventually swing in directly below you and then, after it's hung there for a few seconds, cast it out and swing it again.

When you feel the take, do nothing (other than holding the line firmly)—let the *trout* set the hook.

That's one way to handle a take. Davy Wotton, a real soft-hackle authority, has another (which he also uses for flies called "wet flies"): hold the rod angling up, so the line hangs in an arc; watch the line and when it moves or changes (or you see a fuss where your fly should be), tighten only lightly on the trout that has caused that movement or change; then hold the rod and line firmly and let the trout dart off and set the hook on its own.

Tip 226 Show Fish Something They Haven't Seen Tr-S, Tr-L Lg-L Sm-L, Sm-S Pf-L

Question: Why do new fly designs keep popping up?
Answer: Because fish get wise to the old ones.

I really believe that's how it works—show a fish a fly it hasn't seen, and not only do you avoid tripping its alarm over something it's identified as a danger but you also arouse its curiosity. This creates consumer demand for ever-new fly designs.

But there's another incentive to keep the fly-pattern conveyer belt running: fashion. Human beings are drawn to the latest things—the latest styles in shoes and sweaters, the latest movies. Fly fishers are just as human (and fashionable) as everyone else: They're drawn to the latest flies.

Actually, fashion is part of the problem. The, oh, let's say Gyroscopic Hopper (I made that up) comes out and soon everyone's chattering about how deadly it's been on their local trout stream. It's become a very fashionable fly. Consequently the trout in the river start seeing the Gyroscopic Hopper every day . . . and learning to identify it as trouble. What do you know? Time for a new hit grasshopper fly!

So, do you go with the next hot hopper fly? You could. Or you could go with an old, now largely forgotten hopper pattern once widely trusted. Or you could sniff around for little-known hopper patterns their followers swear by. Of course, both of these last two options will probably require you to tie the flies yourself—any fly not new, currently hot, or both isn't likely to show up for sale.

However you manage it, do try to show *jaded* fish (the innocent ones won't care)—be they bass, trout, or panfish—flies they haven't seen before.

Tip 227 Trout Aren't Usually Selective about Nymphs Tr-S, Tr-L

This is a very general rule, but one that's generally correct: When you choose a nymph for fishing deep in a trout stream or trout lake, any reasonable pattern will probably do the job. Something heavy enough to get down to the fish in a stream (lakes are often about sinking lines, making nymph weight unnecessary), of logical size (maybe a size 16 for a small stream or a size 6 if you're hunting river lunkers). If the trout are moody, experiment; try something bright, something dark, an imitation, an attractor, in a range of sizes. One of these may fish best, but most times on most trout water, they'll all catch fish. It all goes back to how trout usually feed on a *variety* of bugs and such when feeding near the bottom.

Usually . . . Trout *can* get picky about nymphs. If real mayfly nymphs are fussing down there just before their hatching gets under way, your imitation had better be fairly accurate, whether you're fishing it in a stream or lake, deep to just inches below the surface. If stonefly nymphs are creeping to the edges of a stream or dragonfly nymphs to the shore of a lake, both with the goal of climbing up and out to hatch, again, your fly must suggest the natural. Trout keyed on tiny midge pupae inches under the river's surface call for an equally tiny midge-pupa fly. Chironomid fishing in lakes? That's about imitation far more often than not.

So, while any reasonable nymph really will do most of the time for trout, remember: there will be times when your nymph must be right.

Tip 228 Go Weedless for Largemouth, but Do It Right ⋙ Lg-L

If in a dense bed of exposed aquatic weeds there's a little patch of open water a frog or salamander might be foolish enough to cross, there may be a largemouth bass down there waiting to attack. You've found a good place to work your fly, fine—but how do you keep from immediately snagging the fly in all that tangle?

Here's how: Fish a weedless fly.

Even though the concept of a fly that'll slide over logs and lily pads and still hook fish seems way too tidy to work, it does work. Such flies are made "weedless" usually by heavy monofilament looped just outside the hook's point. (There are other kinds, but the loop is the standard.) That loop is called a "snag guard."

Most flies with snag guards are floating or floating-and-diving hair bugs, but snag guards do show up on sinking flies. (Snag-guard flies are sometimes used for smallmouth bass in lakes, rarely used for panfish, and very rarely fished for trout in lakes.)

Weedless flies are useless unless fished correctly. Here's how to fish one correctly: When the fly comes to a branch or lily pad, coax the fly onto and over it—slowly and smoothly. When a bass takes the fly, just the opposite—drop the rod tip, clamp onto the line, and heave the rod tip up and back, fast and hard. This snaps the hook point past the mono and into the bass's jaw. Done.

Consequently, you are now tied to a big, powerful, angry largemouth tucked back in heavy weeds, and perhaps fallen timber. Good luck.

Tip 229 Half-Submerged Emerger Flies Have Advantages ⋙ Tr-S, Tr-L

Half-submerged emerger flies and the half-submerged insects they imitate typically move more trout than flies and insects perched up on top of the water: The part of the fly or bug that hangs below the water's surface is pretty much a beacon to hungry trout. Here's how that works:

That stout monofilament curving below the bend and point of the fly's hook is a snag guard. A largemouth fly fisher's gift from the heavens.

Thanks to its mono snag guard, this hair bug won't catch on this lily pad when drawn across it, but it will catch a largemouth bass.

1. The underside of water is a mirror—fish can't see up through it (except for one little window). I mention that elsewhere in this book, but it's especially significant here.
2. Trout want to expend the least possible amount of energy in picking off an insect (or, of course, fly). To accomplish this with a floating insect (or, again, fly), they just tip up and let the current lift them

The Quigley Cripple and the Morris Emerger on the left each dangle their abdomen below the water; the Compara-dun on the right doesn't. That difference can matter.

gradually to it (in a lake, trout use not current to raise them but momentum). This requires some advance notice.
3. Here's how 1 and 2 function together. Trout may not get that notice from the slight pattern of depression a floating bug (or fly) makes on the water's skin. But a bug/fly with its nymphal or pupal rear half dangling below the reflection? Might as well be a flashing red light accompanied by the wail of a siren.

But it's about this too: Fully hatched mayflies and caddis are ready to go—they may fly off at the last moment, just as a trout is about to take them. Half-hatched insects (the kind half above and half under water), however, are still tangled in their shucks and cannot swim or fly off. Trout know all this—and act accordingly.

Tip 230 Know When to Fish Hopper Flies, and How Tr-S, Tr-L   Lg-L   Sm-L, Sm-S   Pf-L

Even one big grasshopper can go a long way toward filling a trout's belly. A smallmouth or largemouth bass's belly too. (And probably a bluegill's or green sunfish's belly, though I've not seen that.) The long grasses grasshoppers (or just "hoppers") love seem to flourish around water, and water, of course, holds fish with appetites.

Since most of my hopper-fishing experience is on the same water as most everybody's—trout streams—I'll stick with them from here on. But most of what follows applies to lakes and streams both and to any fish that takes hoppers.

Hopper fishing is a summer-into-fall affair. It's a dry-day affair too, starting usually as the day really warms.

Trout may slip to the edges of streams in hopes of finding hoppers any time the big bugs are active, but the best hopper fishing usually includes wind. Wind to startle the big bugs into leaping or flying. Wind to throw them onto the water.

Hoppers aren't made for water and, wind or no wind, generally land on it in a clumsy little crash.

So, here's the whole hopper-fishing thing in a nutshell, the points above and some new ones: (1) mostly it's about trout streams; (2) it happens from summer into fall; (3) dry, windy days are best; (4) expect hopper-seeking trout to hold close to the banks;

Drop your hopper fly in close along grassy banks, but out farther too.

Effective grasshopper-imitating fly patterns abound. From the top, clockwise, are the Rainey's Grand Hopper, Tan; the Parachute Hopper; and the archetypal hopper fly, the Dave's Hopper.

(5) plop your hopper fly down (and maybe twitch it); and (6) try to match the color and especially size of the grasshoppers in your fly, though size and color may not be critical with such a big bug and fly. (See tip 218.)

Tip 231 Dunk a Terrestrial Imitation

Tr-S

Eventually, terrestrial insects—grasshoppers, beetles, ants, etc.—sink. What do we fly fishers do about it? Ed Engle, in his book *Trout Lessons*, says that "it's pretty much a no-brainer that any terrestrial imitation will catch trout below the surface," so, we sink our terrestrial imitations.

On the left is a sinking-ant pattern (the Black Thread Wood Ant) and on the right, a hopper pattern (the Drunken Hopper) that comes with a metal bead to ensure it goes right down.

I'm not suggesting we abandon floating hopper and ant patterns, just that we try sunken ones when the floaters aren't paying off as they should.

You can just leave your dry grasshopper or ant fly undressed with floatant and let it, eventually, go down an inch or a bit more, or you can fish terrestrial patterns designed to sink (though you may have to tie them yourself). There are glossy, hard ant imitations, tied on heavy wire hooks, that sink slowly but start sinking immediately upon touching the water, and there are hopper flies with metal beads for heads that sink with purpose.

Next time your terrestrial fishing is slow, try a subsurface imitation.

Tip 232 Don't Forget the Oldies

 Tr-S, Tr-L   Lg-L   Sm-L, Sm-S   Pf-L

The top flies of earlier eras keep coming back around and that's a good thing—they are, after all, proven fish catchers. Check out the flies in a print-and-paper or online catalog and you might find, among all sorts of snazzy new patterns with trendy or catchy (sometimes lewd) names, the Carrie Special nymph from the 1920s, or the old Renegade dry sporting a hackle-collar at each end. As fly-tying and fly-design theories evolve and cycle, and fly patterns rise to prominence then sink to obscurity, some good stuff gets forgotten.

The fish we seek have, if not truly evolved, have certainly wised up on the whole. Catch-and-release has educated trout, largemouths, smallmouths, bluegills, and maybe even crappies to the fly fisher's deceptions. (No, on second thought, not crappies, those poor, speckled, lovely brain-numb slabs . . .) All this, and yet that Carey Special, a fly

Atop that very old Leonard reel, the Renegade. Lower left, Dave's Eelworm Streamer. Lower right, the Carey Special.

from a time when tippets were of silk and all fly rods had metal ferrules, catches trout in lakes today. I still fish the Eelworm Streamer, a largemouth bass fly that first appeared in *The Fly Tyer's Almanac* (yes, "tyer"—some fly fishers like to spell it that way), published in 1975, and still catch bass on it. Trust me: There's nothing about the Eelworm that largemouths have stopped liking.

So, if someone tells you he really nailed the rainbows on such-and-such lake or the smallies on such-and-such river with some ancient fly pattern, don't smile all smug as he walks away, shaking your head in pity for this Neanderthal stuck in fly fishing's Pleistocene epoch. Instead, consider fishing the pattern he mentioned.

Tip 233 Big Water Doesn't Necessarily Mean Big Flies Tr-S, Tr-L

Oregon's Lower Deschutes is a big trout river. Wading from one side to the other, at any point, even in its lowest flows, is an impossible dream. Much of it is swift. It flows through rugged, rocky desert. Its trout is the Deschutes redside, a stout rainbow with big eyes, a vivid stripe along each flank, and a reckless might and endurance that shocks every new fly fisher it meets.

So, seems like a good place for big flies, right? Overall, nope.

I've had fine days with big nymphs and dry flies on the Lower Deschutes, especially during hatches of such beefy insects as the Salmonfly, Golden Stonefly, and October Caddis. But on average this is nymph water—*little*-nymph water.

I remember my friend Rick Hafele (who's also my coauthor on *Tactics for Trout* and *Seasons for Trout*, along with Dave Hughes) recommending to a guy the nymphs to carry to the Lower D. Rick has fished the river hundreds of times over the past few decades, studied it as an entomologist. The guy opened a box of nymphs, pointed to some size 10 Gold-Ribbed Hare's Ears, and said, "So you're saying little nymphs like these?"

Rick peered around the box until he found a couple of size 14s and said, "No, like these, but mostly smaller."

Rick fishes a lot of size 16 and 18 nymphs in that big, churning water. Experience has taught him that its clever angler-pestered rainbows often refuse nymphs that are larger. Let his experience teach you: Big trout water *can* mean big flies, but it can instead mean mostly small, even tiny ones.

Goes for trout lakes too.

Tip 234 Prefer Flies That Flip for Smallmouth Bass Sm-L, Sm-S

I'm not 100 percent certain about this one, but . . . pretty darn sure: Flies that swim with their hooks upside down hook and hold more smallmouths than flies that swim with their hooks in the conventional upright position. This may also be true for largemouths and panfish, maybe even for trout, but I'm *really* unsure about these species. With smallies, though, I just seem to lock into and land my highest percentage of them when I fish inverted underwater flies, such as the Clouser Minnow and NearNuff Crayfish.

Each of these flies is designed to, and in fact does, flip upside down in water, and each is designed for smallmouth bass (though they're all good largemouth flies too). Top left: Half and Half. Top right: Whitlock's NearNuff Crayfish. Center: Meat Whistle. Bottom: Grim Reaper.

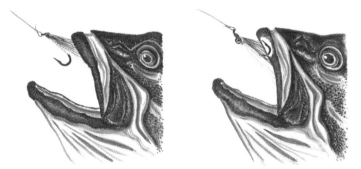

Left, a fly that rides hook down, missing a smallmouth's jaw.
Right, a fly that rides flipped, sinking home.

It's logical that a fly swimming below the level of the angler's rod will tip upward on a hook set so that the inverted-hook fly catches the fish's upper jaw on the way up, while the fly whose hook point is down might miss both jaws. With a floating line, the sinking fly must surely angle *steeply* upward. With a sinking line, especially with a weighted fly, the set is still up and the fly should at least tilt that way.

So why does all this apply only to smallmouths? Not sure why and, again, not sure it does. But if it does, it's probably because smallmouths often take so quickly and usually at the point when a swimming fly is paused.

Floating flies, whose hooks ride upright, hook smallmouths so consistently that I never bother trying to figure out how to get one to flip its hook. No need to flip a buoyant fly fished on a sinking line either, since the fly rides *above* that line—so that setting the hook pulls the fly *down* to give the upright hook a good grab on the bottom jaw.

When you buy or tie a conventional (not buoyant) smallmouth streamer or crayfish fly, prefer a pattern that rides with its hook inverted.

Tip 235 Long Flies: Good for Panfish

 Pf-L

A bluegill's mouth is comically small; a pumpkinseed's mouth is *tiny*. Small and tiny, that is, in relation to the sizes of their bodies. And in relation to other fishes—trout, northern pike, *small*mouth bass, saltwater tarpon and black rockfish, and many more—they give up a lot higher percentage of their body mass to jaws and mouths than do these and some other panfish.

The old Woolly Worm shown here (not the newer Woolly Bugger—its tail's too long for panfish, in my experience) is always tied on a long-shank hook. Consequently the fish usually takes in only the rear part of the fly, leaving plenty of fly outside the mouth for you to grip.

Lots of panfish species have little mouths. You'd expect such fishes to limit their hunting to mayfly nymphs, chironomids, and similarly tiny fare. But nope. Sure, they eat that stuff, but if most panfish find something big they want to eat and can even *possibly* take it in, they'll try. They may succeed—I've caught 7-inch bluegills with half a large bass bug down their throats.

With panfish the problem can be getting your fly back out without harming the fish. Small flies can help solve the problem, or can instead exchange it for another—a little fly may go deep inside a narrow throat, and be hard to see beyond that bitsy mouth. Then you can only cut the tippet, free the fish, and hope it expels the fly soon.

But a bluegill or other panfish can generally take in only part of a fly tied on a long-shank hook, a hook whose straight center section is longer than normal. Or at least take in only part before you set the hook—this leaves the front of the fly exposed, for you to use as a lever or handle.

And that can be a godsend.

Floating panfish flies normally don't need long-shank hooks because you set on seeing the fly go down, before the fish can take it in too far. *Normally* . . .

Tip 236 Organize Your Fly Boxes

 Tr-S,Tr-L   Lg-L   Sm-L, Sm-S   Pf-L

Here's what happens. You start out with one fly box and just put your few flies into it without a thought. No problem . . . yet.

Then you get more flies, and more, and more yet—everyone does—and now you own five fly boxes randomly stuffed with flies. And then you need to find a size 16 Parachute Adams.

Good luck.

You need to take out all the flies—just empty your boxes—then put the flies back grouped by fish (trout, largemouth, panfish . . .), by water (largemouth lake, smallmouth lake, trout creek . . .), by type (nymph, dry, emerger, streamer, hair bug . . .), and perhaps by size too. Now you have them organized. Now you won't have to bring them all every time—just the ones you need—and plow constantly through them in search of that one critical fly.

I, for example, carry a trout-stream mayfly box and a trout-stream stonefly box and a trout-stream streamer box and others in my trout-stream vest; currently, eight boxes in all. Then there are my trout-lake boxes, smallmouth-stream boxes . . .

That's still not systematic enough, though, for me to easily find flies. So my trout-stream mayfly box contains a row of dry and half-floating emergers for imitating Green Drake mayflies, another row for PMDs, another for *Baetis*, and so on. There are rows of imitation mayfly spinners. And the other side of the box (it's divided down the middle into two compartments) holds all my mayfly nymphs lined up in similar fashion.

Tip 237 Ride the Fence for Bass and Bluegills  Lg-L Sm-L Pf-L

When I read about Jack Ellis's Fence Rider floating hair bug (tied always in size 6) in his book *The Sunfishes,* while doing research for my book *The Art of Tying the Bass Fly,* I liked what I read: "The size 6 bug may not be a full meal for the bass, but it's substantial enough to bring him up. Small bream ["bream" refers to some or all panfish] will curiously inspect such a fly but the big boys, the ones we are primarily interested in, will have no problem taking it."

Thing is, largemouth bass water is often bluegill water—what a gift to catch both species on one fly!

Ellis was right. I dove into testing his principle right away, soon proving to my satisfaction that fence riding works.

Fence riding isn't about fly type or pattern, it's really about *hook* size. Ellis uses only one hook for fence riding, the Mustad 3366 in size 6. I measured one: $7/8$ inch from far edge of bend to tip of eye. So, purchase or tie, then fish, a fly on a hook of this length and, baby—you're fence ridin'! (I use the Daiichi 1550, size 6.)

Tip 238 Sculpt a Fly

 Tr-S, Tr-L   Lg-L   Sm-L, Sm-S   Pf-L

The stream is full of plump caddis larvae. You need a weighted fly (probably one with a metal bead for a head) that imitates the larva, but you have none in the right size or color. What to do, what to do . . .

Do this: Find a mayfly nymph imitation (with a bead) in the correct size and color, and trim off its legs and tails—now it's a fair imitation of that larva. A fly that started out imitating a caddis pupa can become a scud if you trim it right. A green Woolly Bugger can become a dragonfly nymph if you shorten its tail, perhaps trim the hackle fibers off its top. A Dave's Hopper looks a lot like a Golden Stone adult once you've snipped off the kicker legs.

A little creative sculpting on flies can make them effective imitations of all sorts of things they were never meant to imitate. And, in turn, save your fishing.

Tip 239 The Glo-Bug Can Work Wonders, Often When It Shouldn't

Tr-S, Tr-L

In Alaska I've watched Dolly Varden char slam through coho salmon ten times their weight to grab a Glo-Bug, a fuzzy fish-egg-imitating fly—the salmon were in the river to spawn and the dollies had followed them up to gorge on the spilled eggs. That makes perfect sense. But here's what doesn't: I've also seen normally cautious trout charge up to grab a Glo-Bug almost the moment it touched the water—an egg-fly that absolutely dwarfed any egg ever laid by a fish in that water, a fly the size of a grape. Odd, no?

On the left is my Predator tied on a size 6 hook of about ⅞ inch total length, fence-riding size. In the center is Ellis's Fence Rider (one I tied). On the right is a full-size largemouth bass bug (Dave's Diving Frog). SKIP MORRIS

The original Adams (not Parachute Adams) on the left. On the right is another just like it, or rather, one that was just like it before cosmetic surgery turned it into a mayfly or stonefly nymph or even a mayfly spinner. Amputate the tail and what remains could pass for a caddis larva or pupa.

I've caught some fine trout in freestone creeks, in spring creeks, and even in the gargantuan Upper Columbia River fishing a Glo-Bug under a strike indicator. Sometimes, when nothing is spawning and no real fish eggs are around, the Glo-Bug just works. Sometimes it works wonders.

And it can work wonders in lakes. More than once on a pond of only an acre or two, it's moved trout fed up with getting tricked and poked and released—it's been the fly of the day. Why? Well . . .

Any fish egg is a ball of protein: serious trout sustenance. And eating their own eggs and the eggs of other fishes may go back so far and run so deep in the collective trout psyche as to be an instinctive response.

Egg yarn, from which Glo-Bugs are made, is buoyant, so you may need weight on your tippet. I tie my Glo-Bugs each with a heavy metal bead at the front. My favorite

A fish egg

Glo-Bugs of orange, red, and pink, not deviled but nevertheless resting in a deviled-egg serving dish

Glo-Bug colors are orange and pink, but red can work, and some sharp fly fishers swear by (really?) green and black.

I'm sure there are other fine egg-imitating flies that will do what a Glo-Bug can do. I just don't know them as well.

Tip 240 Break Off Your Fly without Breaking Your Rod

 Tr-S,Tr-L Lg-L Sm-L, Sm-S Pf-L

Sometimes your fly just isn't coming back—a nymph snagged deep, a dry fly dug well into a high tree branch . . . Then you just pull until the fly breaks off, tie on another fly.

When you have to pull until you break off a fly, don't use your rod to do it. A rod bent too deeply can snap. Instead, point your rod at the fly and pull ever harder on the line until the tippet gives (or you get lucky and the fly comes free). I sometimes just clamp onto the line and walk backward. Another option: peel out a bunch of line, set your rod aside, pull on the line directly, no rod involved.

If you do point the rod, tighten all its ferrules first—otherwise, the jolt of the snapping tippet may pop a rod section free, and then it'll slide down the line and away since there's no fly to stop it.

And, since carelessly leaving flies in or around streams and lakes is littering, recover your flies if you can do so without taking risks or extreme measures.

Tip 241 Bend a Branch, Save a Fly

 Tr-S,Tr-L Lg-L Sm-L, Sm-S Pf-L

We're out there to enjoy nature, not destroy it, so don't go breaking limbs off tall trees or snapping young trees in half. But trees and their limbs *are* tough and flexible—ever see what happens to them in a windstorm? Mayhem. Yet there they remain (most of them, anyway).

Flies get caught up beyond reach in tree limbs, all the time, actually. You may have to break off such flies, but if you *bend* that small tree or limb down, you may get your fly back. Sometimes I'll find a dead tree limb lying on the ground and use it to bend down a live limb holding my fly. Dead limbs often have the remains of smaller broken-off ones that make good hooks.

Never, ever—*never ever*—try to use your rod as a sort of grappling hook to pull down a branch. And never try to *push* your fly free with more than the *lightest* pressure from your rod tip. No fly is worth breaking a rod over.

Often, a tree-caught fly's a goner. I'm just saying, don't give up *too* easily.

Tip 242 Fish the Best Fly

Tr-S, Tr-L   Lg-L   Sm-L, Sm-S   Pf-L

Which fly, out of all the flies in all your boxes, is best, the one most likely to catch fish at any particular moment? It's the one you trust. The more confidence you have in a fly, the more effectively you'll fish it. Obviously, fish will sometimes make you fish flies you don't yet trust. But if fly selection is open because the fish are currently open-minded, fish a fly pattern that's earned your confidence.

Does this mean you find a fly you trust and for the rest of your fishing days fish it alone? I hope not, because that won't work. I've seen fly fishers who, by fishing their one God-sent fly pattern with great care and persistence, came surprisingly close to pulling it off. Surprisingly close, but not very close. If trout are focused on loose salmon eggs tumbling along the bed of a stream, your Parachute Adams, and likely your Woolly Bugger too, won't interest them. You'll need a fly that looks like an egg.

So what I'm saying is, find not one but a small group of flies you trust, prefer them to all the rest, but be willing to leave them for others when you must. Or, of course, if you just want to experiment.

CHAPTER 8
WHAT FISH EAT AND (MOST OF) OUR FLIES IMITATE

Tip 243 You Don't Need to Become an Entomologist to Match Flies to Bugs

 Tr-S, Tr-L — Lg-L — Sm-L, Sm-S — Pf-L

As a trout fisher, you're better off with a good understanding of aquatic entomology, but you can go a long way without it.

Let's say trout are rising on your favorite stream or lake. You *catch* a sample of the insect they're taking; *find* a fly in your box that makes a good match in size, especially, but also in form and general lightness or darkness; and then *watch* how the insects struggle or wave their wings or scurry or rest quietly so you can *imitate* that action (or lack of it) in your fly. You may have no idea your Parachute Light Cahill is passing as the mayfly *Heptagenia elegantula* (which most fly fishers call the Pale Evening Dun), but neither do the trout.

When largemouth and smallmouth bass and panfish are onto hatches (which they are far less often than trout are), everything I said above applies to them too.

Entomology really can help you catch more fish (especially trout)—and it's fascinating—but, often, you can do just fine with only a keen and patient eye.

Tip 244 Meet What Trout Eat in Streams

Tr-S

Here are the bugs and other trout feed common to streams across North America and some other parts of the world.

MAYFLY
Lives most of its life underwater as a nymph, swims up to the surface of the water to escape its shuck in its emerger stage (at least most species swim up), and hatches as a winged adult, a "dun." The fully mature mayfly is called a "spinner." The female spinner

Mayfly nymph

Mayfly dun

Mayfly spinner

returns to the water to release her eggs and die. Mayflies run from tiny to very big, in all sorts of colors.

CADDISFLY

Lives underwater hidden or out hauling around a case it constructs as a larva, transforms into a pupa, and then swims up to the surface of the water to slip from its shuck as an emerger (some swim to shore), becoming, finally, a winged adult that looks something like a moth. Caddisflies run a big range of size and coloring.

Caddisfly larva

Caddisfly pupa

Caddisfly adult

STONEFLY

A stout insect that's first a nymph, living in at least fairly swift currents, then a winged adult. It climbs out on the bank to hatch. Tiny to huge, lots of colors.

Stonefly nymph

Stonefly adult

MIDGE

A tiny aquatic insect that lives as a larva, rises as a pupa, and hatches openly as an adult that looks like a mosquito. Tiny in *streams*—in lakes it can run large and, there, is usually called a chironomid. Colors vary. The diminutive midge can hatch in such mobs as to move large trout to take size 22 flies.

Midge larva JIM SCHOLLMEYER

Midge pupa JIM SCHOLLMEYER

Midge adult

TERRESTRIALS

Bugs that live on land but can fall onto water. Grasshoppers, ants, flying ants, and beetles are the main ones.

Grasshopper

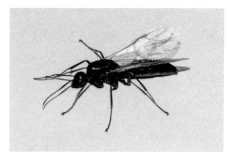

Flying ant

Ant

Beetle

THE REST

Shrimplike scuds and less shrimplike sow bugs can flourish in slow, weedy streams. Aquatic worms look like earthworms but live underwater. All sorts of small fishes feed trout in streams: sculpins, *baby* trout, blacknose dace . . .

Aquatic earthworm

Sculpin JIM SCHOLLMEYER

Tip 245 Meet What Trout Eat in Lakes

Tr-L

Here are the creatures trout primarily eat in lakes.

CHIRONOMID

Called a midge when it's in a stream. Stream or lake, same bug, but always tiny in streams while often fair-sized to even large in lakes. Color runs a big range, with brown and black most common. Chironomid stages: larva, pupa (that squirms slowly to the surface of the water), emerger, adult (the female buzzes on the water, releasing her eggs).

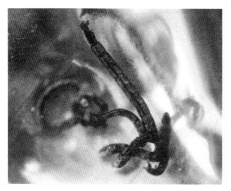

Chironomid larva

Chironomid pupa

Chironomid adult

MAYFLY

Fewer species in lakes than in moving water. Stages are nymph, emerger, dun (new winged adult), spinner (mature adult). Tiny to huge, varied colors. The most common mayfly of lakes is *Callibaetis*.

Mayfly nymph (Callibaetis)

Mayfly dun (Callibaetis)

Mayfly spinner (Callibaetis)

CADDISFLY

As in streams: larva hidden or out hauling around its case, upward-swimming pupa, emerger, finally the adult that's like a moth. Typically a lake caddis hatch is about twitched and skimmed dry flies, sometimes about imitating the pupa. Big size and color range.

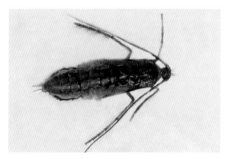

Caddisfly pupa JIM SCHOLLMEYER

Caddisfly adult

DAMSELFLY

Slim nymph, usually some shade of green, swims up to within a yard of the lake's surface, then swims toward shore, climbs out on reeds to hatch. Winged adults (blue, some are olive) flitting in abundance can occasionally move trout.

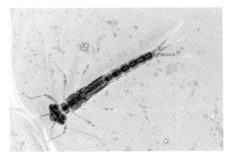

Damselfly nymph

Damselfly adult

DRAGONFLY

The beast of a nymph crawls underwater to shore, crawls out, hatches, then flies around like a helicopter/jet fighter hybrid that trout rarely eat. Two common lake dragons: one big, the other huge.

Dragonfly nymphs

SCUD

Like little shrimp. Often abundant in rich lakes. Never hatch, just putter about to fill trout bellies.

LEECH

Slick and disgusting. In addition: big, stout, elongated, eyeless, squishy, and swims in a serpentine fashion turned vertical. Brown, black, olive, or tan. Some are spotted. A real meal for a trout.

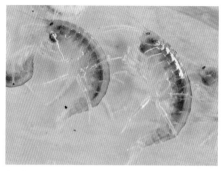

Scuds

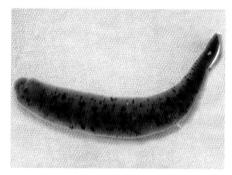

Leech

THE REST

Water boatmen and backswimmers have teardrop bodies equipped with two long stroking legs. Never hatch but swim, scurry across the water, or fly. They go on swarming flights in spring and fall. Flying ants of all sizes in black or brown or red drop onto lakes. Other terrestrials (beetles, grasshoppers, etc.) can too. Little fishes feed trout in lakes, of course.

Water boatman

Flying ant

Tip 246 Remember: Bugs Run All Ages and Sizes 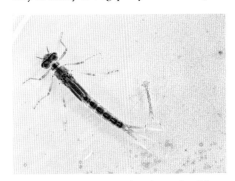 Tr-S,Tr-L Lg-L Sm-L, Sm-S Pf-L

I believe that most fly fishers see bug size in the following neat and simple way: If the adult matches a size 14 hook, so must the nymph or larva. Sorry, too neat. And *way* too simple.

Some nymphs grow for three years before hatching. So, *right now*, there may be dinky first-year, substantial second-year, and gargantuan third-year dragonfly or Golden Stonefly nymphs all sharing the same lake or stream.

The one-year life cycle of most insects doesn't help. Six months before hatch time, the larvae or nymphs are only half grown; right after the hatch, the babies will barely have *started* growing.

Fly fishers seem to assume that all nymphs and larvae of a type always run one size because the adults that hatch from them all run one size. But this one-size-matches-all business is silly when you try to apply it to insects in their underwater forms. Are you the same size today as on the day you exited the womb? Hope not.

So what does all this mean to you, the fly fisher, in practical terms? It means that (1) you can loosen up in general about fly size for nymphs, and (2) if a particular nymph or larva is prevalent in a lake or stream so that the trout are eating it often, you may need to catch a sample and see what size it's *currently* running before selecting your fly.

Of course, if there's a hatch and the trout are taking the nymphs or pupae just before they emerge, those nymphs or pupae will all be full grown, all of a certain size—a size you'd better match in your fly.

Since largemouths (occasionally) and smallmouths (fairly often) and panfish (probably all the time) feed on nymphs and larvae, everything above *can* apply to them too (though they're rarely as bug-picky as trout are).

This full-grown damsel nymph is obvious, but did you notice the tiny juvenile one next to it? Trout will.

In early summer, when the first tiny grasshoppers appear, who cares, who notices? Trout, that's who.

Tip 247 These Are the Main Tiny-Fly Insects and Hatches Tr-S, Tr-L

You need to know the tiny insects that trout, sometimes *large* trout, sometimes concentrate on eating so that you can bring the right flies and know what to do with them. Here those bitsy bugs are, in (sort of) order of importance.

MIDGES

The larvae, pupae, and adults match size 20 (possibly 18) hooks down to as small as fly hooks go. During hatches, trout rising in streams may take dry flies, but more likely emerger flies; sometimes an imitation of the pupa just below the water's surface can kill.

MAYFLIES

There are mayflies matching hooks of size 18 and smaller—and some of them are common and hatch in abundance. (The Blue-Winged Olive is the most common, hatching from North American coast to coast.) As with midges, a dry or emerger fly can work for imitating various bitsy mayflies, but sometimes a nymph suspended below a dry fly or little indicator works best on either a lake or stream.

Fly fishers see the midge as a symbol representing all dinky insects. Perhaps because it is, in fact, always dinky.

CADDISFLIES

Some call the tiny ones "microcaddis." A floating emerger, a twitched or dead-drift dry fly, or a pupa imitation on the swing—any of these can do the trick whether you're fishing a stream or a lake. Watch the feeding trout. Experiment.

TERRESTRIALS

I've seen trout rise to tiny wingless ants and tiny winged ants on streams and lakes. I've heard about tiny beetles but have not seen (or at least noticed) them yet. There *are* tiny grasshoppers. (See tip 246.) Imitate these insects with dry flies fished dead drift on a stream and still on a lake (and *maybe* with the tiniest twitches).

A Tricorythodes mayfly spinner. Baetis may be the best-known of tiny mayflies, but the "Trico," shown here, probably comes next. If you can't see its freakishly long tails in the photo, look for their freakishly long shadows. Only the male Trico is crazy enough to drag around tails like those. The Trico hatches from both streams (the slow parts) and lakes. Few mayflies do.

CHIRONOMIDS

If a chironomid in a stream is tiny (which it always is) and we call it a midge, but we call a large chironomid in a lake a chironomid, do we call a tiny chironomid in a lake a midge? Ponder that. Anyway, although midges/chironomids often run large in lakes, tiny ones do hatch there and trout will rise to the minuscule adults and, especially, go after the bitsy squirming pupae near the surface.

Tip 248 Some Mayflies and Caddisflies Cheat  Tr-S,Tr-L Lg-L Sm-L, Sm-S Pf-L

Mayflies are beloved by fly fishers (by trout and smallmouths and other fishes too) for their open-water hatching—their shimmying up, their wriggling from their shucks, their resting on the water before flying off. It's everything up to the flying-off part that interests fish and fly fishers. Mayflies do this in both streams and lakes.

Caddisflies do something similar. They swim up in strong pulses, pop from their shucks, and, sometimes, rest or scurry on the water before flying off. Also in streams and lakes.

That's what *most* kinds of mayflies and caddis do.

Some kinds, that live in lakes or streams, don't. Some kinds of both these insects swim not up but off, toward shore, and then climb out of the water and shed their shucks there. Clearly, such mayfly nymphs and caddis pupae can be important to imitate during their swim in, but their hatching is up on land, meaningless to the fish. The fish do get another shot at these mayflies and caddis when the mature female insects return to the water to release their eggs.

Here's where a little time spent with a fly fisher's entomology book can really pay off—look up which mayflies and caddis are open-water hatchers and which are

On the left side of this stone is the shuck that mayfly wriggled free of. Most species of mayfly hatch out in open water. A few, like this one, climb out to hatch.

shore hatchers and then come to the water prepared with the proper flies and fishing approaches for both.

But it doesn't end there. Brace yourself for this: Some mayflies don't escape their shucks at the water's surface or on shore, but just *under* the surface. We fly fishers are still figuring that one out.

Sure, all this is mostly about trout. But smallmouths and largemouths and panfish do eat mayflies and caddis, so . . .

Tip 249 It Matters That Different Bugs Hatch in Different Ways

 Tr-S, Tr-L   Lg-L   Sm-L, Sm-S   Pf-L

Insect hatches can get confusing because they vary so much. But hatches are a major part of trout fishing—the finest trout fishing often accompanies them—so it's import- ant you understand them. (They can matter with smallmouth bass too. Less often with panfish and largemouths.)

The classic hatch is a mayfly hatch: the nymphs swimming up in open water to strug- gle from their shucks at the top; the slender duns riding sedately on the current and displaying the elongated soft triangles of their new wings. The classic fish feeding on a mayfly hatch is the trout, taking down the duns in rhythms. It's easy to get sentimental over all this, but it *is* awesome.

If all insects hatched this way it'd be just so neat. But it isn't, because they don't. Caddis sometimes pop out and fly away so quickly that swung pupa flies may outfish dry flies. All stoneflies and a few mayflies and caddis swim or crawl to the edge of the water before emerging. Damselfly nymphs swim *nearly* up, then in toward shore to climb up reeds and hatch.

Some bugs wind up on trout water well after they're done hatching; others that wind up there never hatch at all. Flying ants fly out and drop onto lakes and streams; wingless ants fall in too, along with grasshoppers, beetles . . . Female mayfly spinners drop to the water, dying, to release their fertilized eggs.

My point is that you need to adjust flies and tactics to the insects and their behav- ior—you fish imitations of terrestrials along stream and lake edges, stonefly imitations along the edges of streams. You swing caddis-pupa flies if emergers and dries fail. You swim damsel nymph patterns a foot or two under a lake's surface around the reeds the naturals seek. You fish imitation spinners dead drift during a spinner fall. You adjust, based on knowledge and observation.

 **Bonus Tip** Windy Days Can Be Terrestrial Days

Tr-S, Tr-L   Lg-L   Sm-L, Sm-S   Pf-L

A winged ant flying, a beetle on a streamside spear of grass, a grasshopper flying or hopping—one good gust of wind can toss these and other terrestrial insects onto a lake or stream. If it's terrestrial time (usually midsummer into early fall), hope for wind and, if you get it, go fishing.

Tip 250 Here's How to Connect with Insect Hatches Tr-S, Tr-L Lg-L Sm-L, Sm-S Pf-L

Insect hatches get a lot of press. Read enough about them, and you can get the sense they're just going on everywhere all the time.

They aren't.

You connect with insect hatches in two ways: (1) luck and (2) research, planning, timing, and luck.

Sure, I've stumbled across damselfly hatches on trout lakes and caddisfly hatches on trout streams (and hatches on smallmouth streams and largemouth, panfish, and small-mouth lakes—as I discuss elsewhere in this book, hatches can inspire these fishes too). But more often my stumbling puts me on a lake or stream with nary a bug on the move. Hatchless water can provide excellent action, but if your heart's set on meeting a hatch, you need to reduce the luck factor.

You can target a specific hatch, or just a promising time of the season for hatches in general: springtime into early summer on lakes, and late spring into early fall on streams.

The legendary Salmonfly hatch of the West, a specific hatch, is easy to time because . . . because it's *legendary*. Information, general and current, is all over the internet. But lesser-known hatches can be wonderful, and you can often learn about them regionally on fly-shop websites.

Say your trip for hitting the Western March Brown mayfly hatch is set. Will all your planning and research get you into those March Browns? Probably . . . Nevertheless, your odds in general of connecting with a particular hatch go way up when you choose option 2 over option 1.

Tip 251 When Trout Feed on Top, Here's How to Figure Out Which Bug They're Taking Tr-S, Tr-L

When two or three or even more hatches come off at once on a stream or lake, as Pat Dorsey says in his book *Fly Fishing Tailwaters*, "First, you must decipher which species (midges, mayflies, caddis, or stoneflies) the fish are feeding on." (I could have just said that in my own words, but I like the backup.) Of course, some of those bugs might not actually be hatching at all—dropping mayfly spinners or flying ants, scurrying caddis adults releasing their eggs . . . But the point is, bugs get on the water, and sometimes trout have a lot of them to choose among.

Sometimes they just take it all, especially, I find, around sunset. But usually, the bulk of them will pick out *one* particular insect in *one* form (nymph, emerger, spinner) and ignore the rest. When that happens, you need to pay attention.

Collecting a bunch of sample insects is wise. I always carry an aquarium net for this purpose, in the back pouch of my vest or in the tackle box in my boat.

Let's say you're down to two likely suspects: a caddis and a mayfly, both matching about a size 16 hook. Now zero in on a rising fish and try to spot each bug as it drifts up, and see which ones the trout takes.

If you can't catch a sample or see what bugs the trout are taking, make a guess, and then experiment until you find a fly that works.

Tip 252 When Trout Feed on Top, Here's How to Figure Out Which *Stage* of a Bug They're Taking Tr-S, Tr-L

Your odds of hooking trout feeding at the surface of a stream or lake go up if you can figure out not only what insect but what *stage* of that insect they're most interested in.

Example: Trout are showing on top and you've done the right things to figure out what insects are out there with them. You're pretty sure a small mayfly is the hot item on a menu of caddisflies, mayflies, midges, and big clumsy stoneflies. You're closing in.

Now comes a process of elimination. First, are your mayflies in the helpless-atop-the-water spinner stage? If you see that the insects' wings are transparent and one or both lie flush on the water, and their bodies are down on the water, they're almost certainly spinners.

No? Then spinners are (probably) out.

Next, remember that insects only partially free of their shucks (emergers) are more vulnerable than ones fully hatched and that trout know it. So, it makes sense to prefer an emerger fly.

But before you decide, study the rises (if you haven't already) and note the *way* the trout rise; that narrows the possibilities. (See tip 9.)

You're now convinced that those rises are really not rises at all but are the swirls of trout taking the mayflies just below the water's surface as nymphs. Well done—you've got your bug and its stage the trout want all figured out! Perhaps . . . The soft-hackle seems like the logical solution, so you fish it a while. Nothing. Oh, well . . . Better keep experimenting. And eliminating options. It's often a messy process, sure. Intriguing, though.

Tip 253 Hatches Can Matter for Warmwater Fishes Too

 Lg-L   Sm-L, Sm-S   Pf-L

Yes, hatches are mainly about trout. But if you forget about hatches and the warmwater fishes, Fate will throw that combination at you again and again. Fate can be nasty that way.

Smallmouths feed as largemouths feed, on gut-filling stuff—leeches, their own babies, crayfish, and such—but feed on much smaller trout stuff as well—caddis larvae, stoneflies, mayfly spinners . . . I've seen smallies rise steadily to Pale Evening Duns, mayflies matching size 14 hooks. (Once, to my amazement, I found them sipping down minute Trico mayflies—matching size 22 hooks—along a lazy current seam. I showed them flies on size 22 hooks. They took them.)

Late every summer a lake near my home gets largemouth bass rising sedately to termites. The rainbow trout rise among the bass, both out as far as 50 feet from shore. When I set the hook on my termite dry fly, I never know which fish I'm hooking.

Termites flying out from a forest isn't technically a *hatch*, but the effect is essentially the same: identical bugs on the water.

Oddly, I've yet to find bluegills or crappies or other panfish really focused on hatching bugs (or non-hatching bugs, like termites), though I know it happens. In *The Sunfishes: A Fly Fishing Journey of Discovery*, author Jack Ellis talks about bluegills focusing on fallen bees and wasps and hatching chironomids and mayflies and more.

Hatch matching isn't the norm in warmwater fishing, but warmwater fish can make the practice mandatory. When they do, just fish as you'd fish for hatch-focused trout.

Tip 254 Trout Love Dragonfly Nymphs— Use That  Tr-L

Dragonfly nymphs offer more to trout than just their whopping-dollop-of-protein bodies: They offer availability. Thing is, dragonfly nymphs, like trout, are hunters, out searching for other, smaller critters to eat. Most of the nymphs and larvae in a trout lake spend the bulk of their lives hidden among waterweeds, under waterlogged bark, in silt, or under stones. While most of them are tucked safely away, dragonfly nymphs hunt them, out in the relative open.

Here's something trout love: a stout, meaty full-grown Green Darner Nymph.

I'm a dragonfly fan—if no trout are rising and no bugs are hatching or showing on a lake, my first thought is an imitation dragon nymph. I'll usually fish it either by trolling or with the countdown method.

Trolling is trolling: full-sinking line, rowing or working swim fins . . . But I tailor the countdown method to make my fly move like the real nymph. Since dragon nymphs move quicker than most other nymphs, I fish a type III (or IV) full-sinking line so that I can keep the fly down. Then I retrieve the fly in short strips of the line, neither quick nor slow. If that isn't working, I try the same but interspersed with long, quick strips— dragonfly nymphs can dart with real speed when they have reason to, and a trout closing in is a fine reason. Trout often react to fleeing food by attacking it.

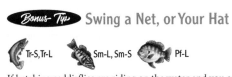

Bonus Tip Swing a Net, or Your Hat

 Tr-S, Tr-L   Sm-L, Sm-S   Pf-L

If hatching caddisflies are riding on the water and you can't get out far enough to catch one, or doing so will put down your rising trout, catch one that's flying. An aquarium net can do it; a real insect net, an *aerial net*, is best, but large and awkward to carry fishing; or you can use your hat—swing it at a bug until you catch the bug in the crown, the cupped top part of the hat. A sample bug from the prevailing hatch is a great asset in selecting an effective fly.

There are two dragonflies common to trout lakes: Libellulidae and Aeshnidae (commonly called the Green Darner). The former's the smaller and generally lies in wait for prey; the latter's truly big and an aggressive hunter. Libellulidae in strong numbers can focus trout, but it's the Darner that gets most of my, and the trout's, attention.

Tip 255 Bass Love Dragonfly Nymphs Too  Lg-L Sm-L, Sm-S

There's long been chatter about dragonfly nymphs and trout lakes, but not so much about dragons and smallmouths, and even less about dragons and largemouths. That needs to stop—now. It's time the topic of dragon nymphs and bass got some respect.

Yes, trout in lakes watch for dragonfly nymphs all season long. But bass, smallmouth and largemouth both, live in lakes too.

Concerned bass lakes are too warm for dragons? Don't be. Lakes that hold dragonfly nymphs range from cold climates clear to the sizzling equator—almost wherever there's standing fresh water, there are dragons. Hardy bunch.

Smallmouth bass eat insects all the time, so they're a shoo-in. Largemouths like big stuff such as frogs and leeches—but if they're going to eat bugs at all, they're going to go for the biggest, meatiest insect entrees on the menu. Dragonfly nymphs are in many lakes the biggest of all the aquatic insects.

In a smallmouth or largemouth lake I typically fish imitation dragonfly nymphs down along the bottom on a fast-sinking, full-sinking line with modest strips, sometimes mixed with long, quick ones. Or I troll.

There are lots of dragonfly nymphs in some smallmouth rivers too. I fish one that's loaded with them. I fish a weighted imitation on a floating line in shallow water or an unweighted one deeper on a sink-tip line.

Want to know more about dragonfly nymphs? Read the previous tip (254).

Tip 256 Adult Dragonflies Can Make for Exciting Fishing

Tr-L   Lg-L   Sm-L, Sm-S   Pf-L

In *Fly Fishing for Western Smallmouth*, author David Paul Williams says, "Dragonflies are a smallmouth favorite. Nymph patterns catch fish but adult imitations are great fun to fish." Amen to all three points, David, but especially to your last.

I remember the final 20 minutes of my final day on a desert smallmouth river a couple of years ago: Twelve times I slapped a foam dragonfly onto the tail of a big pool, nine times it went under with the swift smack of a bass. It can be that good.

Largemouth bass go after adult dragons too. They'll hunt the big bugs around the shallows, leap to snap them out of the air or off reeds, grab them when they get caught on the water, and ignore flies that don't look like them or act like them.

The trick with a dragon-adult fly for largemouths and smallmouths both, I've found, isn't to get a fly of just the right size and shape and color; it's to get a fly of roughly

A water-caught dragonfly adult: big, helpless, and (to fish) a fine big snack—or full meal

An adult dragonfly. The adults run a considerable range of size and color.

Yes, this Bett's Foam Dragon matches well the coloring of the real dragonfly adult above. But you won't find this particular fly for sale; I had to tie it and color it myself. You will find lots of fine adult-dragon patterns of all kinds and colors out there for sale, however, and they'll probably work just as well.

comparable size and shape (color seems of minor importance), drop or slap it down amid the action, and then make it *act* like the insect: This means twitches, pauses—all of it subtle.

That's also how it worked the *one* time I found trout in a lake chasing adult dragonflies.

Damselflies are essentially smaller, daintier version of dragonflies, and both basses—*and* panfish—will get onto them. Just follow the rules I laid out for fishing dragon-adult flies, but tone down the movement even more.

Tip 257 Hatches Can Be Easy to Miss

 Tr-S, Tr-L   Lg-L   Sm-L, Sm-S   Pf-L

Hatches of midges and mayflies, flying ants and mayfly spinners dropping onto the water—such events can, often *do*, go on all around our waders or boats without us

A heavy hatch is a marvel—the bugs everywhere, on your glasses, in your ears, bumping your face, swarming and flying all around you (and flattening against your truck as you drive alongside the river). But not all hatches are heavy.

A lonely mayfly on the still surface of a trout lake, not another for 10 feet. A sparse hatch, but if the insects are at least fair-sized (as this one is), the trout will probably notice them. You'd be wise to do the same.

noticing. The fish, however (perhaps either of the basses or some panfish or other, but most likely trout), will notice. It's their job to notice, they were designed to notice, in order to survive they must notice, and they're good at noticing insect activity or *anything* going on with *anything* that might involve food.

So, we need to notice too.

Observation, in all its forms, is invaluable to the fly fisher, and this particular form is as important as any. Look near, at the water and along the shoreline, and far up in the air to see what's flying and what's dropping. Scan the water's surface for any sign of insects on it. Lower your eyes to within inches of the water to see if nearly invisible creatures lie tiny or low or both tiny *and* low atop it, and look down into the water in case a damselfly nymph is snaking along inches below.

I've often pointed out a quiet hatch or some other fish-feed event to new fly fishers who hadn't noticed it, and then watched these anglers' fishing fire up once they changed flies and tactics to imitate the feed. How many hatches have gone on right under my rod that I, personally, have failed to notice? Probably an embarrassing number.

Tip 258 Hatch Density Is a Big Deal

 Tr-S, Tr-L   Lg-L   Sm-L, Sm-S   Pf-L

Caddisflies, midges, or mayflies hatching, beetles falling onto the water or female adult stoneflies dropping onto it to release their eggs—such events as these (all of which fly fishers may refer to as "hatches," even though some aren't) can run from a few isolated insects up to hordes of them. Of course, fish (mainly trout, but definitely the basses and panfish at times) normally go nuts for the heavy stuff. But often, they'll move for even really sparse hatches.

That's a lot of dinky mayfly duns per square foot—a heavy hatch.

So don't be quick to write off the sort of hatches where you may only see a bug every few minutes—currents may gather those few in sufficient numbers in certain places to interest the fish. And perhaps there are more insects than you're noticing.

With really big insects, such as giant stoneflies, it won't take many to fire the fishing up—each fish wants its meal-in-a-bug.

A steady, middling hatch is usually the best (or pseudo-hatch, such as moths falling on the water). There's plenty to hold the fish's interest, but not so many insects your fly is lost among them.

The truly dense hatches, the kind in which bugs seem everywhere on and above the water, can be tough. With these, the best fishing usually comes early, before the numbers really build, and sometimes again when they thin at the end—if by that point the fish are still hungry enough to feed. During a dense hatch, you'd better get your fly right in front of a fish; that fish isn't likely to move far for your fly with such plenty so close.

Tip 259 Insects in the Air May Only Be in the Air Tr-S, Tr-L

Elsewhere in this book, I suggest that you become a fly-fishing detective. And as a detective, you may see a swarm of mayflies hovering and flitting, and then proudly proclaim that you've found a clue. You have, but it may be a false one.

Every seasoned trout fisher's been fooled by this. The problem is, insects only matter to trout if they're *available* to those trout—even if teeming winged caddisflies form a hazy cloud, none of them may be touching the water. If they're not on or in the water, trout won't care about them. And why should they?

That's always the key: Are these bugs where the trout can get them?

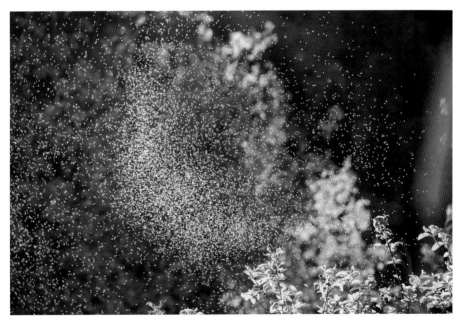

A cloud of adult aquatic bugs. Exciting for you, sure. But for the fish? Perhaps . . .

You need to know this: Most hatching aquatic insects have life cycles that include activity near the water but not actually on or in the water. The off-water stuff is mating business, usually.

So notice first, are these insects over land or over water? Over land? Probably meaningless. If there's a swarm of insects over the *water*, however, at least a few *may* be touching down. Or not . . .

Notice second—and this takes some patience with your eyes down close—do you actually *see* the insects atop or awash in the water?

Third, if the bugs *are* on or awash in the water, are the trout working them in slashes or rises?

It's not just about insects that hatch. Grasshoppers leaping from streamside grass, stoneflies scrambling over tree branches overhanging the water—it's all just peachy, but none of it matters unless trout are getting their shot.

Tip 260 Here's the Deal with Instar Nymphs Tr-S Sm-S

Instar. Title of a sci-fi movie? Nope. The word refers to a bug that recently shed its outer skin . . . or so lots of fly fishers think.

My professional-entomologist friend Rick Hafele (author of such titles as *Nymph-Fishing Rivers & Streams*) says an instar stage is actually—surprise!—when a nymph (or larva) is *not* molting. Instar periods are growth periods for a larva or nymph; they end when the insect has grown too large for its exoskeleton and must shed it. It's the molting stage, when an underwater insect is out of its old exoskeleton but hasn't yet grown the next one, lasting only several hours, that's the point here.

Stonefly nymphs. The pale one molted recently.

So what's the big deal about a nymph (or larva) without its self-made body armor? It's that such an insect is (to a trout) soft, succulent, scrumptious, and pretty darn helpless. Imagine yourself with no skeleton—how well could you evade a charging rhino?

A recently molted nymph (or larva) is also easy to spot: If you're a trout with a molted-nymph hankering, all you need do is look for the really pale ones—I mean light tan to nearly white.

I've heard it said that trout in streams will lock onto molting nymphs and ignore all else. I haven't seen exactly that, but I sometimes do very well on trout streams by fishing creamy nymphs. I think bringing along a few such imitations is a wise move.

River smallmouths and molted nymphs? Sure, why not? I've caught river smallies on pale nymphs, and I can't imagine why they wouldn't they savor those little delicacies that go down so smoothly.

Molters in lakes: not an issue. At least that's how I figure it. Soft molted nymphs try to stay hidden in their vulnerable form, and with no currents to sweep them out into the open, probably do.

Tip 261 Damselflies Can Be a Big Deal in Trout Lake Fishing

 Tr-L   Lg-L   Sm-L, Sm-S   Pf-L

The damselfly hatch can generate some remarkable fishing: trout swirling after the slim, sculling nymphs, then grabbing them in close to the reeds the insects seek to climb, and finally even banging into reeds to knock the climbing nymphs back to the water. Legendary stuff.

Damselflies hatch mornings from late spring into summer. The nymphs swim up to within three feet of the water's surface, then turn and swim toward shore. You anchor, tie an imitation onto your tippet, toss it out amid the action on a floating or

Damsel adults crowded onto the stalks of flooded grass: a clear sign this lake carries a big damselfly population.

A typical adult damselfly. Most are blue, like this; some are olive.

Two among the many reliable imitations of the damselfly adult. New ones keep appearing.

A typical damselfly nymph: slender, large but not big, some sort of olive or green

When enough of them are flying around, adult damsels regularly wind up caught on the water, and the fish learn to hunt them. Occasionally giving your floating imitation a light twitch can make it especially convincing.

slow-sinking line, and work it slowly back—a hand-twist retrieve is perfect for this—with pauses.

Some fly fishers position themselves near and, later, *among* the reeds so their flies swim toward shore, like the naturals.

Far less common than damsel-nymph trout fishing is trout chasing *adult* damselflies on lakes. But it's worth hunting down. Here's what I've figured out about it. It's localized: One shallow bay, a pocket sheltered from the wind behind a small rock point—places like these may offer damsel-adult dry-fly action while the rest of the lake doesn't. It usually happens only when there are *lots* of damsels flitting about the water. It often happens next to the exposed tops of aquatic weed beds—the adults rest on the greenery, fall in.

This fishing: captivating.

I've only seen stream trout after adult damselflies once. But I have seen largemouths and bluegills get onto them in lakes and smallmouths get onto them in streams, and I've read about all three fishes going after the nymphs. Damsels may be mostly about trout in lakes, but not entirely.

Tip 262 Catch a Sample Bug

 Tr-S, Tr-L   Lg-L   Sm-L, Sm-S   Pf-L

Here's the thing: From a distance, all flying insects tend to look pale. Those trout are rising away out there to what look to be creamy mayflies matching a size 14 hook. You, logically, tie on a Parachute Light Cahill in size 14 and toss it upstream of a rising fish. All set, right? Look out, trout, here it comes . . .

Oh, and bugs tend to look *bigger* from a distance too. So thanks to these two tendencies, you get to spend a pleasant afternoon casting a fly too pale and too large to trout that won't take it. Lucky you.

Let's rewrite that story.

You see mayflies coming off the stream, so you . . . catch one. It takes a little fussing, but you slip up next to the edge of the water, crouching, downstream of the rising trout, and scoop up a sample as it drifts near. You hold the tiny mayfly by its wings and inspect it closely—how about that? It's *tiny*—and the underside's brown. Turns out you need a size *18* dry fly much darker than a Light Cahill.

So you tie on a size 18 Parachute Adams.

It works.

You're always far better off inspecting a sample of what trout are eating close up than trying to guess from five, eight, or more feet away. Same goes for nymphs and larvae: turn some rocks or scan the shallows, find samples, match them well with your fly.

Matching hatching bugs is mostly a trout thing, but occasionally it applies to warmwater fishes.

Tip 263 Net a Bug

Tr-S,Tr-L   Lg-L   Sm-L, Sm-S   Pf-L

When trout (and sometimes bass or panfish) are fussy, it's usually because they're locked into eating just one particular insect or another. If you can catch some samples of the predominant insects living in a lake or stream, or a sample of one that's hatching, you may have your solution, or at least some promising clues (and as I say elsewhere in this book, good fly fishers are detectives—and detectives work with clues).

So how do you catch those sample insects? In the shallows of a river or lake you can find stones and sunken wood to raise and inspect for clinging insects. You can catch floating insects in your cupped palm, but it's difficult—the water parts around your hand and the bug rides off down one side or the other. Your hat might work better, if you don't mind soaking it.

A net is best.

There are collapsible seines, "kick nets," marketed especially for fly fishers, and they're great for underwater collecting—just hold the net down in the current or sweep it through the standing water of a lake, kicking up the bottom to dislodge bugs. Kick nets are okay for catching up floating insects.

Another option is an aquarium net. These nets are inexpensive and especially good for collecting bugs floating on the water.

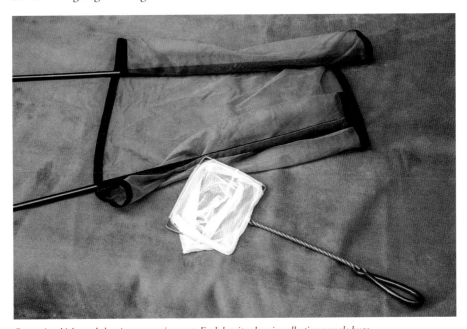

On top is a kick net, below it an aquarium net. Each has its place in collecting sample bugs.

Tip 264 Bug Bodies Often Come in Two Main Colors

 Tr-S,Tr-L   Lg-L   Sm-L, Sm-S   Pf-L

A classic error: We look at, say, a Salmonfly stonefly adult drifting atop a stream, see its body, legs, tails—all so near true black that it's hard to tell if a little dark brown is mixed in—and set out to imitate it with a black fly. So neat, so logical, what could go wrong?

This: The *underside* of the Salmonfly is *orange* (pinkish orange, reddish orange . . . in any case, still orange). Since fish see only the underside of a floating bug, you've got a problem. Will the trout ignore the color difference and take your all-black fly? Probably,

Here's a Western Golden Stonefly adult: head, thorax (what little of it shows), and legs all dark brown, wings dark. Flip it over . . .

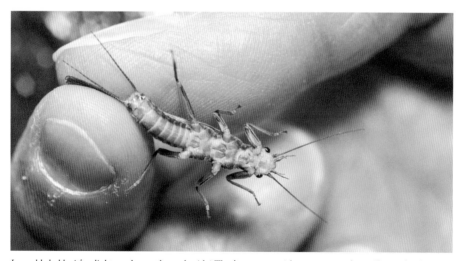

Lo and behold—it's a lighter color on the underside! That's common with trout-stream bugs. Get used to it.

if the fly is presented well—color is low on the list of factors that determine if an imitative fly passes muster with fish. Still, for the cagiest fish, color starts to count.

So if your smallmouths or trout or bluegills or whatever are on floating bugs—stoneflies, caddis, mayflies, midges—catch a sample, and then turn the bug over to see its underside, the side the *fish* see. After that, you can choose your fly wisely.

Tip 265 Spinners and Failed Hatchers: Watch for Them, and Carry Imitations

Tr-S, Tr-L   Lg-L   Sm-L, Sm-S   Pf-L

Mayfly spinners—dying, their bodies awash in the water's surface, their clear wings down—are difficult for fly fishers to see on shifting, complex stream currents. As are mayflies and caddisflies and midges that fail to properly hatch. That's surely why lake fishers, looking onto still water, more often than stream fishers, give spinners (and sometimes failed hatchers) the attention they deserve. (Note: "Cripple" was, still is, the standard term for a bug whose hatching went wrong, but a controversial word today. Hence "failed hatcher.")

Spinners and failed hatchers do deserve anglers' attention. (They always get the attention of trout.) If spinners, tiny to big, fall in sufficient numbers, trout will come up for them. (And falling is exactly what they do. In fact, when spinners are dropping to the water, it's called a "spinner fall.")

If failed hatchers collect in eddies and along foam lines, trout may feed on them well after the hatch is essentially over.

Female spinners, half floating, dying as they free their fertilized eggs, are truly helpless. Trout like that about them. Failed hatchers are helpless too.

Spinner and failed-hatcher flies are usually fished dead drift on streams, though a little very light twitching can increase their attraction on lakes. Standard emerger fly patterns pass well as failed emergers.

A mayfly whose hatching went haywire and a typical mayfly spinner—both are easy marks for trout.

The spinners of most mayfly types are a rust color underneath (the side trout see), with clear wings, so carry mostly rust-colored imitations. (Though the most important spinner of lakes, *Callibaetis*, is light gray along its underside, so don't get cocky about the rust.)

I've not seen largemouths or panfish locked onto spinners or failed hatchers *yet*, and smallies only once, but spinners drop onto their waters and insects hatch from them too, so it makes perfect sense they would go for them—in fact, they must eat them. They *must*.

Tip 266 Smallmouths *Crave* Crayfish

 Sm-L, Sm-S

I used to fish a smallmouth river in southern Oregon whose sandstone bed was in many places a wild topography, dividing its flow into chutes, near-dead bowls, long side channels, and about every imaginable shape a river could take. Lots of good places in all that to find smallmouths.

There was in all that a lot of water that suited a crayfish fly worked on the bottom. Peering, perhaps, over the top of a boulder a few feet back from the water, I'd toss a small, weighted crayfish fly out into some quiet spot and let it sink. Then I'd creep the fly just slightly, let it sit, then creep it again—that's usually about as far as it got. A small-mouth would scrape the fly off the bottom right before my ecstatic eyes.

The intensity, though—those smallmouths seemed so . . . lustful. Sometimes they'd charge in from 10 feet off; stop within inches, working all their fins in anticipation; and grab.

That's one way to fish a crayfish fly in a stream, though an uncommon one. Typically you cast out the heavy fly (on a floating line in water shallow, slow, or both; on a sink-tip

A crayfish—hard-shelled, hard-nosed, and nearly irresistible to smallmouth bass

The Clouser's Crayfish is one among many proven crayfish-imitating flies.

line in water deep, quick, or both), let it sink, and then tug it back low, close to the river-bed, in darts separated by brief pauses.

In *Fly Fishing for Smallmouth in Rivers and Streams*, author Bob Clouser describes dead drifting his Clouser Crayfish fly like a nymph, and giving it an occasional twitch. It's on my list to try.

Lakes? I fish smallmouth lakes but none with serious crayfish populations. But crayfish can thrive in lakes. I'm confident that smallies go mad for the surly crustaceans there too.

Tip 267 Take Advantage of the Insect Drift Tr-S Sm-S

In streams, the larvae and nymphs of aquatic insects just let loose, let the currents carry them off downstream, fully exposed, three times daily. You can imagine what trout and smallmouth bass think of this.

Actual degree-sporting entomologist Rick Hafele understands the bug drift far better than I ever will. In his book *Nymph Fishing Rivers and Streams*, he asks, How do imma-ture underwater insects "find new sources of food, minimize competition for food, avoid predators, and find the right habitats to live in?" Then he provides the answer: "Let go and drift."

Rick goes on to say that insect drift goes on all the time, but describes three peak periods: (1) morning, about an hour before and an hour after sunrise; (2) evening, about an hour before and an hour after sunset; and (3) from around midnight until 2:00 a.m.

Which insects drift most in streams? Rick says studies show that little to tiny Blue-Winged Olive (*Baetis*) mayflies and bitsy midges, both common in streams across North America, top the list. Next come scuds and several species of caddisflies.

What do you do about it? This: Fish nymphs in streams around sunrise and sun-set (and in the bloody middle of the night if it's legal on your stream and you're a tad unstable). The problem with evening drift is that there may be an evening *rise*—if trout are rising at sunset, good luck getting *me* to fish a nymph.

Does the drift apply to smallmouths in streams? Personally, haven't seen it. Still, smal-lies eat nymphs, so . . .

Tip 268 Swing Flies for Caddis Hatches

 Tr-S, Tr-L

Caddisfly hatches, the moth-looking adults popping out all over the water, always seem like fine opportunities for fishing dry flies or at least half-floating emerger imitations. Trout, however, often disagree—they typically pass on floating caddis and floating flies to concentrate instead on the pupae swimming up to hatch.

Is this subsurface preference perhaps due to the pupae being easier to catch than adults? I don't know. But I do know that I'll typically catch more trout during a caddis hatch on a stream by fishing a pupa imitation (perhaps one weighted at its core or with a metal bead) or a soft-hackled fly than by fishing a dry. That said, if caddis are hatching sedately—taking their time in sloughing off their shucks, drying their wings—an emerger, and possibly even a dry fly, may be best.

Adult female caddis return to streams to release their eggs, and when they do, a dry fly given an occasional twitch is right.

I normally fish dry flies during caddis hatches on trout lakes and typically do well that way, but I have seen lake trout stubbornly refuse all dry-fly imitations matching the hatched adults while eagerly grabbing a pupa fly retrieved on a sinking line.

My point: Especially if you're fishing a trout stream (and sometimes a trout lake) during a caddis hatch, keep the swung (or retrieved, for lakes) pupa imitation in mind. It could be killing.

Tip 269 Remember: Largemouths Don't Feed Often, but They Needn't Feed to Be Caught Lg-L

I know a little largemouth lake that's dynamite around the middle two weeks of August on a dry day under dark, still, packed-tight clouds. On such a day I'll fish the entire shoreline, once around, hooking bass after bass, and then go around again and catch nearly as many as the first time. Fifty, 60, 100 bass landed? Never counted, too busy catching bass, but somewhere in that range. Under normal circumstances the lake is exactly good: 8, 10, maybe even 20 bass in two or three earnest hours of working the shoreline. So what happens on those glory days?

I know what happens: *All* the bass feed.

That's the thing about largemouth bass: Outside of those occasional events when they go on a group binge, they spend a good chunk of their time ignoring food. When few largemouth bass are feeding, you're left with three choices: (1) accept that you won't catch many, and mainly just enjoy being out on the water; (2) wait for better conditions (morning, evening, cloud cover, stable weather, etc.); or (3) goad bass into taking a fly. Largemouths will hit a fly for several reasons having nothing to do with feeding, including anger, the defending of turf, reflex, even curiosity. That's why some of our bass flies are so . . . well, just weird—ever see Pat Ehlers's chartreuse Grim Reaper fly?

The inconsistent feeding of largemouth bass also means you shouldn't write off largemouth water quickly—that lake that was lousy today may be alive with hungry bass tomorrow.

The Grim Reaper (in its lovely, vibrant Fire Tiger color scheme), waving its chartreuse-and-orange tentacles, sparkling through its chartreuse body, its hidden glass rattle clicking away, must just irk a largemouth cross-eyed. But if a largemouth won't feed, well . . .

Tip 270 Don't Forget the Other Terrestrials Tr-S, Tr-L Lg-L Sm-L, Sm-S Pf-L

The grasshopper gets all the fanfare from anglers it should—it can run huge for a trout bug, and it leaps and flies across grassy meadows announcing itself. It can make for some wonderful, intriguing late-season trout-stream fishing. But the grasshopper's not

Wasps, bees, hornets—on occasion, if enough of them are around, fish will notice. Honest: I've seen it. And at such times I've caught trout on imitations.

the only terrestrial bug trout eat. Though sometimes you might think so, the way fly fishers go on about it.

Ants (both winged and wingless) and beetles round out the rest of the top-tier terrestrials, the attention-getters.

But caterpillars and inchworms fall from streamside and lakeside tree branches too. Hornets out in abundance in hot early fall drop onto lake edges. And the alternative-terrestrial list goes on: cicadas, caterpillars, honeybees, moths . . .

Each of these lesser-known bugs is worth knowing. But if you don't know them, watch where they land—out in mid-lake, close to the stream bank, directly under a tree limb . . . Watch what they do on the water and make your fly do the same, using a fly that looks pretty much like them and more or less matches their size.

Terrestrial action is usually a mid- to late-summer thing, the hot months, though I've seen flying ants out in late spring and beetles active on cool fall days.

Terrestrial insects are mainly about trout, but I've found largemouths focused on big flying ants (termites, actually). Smallmouths and panfish will go for terrestrials too.

Tip 271 Experience the Hex Hatch, at Least Once (or Twice) Tr-S, Tr-L

The *Hexagenia* mayfly is a yellow giant. You mostly hear about it hatching in the Midwest, but Hexes hatch in the Far West too. Apparently various species hatch in the East and even down into the American South.

A Hex hatch can be inspiring. Stout mayflies whose bodies cover half a man's thumb, fluttering all around; trout, perhaps truly *big* trout, up swirling in a silvery gleam from the last sliver of the day's light; a profusion of the great yellow bugs scattered across black water . . .

That last sliver of light is part of the bargain: Hexes normally wait until near dark to appear (although they can start earlier on really cloudy, perhaps drizzly days). This means you're out on a river or a lake from almost full night to, in fact, full night—so

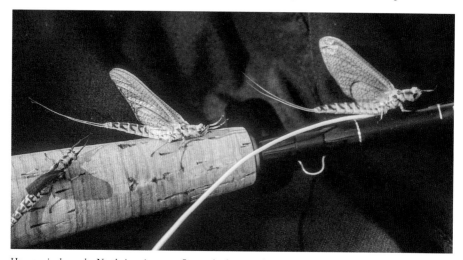

Hexagenia *duns—by North American mayfly standards, mastodons*

know where you're going to fish and go out and come back wisely and safely. (Hexes hatch from lakes and rivers both—from wherever, as burrowing nymphs, they can find that perfect silt they require.)

You'll need big flies that look like *Hexagenia*, typically nymphs, emergers, and dries in the West, but often imitations of the spinner, I've often read, outside the West. (I don't know why the difference.) And the flies need to approximate the size of the huge bugs; hooks should be at least size 8, 2X long, up to—*gasp*—size 2, 2X long (one of my books says *4X* long).

You arrive a bit early, launch your boat or inflatable craft or sit where you can stake out your wade-fishing water, and finally (at least when I chase Hex hatches) about the time you've given up hope—they come.

Tip 272 Know Your Shucks

 Tr-S, Tr-L   Lg-L   Sm-L, Sm-S   Pf-L

I suggest in tip 77 that you become a fly-fishing detective, and detective work is about clues, right? In a murder case, a clue might be shell casings; in fly fishing, perhaps the cast-off casings (the *shucks*) of hatched insects. But neither casings nor shucks are of much use if you can't identify them.

Clear shucks are lost among currents and swept away in streams. But lakes? Discarded shucks float plainly on that still, dark water.

Shuck ID is about trout, mainly, because trout are real hatch-addicts, though it *can* be about warmwater fishes.

Shucks on lakes will almost certainly be from chironomids, mayflies, or caddisflies. So, when you do find shucks floating on a lake:

Identify the insect. For example, a chironomid shuck is a segmented tube swollen at one end, with a white beard (the former gills). No tails or legs. A mayfly shuck looks like a mayfly nymph (tails, slender abdomen and fuller thorax, legs). A caddisfly shuck looks like a caddis pupa (long legs, stout cylindrical body).

Expect airborne—and hope for waterborne—adult stoneflies if you see their shucks on streamside stones and trees.

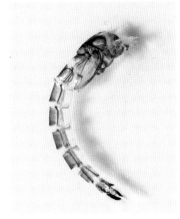

The shuck of the chironomid, the most important, to trout and fly fishers both, of all the insects that hatch in lakes

Note the size.

Select a fly that matches the insect and its stage (a chironomid pupa, for example) and size.

A shuck won't tell you the color of the shuck's former inhabitant, so go with something neutral—medium brown or gray—until you can find a live sample. No biggie, though—color is the least important factor in matching insects with flies.

Insects that hatch by crawling from the water—dragonflies, damselflies, a few mayflies and caddis, stoneflies on streams—leave shucks along the shoreline and on reeds and other water plants. These shucks can also be useful clues. Just apply the previous three steps to shucks you find up out of the water.

Tip 273 Don't Assume It's the Big Bug

 Tr-S, Tr-L

It happens all the bloody time: Middling to hefty mayflies, caddisflies, or stoneflies are showing but the trout are eating only bitsy hatching midges.

Honest.

In *Fly Fishing Strategy*, authors Doug Swisher and Carl Richards chalk up this odd behavior as another mystery of the universe. After describing a day when trout ignored mayflies matching size 18 hooks to go for mayflies matching 24s, they add, "For some reason, the fish often prefer the smaller fly." It's clear from the surrounding context that by "fly" they mean "insect."

Mike Lawson in his book *Spring Creeks* offers at least a partial explanation: "Trout have individual habits and behavior traits. One trout may prefer one kind of insect while other trout are feeding on different insects."

I tend to think that when there are various kinds of bugs on or in the surface of the water, trout choose the one that offers the strongest combination of high numbers and ease of capture. But sometimes trout seem to just blow off that notion altogether.

Ultimately, does it matter why trout will dodge around big, yummy caddisflies to pick off speck-sized mayflies? Not really. What does matter is what you do about it.

Here's what you should do about it. Don't *assume* the big bug is the one trout want.

CHAPTER 9
RIGS, RIGGING, AND TACKLE

Tip 274 Line Your Rod This Way

 Tr-S,Tr-L   Lg-L   Sm-L, Sm-S   Pf-L

As a kid, I always lined my rods by working the point of the tippet up through the guides, the line following. Seemed logical, but was always *frustrating*. That fine tippet, under the weight of the hanging line, kept escaping so that I'd have to start all over. *Too many years later* I watched a friend, who worked in a fly shop, double a line and push its pinched-narrow loop up through one rod guide after another.

I wanted to slap myself—such a simple solution!

So, to line a rod, double the line just below where it's attached to the leader, hold the line just back from its pinched-narrow looped end, push the loop up through each guide and finally out the tip guide, and then pull the rest of the loop out the tip along with more line and the leader and tippet.

So efficient. So practical. So embarrassing that I never figured this out on my own.

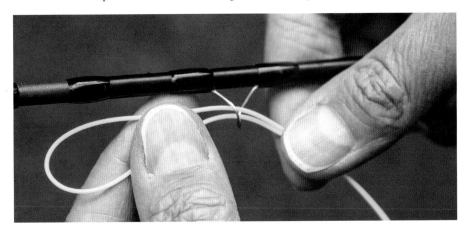

Tip 275 Here's Your Basic Dry-Fly Rig

 Tr-S,Tr-L   Sm-L, Sm-S

The following is a middling sort of all-purpose rig for average streams and lakes and average-size floating dry flies and floating emergers: 9-foot 3X tapered leader, 3 feet of 4X standard tippet (not fluorocarbon). This would be the first rig I'd consider for both trout and rising smallmouth bass.

For really crafty trout in clear lakes or slow, clear currents, the leader could be lengthened to 12 feet (or at the extreme, even beyond 12) and dropped to 4X or 5X, and the tippet lengthened to 4 feet and reduced to 5X (which most fly fishers would say is

Bonus Tip — Always Tie on a Fly

Tr-S, Tr-L   Lg-L   Sm-L, Sm-S   Pf-L

You're plowing through brush to get to the river, rowing your boat—*whatever* you're doing, if you've got one or more assembled rods with you, it or they should all have flies tied to their tippets. Rod ferrules open on their own sometimes, and with no fly to stop it, a rod section (or two or three) is free to just slide down line, leader, and tippet and off to the great unknown. Done that, *deeply* disliked it.

average for trout) or 6X. I've gone to 7X or 8X (once clear down to *10X*) with tiny flies, but only on rare occasions for the very fussiest of trout.

For eager, innocent trout and smallmouths, especially on streams that are small, choppy, or both, I go with a 7½-foot 2X leader and 2½ feet of 3X tippet. For big dry flies, I go with 3X tippet, if the fish will play along.

Tip 276 Here's How to Rig for Indicator Nymph Fishing Tr-S

A strike-indicator nymph-fishing rig for streams begins with a weighted nymph, often one with a heavy metal bead for a head to help the fly quickly sink. Above that is a long tippet; tippet is the slimmest filament in your leader system and therefore allows your nymph to sink quickly. I usually go with 3 to 4 feet of tippet for an average-size trout stream or river, 2½ feet for small streams and creeks.

Opinions about leaders for indicator nymphing vary widely. I, personally, like a 9-foot tapered leader for larger streams and rivers, a 7½-footer for small water.

Usually, I nymph with a 4X tippet on a 3X leader, sometimes 3X tippet and 2X leader, but I'll go up or down for lighter or heavier flows and by fly size.

Added weight up from the nymph is optional (usually split shot crimped onto the tippet with pliers or forceps). The standard recommendation is to fix the weight 8 to

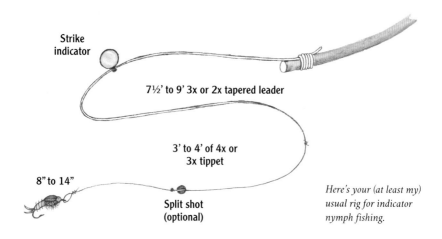

Strike indicator

7½' to 9' 3x or 2x tapered leader

3' to 4' of 4x or 3x tippet

8" to 14"

Split shot (optional)

Here's your (at least my) usual rig for indicator nymph fishing.

10 inches up from the fly. I go at least a foot. Something has to block the weight from sliding down to the fly; an overhand knot in the tippet does it, as does cutting the tippet and tying it back together with a surgeon's knot.

Next comes a strike indicator. I currently prefer the indicators with screw-on tops.

Now you're set . . . almost. You've got your floating line, leader, tippet, indicator, weight, and nymph all put together—but how far should you fix your indicator up from your nymph? Easy: one and a half times the depth; for example, $4\frac{1}{2}$ feet up for water 3 feet deep. In really quick water perhaps twice the depth, in slowish currents only slightly past the depth. See? Easy.

Tip 277 Here's Your Basic Trout-Streamer Rig Tr-S, Tr-L

The way you rig for fishing a streamer will vary—*should* vary—by (1) the size of the streamer (heavier leaders and tippets for the biggest streamers and lighter for smaller ones); (2) the size of the trout (heavier leaders and tippets if really big trout are possible and lighter if not); (3) the clarity of the water (heavier and shorter for tinted water and lighter and longer for really clear water); and (4) the speed of the currents if you're fishing a stream (heavier and shorter for quick, churning currents and longer and lighter for slow currents).

There's no single always-appropriate formula for leader and tippet length and weight for fishing trout streamers. But there's a standard formula I use most of the time, and you can use it most of the time too, then vary it to suit. (It's longer than what most like for streamer fishing, but I want to keep the fly well away from the line, and my rig *does* work . . .) Here it is: $7\frac{1}{2}$-foot 1X tapered leader with 2 feet of standard 2X tippet (fluorocarbon tippet optional).

Tip 278 Here's Your Basic Smallmouth Bass Rig Sm-L, Sm-S

A smallmouth bass will typically put up a strong, fast fight of stunning endurance. A largemouth bass fights hard too, but not for very long. This suggests that smallmouth fishing requires heavier leaders and tippets than does fishing for largemouth bass.

Sorry—not so.

Largemouths are dirty fighters, street fighters. They burrow into weed beds, wind tippet around fallen trees . . . and on top of that they love to hang out right in the thick of such clutter. Not so, smallmouths. They're super athletes, but fine sportsmen: They generally just run out into open water. That is, they (usually) fight fair. (If any fight between a 175-pound man and a 2-pound fish can be called fair.) So leaders and tippets tend to run lighter for smallmouth than for their largemouth cousins.

Here's my standard smallmouth rig, for poppers or streamers or crayfish flies, floating lines or sinking: $7\frac{1}{2}$-foot 1X pre-tapered leader with 2 feet of standard 2X tippet. Think of that first, but don't hesitate to lengthen and lighten your leader and tippet for low water, clear water, fussy fish, smaller dry flies, or all four. I've gone down to 5X tippet for smallies at times.

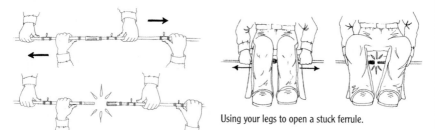

Using your legs to open a stuck ferrule.

Bonus Tip Here's How to Open Stuck Ferrules

Tr-S, Tr-L   Lg-L   Sm-L, Sm-S   Pf-L

If you try to force open a stuck ferrule the wrong way, you may break or damage your rod. When you do pull a ferrule open, never hold the rod over or even near a guide.

The two solutions in the illustrations below work great. I prefer the two-person approach myself.

If you have a friend handy, stand facing each other. Each of you hold the rod on both sides of the ferrule, and pull.

And you can go to leaders and tippets heavier than my standard rig for big small-mouths, especially in big rough water. Bob Clouser, in his book *Fly-Fishing for Smallmouth in Rivers and Streams*, recommends tippets up to 15-pound test—now that's just . . . *rope*.

Tip 279 Here's Your Basic Largemouth Bass Rig Lg-L

It's difficult to generalize about leaders and tippets for largemouth bass, because largemouths run such a broad range of size and hang out sometimes in open water, sometimes back in the heaviest shoreline tangles. Still, it's easier to generalize than to be specific—as the chap who's writing this tip, I at least have that advantage . . .

So, for medium-small to fairly big largemouths, in open water and in shallow water among lily pads or fallen timber, with floating lines or sinking, here's my standard leader-tippet setup: a 7½-foot 0X pre-tapered leader with 2 feet of 1X standard tippet.

As I say in the other tips about rigging, you could go lighter for smaller bass (as light as 3X tippet and a 2X leader), heavier for really big bass (as heavy as 0/2X tippet, with a leader one size heavier), and longer for really clear water. Just use my average rig when you have no reason to do otherwise; then, when you do have a reason, use whatever makes sense for the fish and conditions.

Tip 280 Here's Your Standard Rig for Panfish—and Don't Go Too Light

 Lg-L Pf-L

Follow the logic. Most panfish—bluegills, green sunfish, pumpkinseeds, and crappies, among others—live in ponds, lakes, and reservoirs along with largemouth bass. Most panfish feed frequently around shoreline cover and in and around fallen timber and beds of aquatic weeds, as do largemouth bass. Fly fishers go after panfish around cover and weeds by throwing small poppers and other flies seemingly too small to interest hefty largemouths—yet hefty largemouths sometimes grab such flies. Conclusion: When you're fishing for 6-inch bluegills, you may hook a 3-pound largemouth bass.

So, if you fish a 2-weight rod that lets you really feel those spunky little bluegills pull and dart, you'll have a merry time—until the panicked moment you feel something big and angry try to jerk that flimsy rod out of your hand, or try to snap it in half. And *that's* why I recommend you go after panfish with *at least* a 6-weight rod and *at least* 3X tippet. A logical conclusion.

A 6-weight rod and 3X tippet is still a light setup for most largemouth fishing, but I've landed 5-pounders on them. Yet such a rod and tippet will comfortably throw panfish-size poppers and nymphs and streamers; and a 6-weight rod won't feel even a smidge too light when a 9-inch bluegill is boring down against it. A sound compromise. But if you think your odds of a hefty bass taking your little fly is reasonably high, fish a 7-weight rod and line and a 2X or even 1X tippet. One truly big crappie or green sunfish on the line, and your tackle will seem perfectly sporting.

All that said, what exactly, then, is my recommendation for an all-around panfish leader and tippet? It is: 7½-foot, 2X tapered leader and two feet of 3X standard tippet.

Tip 281 Rig Right for Trolling

 Tr-L  Lg-L Sm-L Pf-L

Lake trolling starts with a *full-sinking* fly line with a quick sink rate, a type III line, even a type V. Next: Leaders.

Many anglers troll with short leaders and tippets, the idea being that the fly follows the line down closely and gets down to the fish quickly. True . . . But a longish leader (and some tippet) puts real distance between a fish and that highly apparent line, which makes sense to me.

Lots of potential snags down there along a lake bed, and you'll hook more big fish when fishing a dozen feet down than when fishing shallow. Also, the deeper you go down in water, the less light gets through to illuminate your leader and tippet and reveal them to fish. That's why when I troll, I go heavy on leader and tippet both.

So, I normally troll for trout and panfish with a 7½-foot (9-foot in very clear water) 2X tapered leader and 2 to 2½ feet of 3X tippet. For both basses, same leader and tippet length but considerably heavier—usually a 0X leader and 1X tippet.

Most of my trolling flies are unweighted, and sort of hover down there. My flies that imitate real swimmers, such as leeches or small fishes, are weighted in front to make them raise and dip their heads. Some of the flies I troll are actually buoyant, but that's a matter for another tip (tip 113).

I always tie trolling flies on with a loop knot.

Tip 282 Try a Trailer Nymph Rig

Tr-S

The standard nymph rig for trout streams these past few decades is one nymph below a strike indicator, perhaps with some weight on the tippet (although Czech nymphing grows ever more popular). To fish two nymphs, there's always the snarl-loving but very effective (when not snarled) dropper rig (see tip 283), which guides don't like. Guides don't like spending half the day untangling or retying dropper rigs for their clients, so guides (I assume, seems like something they'd cook up) created the trailer nymph rig. It'll still ball up just fine, but not nearly so easily as a dropper rig will.

Typically this rig starts with a large, heavy nymph—the one that does the serious sinking—and then a smaller nymph goes onto some tippet tied to the bend of big nymph's hook. In his book *Fly Fishing Tailwaters*, Pat Dorsey recommends 14 to 16 inches for the trailer tippet, which is about what I use. I generally use 3X tippet for the big nymph, 4X or 5X for the trailer nymph, so that if the trailer gets snagged I can get at least one fly back. I tie on the big top fly with a Skip's clinch and give the little trailer nymph a chance to swing around on a loop knot.

I've seen guides put the heavier fly on the end. I've also seen them rig three nymphs this way, bend-to-hook-eye tippet sections all the way down. I've seen these variations work too.

Your basic trailer nymph rig. Simple enough, yes? There are other versions.

Tip 283 Take a Second Look at the Old Dropper Rig  Tr-S

If you've ever fished a true dropper-nymph rig in a trout stream—and I do *not* mean a far more manageable trailer nymph rig—you've suffered. That dropper nymph, dangling on a few inches of tippet above the big point nymph, loves to swing around and tangle with the strike indicator, the tippet—whatever it can grab. Its bird's nests are legendary.

To keep a dropper rig from tangling, you must concentrate—a moment's distraction is peril—making broad line loops and long casting strokes of the smoothest possible acceleration, making pickups from the water of the whole wobbly mess as smoothly as the strokes. Good God—is all this worth it?

Fair question. But consider what a *single* weighted nymph does down near the bed of a stream: It gets dragged on through. The unobstructed surface water, where the strike indicator rides, flows quite faster than the current down winding through boulders and stones, down where the nymph goes. So the nymph is *rushed* downstream.

Sure, most real nymphs and pupae swim, some quite well (though larvae only wriggle), but *zipping* downstream? Suspicious behavior.

With the dropper rig, sure, the heavy point nymph gets hurried along. But its sheer weight helps slow it so that the lightweight (if not altogether unweighted) dropper nymph leads it, facing upstream, seeming to struggle, to swim, against the current.

I've watched a dropper do exactly this in light current and clear water—it looks perfect. The effect may not be the same or as good in swift currents—can't say, too hard to see through the chaos—but a dropper rig has caught me scads of trout in currents of all speeds.

A dropper rig. The strike indicator goes on somewhere above it. (How far above it? See tip 276.) SKIP MORRIS

I like a dropper tippet of only about five inches, one tag-end of a surgeon's knot meeting the main tippet at least a foot up from the point fly.

Jason Randall (describing only a mild variation of the standard dropper-nymph rig) sums up the advantages of the dropper nymph in his book *Nymph Masters*. He says that "the lighter dropper fly . . . floats several inches above the bottom" and, being similar in weight to a real nymph, is "free to interact with the current in a natural manner." I'm with you, Jason.

Tip 284 Drop Shot Makes Sense

 Tr-S

Which would be the *least* likely to snag the bottom of a trout stream, (1) a heavy nymph with a sharp hook point or (2) a hookless split shot? Here's a hint: a hook is just looking for something to catch or bury itself in down there while a round split shot wants to skim and dance over stones and sunken logs and branches. Your answer?

No sane fly fisher wants to snag up while nymph fishing a stream. Enter: the drop shot rig.

There are lots of opinions about this setup—how long the dropper tippet should be, how far up it should be from the shot, if there should be a nymph tied directly to the center of the tippet that runs from the dropper to the shot. Nearly everyone, however, seems to agree on the following: (1) at the point, or tip, of the rig should be one or more split shot crimped on just above a stopper knot to keep the shot from slipping off (mostly I see a plain overhand knot recommended), and (2) this rig hangs up on the bed of a stream far less often than does a rig with a nymph on the point.

Consider, too, that the shot is *below* the dropper nymph (or nymphs)—you feel the nymph first, when a trout takes it, rather than having to feel the nymph up through the heavy split shot, a real sensitivity killer.

I drop-shot fish with a standard dropper rig (see the previous tip, 283) but I replace the point fly with one (or more) spit shot.

Really, "drop-shot fishing" isn't a style of nymph fishing at all, but a rig—a rig you can use for fishing with a strike indicator or for Czech nymphing.

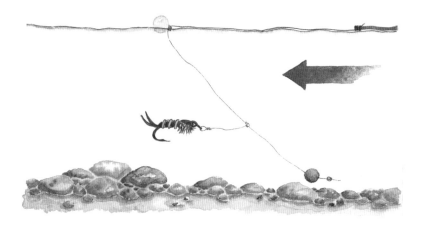

Tip 285 Know Enough Knots

 Tr-S,Tr-L   Lg-L   Sm-L, Sm-S   Pf-L

There's no avoiding it—if you're actually going to go out and try to catch a fish on a fly, you need the backing attached to your reel, the line to the backing, the leader to the line, the tippet to the leader, and the fly to the tippet. You accomplish all this with . . . *knots*. So, here are some standard, proven knots fly fishers use for all this mandatory attaching. (The loop knot is an option, a specialty knot—a valuable knot in my view. Its advantages and uses and tying are covered in tip 286.)

Backing-to-reel knot

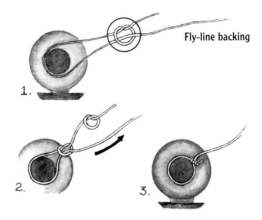

Fly-line backing

1.

2.

3.

Nail knot

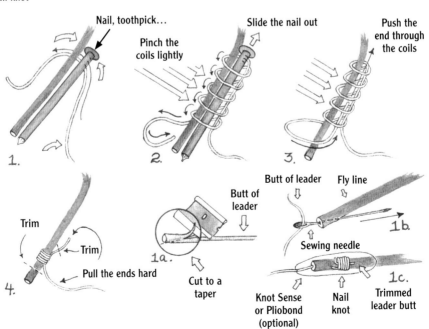

Nail, toothpick...

Pinch the coils lightly

Slide the nail out

Push the end through the coils

1.

2.

3.

Trim

Trim

Pull the ends hard

4.

Butt of leader

Cut to a taper

1a.

Butt of leader   Fly line

Sewing needle

1b.

Knot Sense or Pliobond (optional)

Nail knot

Trimmed leader butt

1c.

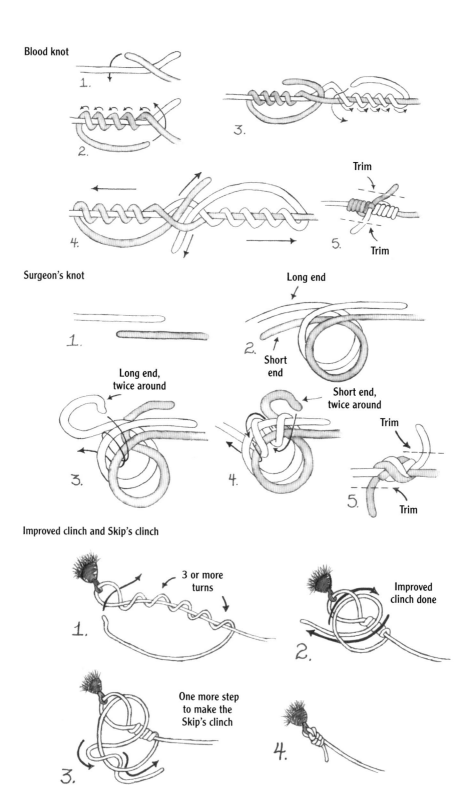

Blood knot

1.

2.

3.

Trim

4.

5.

Trim

Trim

Surgeon's knot

Long end

1.

2.

Short
end

Long end,
twice around

Short end,
twice around

Trim

3.

4.

5.

Trim

Improved clinch and Skip's clinch

3 or more
turns

1.

Improved
clinch done

2.

One more step
to make the
Skip's clinch

3.

4.

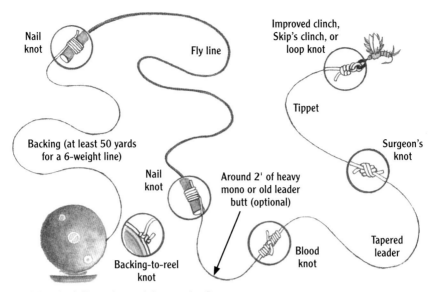

The whole knot kerfuffle neatly tamed, from spool to fly

Tip 286 Embrace the Loop Knot

Tr-S, Tr-L   Lg-L   Sm-L, Sm-S   Pf-L

Water is dense enough to bend tippet and twist a nymph around down in river currents. But imagine if that nymph were *not* connected to a tippet—free of its monofilament shackles, tumbling, turning, doing somersaults. So *alive*. But how do you catch fish on a fly that's not attached to your tippet? You don't, of course. But you can come close to capturing that tippet-free vitality just by tying the fly on with a loop knot.

A loop knot forms a circle of tippet below it for the fly to swing around on. The alternative is the sort of knot all us fly fishers used to always use, one that locks tippet to the fly as though welded to it.

Nymphs, streamers, even big dry flies spring to life when they can swing free on a loop knot.

Morris loop

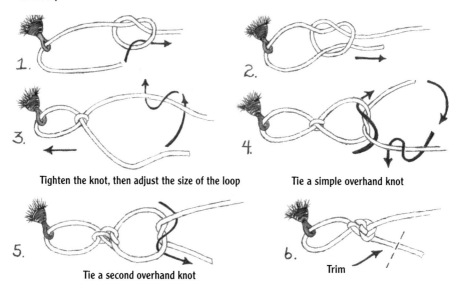

1.

2.

3. Tighten the knot, then adjust the size of the loop

4. Tie a simple overhand knot

5. Tie a second overhand knot

6. Trim

There are several standard loop knots, but mine suits me best. Might suit you the same.

Actually, a rigid old-style knot is still fine for most dry flies and half-floating emerger flies, still the standard. But nymphs? An artificial nymph in the currents of a river or the quiet depths of a lake should mimic the movements of life. Streamer flies, meant to swim like little fish, also swim better on loop knots. And big dry flies, size 8 (or 10, with a long-shank hook) and up, fished on streams, seem to pick up some real-bug attitude when tied on with loop knots.

There are several widely trusted loop knots out there—the mono loop knot, the Rapala loop knot, the Duncan loop knot . . . I now fish only my own (the Morris loop knot), as I find it the easiest to tie and easiest to adjust of them all. I discovered after fishing it for a few years that it's similar to some versions (there are several) of the Homer Rhode knot, but different in ways I prefer (though the Rhode knot is excellent). Pick a loop knot, use it.

Tip 287 When Tying Knots, *Almost* Anything Goes

 Tr-S, Tr-L   Lg-L   Sm-L, Sm-S   Pf-L

When you're tying a nail knot in the butt of a leader on the tip of your fly line or a surgeon's knot to add some tippet, you can hold the monofilament (or fly line) in the normal way, between thumb and first fingertip, but, really, in any way that works—between two clamped fingers, wound around one finger pressed against another, between fingertip and palm . . . Fly fishers go through all sorts of goofy hand contortions to make their knots easier, quicker, and more efficient to tie.

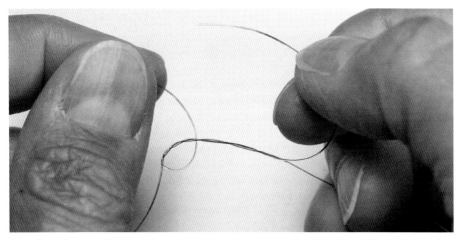

Here, I'm working on a blood knot. I've got monofilament between thumb and first finger of both left and right hands, between second and third fingers of both hands. That's how knot tying goes—you just do what you need to do.

The one way to hold an end of a knot I recommend *against* is in your teeth or mouth. Who knows what sort of chemicals are on fly line or mono fresh from the factory? And wet tippet or leader? Even a remaining drop of stream or lake water could give you the nauseating, gut-cramping misery of giardia or perhaps some other parasite, bacteria, or virus.

So, other than including your mouth or teeth, do whatever works when it comes to tying knots.

Tip 288 Tighten, Compress, and Retighten Knots (and Don't Trim Them Too Close) Tr-S,Tr-L Lg-L Sm-L, Sm-S Pf-L

You do everything just right. You make a graceful cast that drops your size 16 Parachute Adams (which is currently just the right fly in the right size) on the right current line just the right distance above that rising trout with just the right amount of slack. The trout takes in your fly just as it should. You set the hook after just the right pause. You play the trout perfectly with just the right pressure.

It's all just . . . so just right. Until . . .

Your stupid knot lets go!

 **Bonus Tip** Try a Trailer for Bass Lg-L Pf-L

Especially in the confines of hard-fished ponds, largemouth bass and panfish can get . . . difficult. They've had enough of us and our stabbing flies. But if you tie on a popper or hair bug, tie a foot and a half or two feet of tippet onto that fly's hook bend, and then tie onto that tippet a smaller sinking fly, a nymph or small streamer, you may see your popper (worked slowly, with pauses) jerked back and down by a smarty-pants bluegill or largemouth bass a foot below.

That's just wrong.

Knots take a little time to properly tighten, but the little time they take pays off in fish landed and flies saved. A knot that continues tightening on its own can open up, usually because a fish is pulling on it.

Once a knot, any knot, is tied: (1) pull firmly on all its ends, (2) compress the knot by holding the tippet as you push the knot at the fly with your thumbnail and finger, (3) pull on all its ends again, and (4) maybe repeat steps 2 and 3. *Now* you can trim off the tag end and then fish the fly.

I never trim the tag end right up to the knot, as some do, because if that knot slips even a little . . .

Many fly fishers wet a knot just before tightening it in hopes the tightening won't abrade and weaken the tippet. Okay, makes sense.

Tip 289 The Hat Trick

 Tr-S, Tr-L   Lg-L    Sm-L, Sm-S   Pf-L

How many times have I dropped a fly I'd just clipped off or one I was about to tie on, or a split shot I was crimping onto my tippet? Answer: so many times that if they were somehow tallied before my eyes, my face would glow red with embarrassment.

I still drop stuff, but now when I do, I seldom lose it.

No one likes to interrupt the pleasant rhythm of fishing by wading ashore or clearing a space on a boat seat before fiddling with the little things we can so easily drop; but losing them doesn't just interrupt a fishing rhythm—it *kills* it. It inspires great cursing and guttural sounds of dismay and vexation. It sucks.

So pause, and find a clear, flat surface for screwing the tiny nut onto a strike indicator or tying on a size 22 Griffith's Gnat. Hold everything low, so that if (or should I just say *when?*) you drop something, it won't bounce away. A flat rock is good. So is a boat seat or a clear patch of ground.

Best of all is your hat. Turn a hat upside down and it becomes a container—very difficult for a fly or split shot to bounce out of that. You can set your hat on the ground, on a tree stump, on anything, then go about your business with the pulse of your fishing rhythm still echoing pleasantly in the background.

Tip 290 Here's How to Shop for a Line, Rod, and Reel and Why They Should Probably Be a 6-Weight Combo

 Tr-S, Tr-L   Lg-L    Sm-L, Sm-S   Pf-L

It's logical to select your fly rod, then find a line that matches it. Logical, yes, but wrong—line weight is *everything*. Well, almost everything. Whether the line sinks or floats, the rate at which it sinks if it sinks, taper . . . these and other factors are often crucial.

Still, line weight comes first. So you choose your line, and *then* buy a rod to suit it and a reel to hold it. Buy a heavy-duty 8-weight rod and the 8-weight line it calls for and

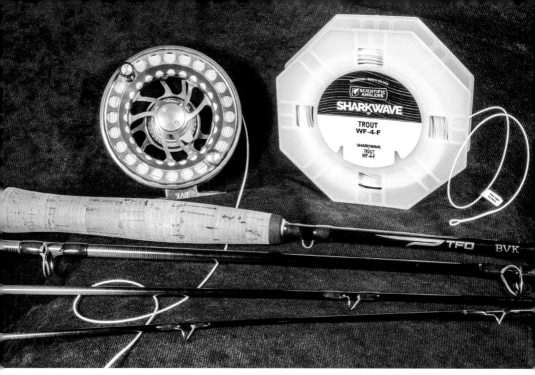

Six-weight rod, line, and reel, perfect for a beginner's outfit and for all sorts of fishing

then go for 8-inch creek trout? That's like a Sherman tank in a bumper-car rink: way . . . too . . . much. If you just pick out a rod you like without first deciding on line weight, you tend to go too light or too heavy.

So, what line weight? If I had to choose one line and rod for all my fishing for trout, bass, and even panfish, floating or sinking line regardless? No question: 6-weight.

With a 6-weight rod and line I can set a size 22 emerger on the slick tail of a pool with barely a disturbance. But with that very same rod and line I can battle a 20-pound Alaska silver salmon to the net. With 6-weights I've done both.

Sure, both of these scenarios asks a 6-weight rig to push itself, but not terribly far— and good casting is nearly always more important than having the right rod or line. No rod and no line will compensate for a clumsy hand.

My advice: Make your first line and rod 6-weights. And pick out your line before shopping for a rod.

Tip 291 You May Need a Clear Fly Line, or Just Want One

 Tr-L Lg-L Sm-L  Pf-L

Some lakes are just so *pure* . . . Imagine what happens when you've got a typical opaque-as-a-snake sinking line down in that invisible water. Yes, your line is a dark green or dark brown to blend with the lake bottom's silt or vegetation, shadows, and waterlogged timber. But what are the odds a trout gets suspicious when it comes close to your

Clear lines, sometimes called "lake lines" or "slime lines," are tough for fish to see. Not fair, right, fish?

plain-to-the-eye line down there? To miss noticing your line, the trout will have to come from behind the moving fly, or at least from the side at just the right moment.

Ever see the movie *Predator*, with the extraterrestrial warrior that turns almost transparent, making just a slight distortion of its background that's noticeable to only the most patient, watchful eye? That's how I imagine a clear fly line looks down there: nearly invisible. That stealth line can slide along near a trout and go unnoticed so that your fly, when it slips up, *will* be noticed. That is, the trout won't get spooked by the line, so it'll still be there when your fly appears.

I really believe I catch more trout—more largemouth, smallmouth, and panfish too— with a clear rather than opaque line when I fish a clear lake. Usually, I fish such a line using the countdown method from an anchored craft, but casting to the shallows and edges of a lake with a clear line works too. And if I troll slowly enough—*really* slowly—a clear line will get and stay a dozen feet down. Clear lines are fairly slow sinkers, but they get down there.

Tip 292 Keep Your Leaders and Tippets Straight Tr-S,Tr-L Lg-L Sm-L, Sm-S Pf-L

It's a smaller problem with today's large-arbor reels than it was with the old narrow-arbor ones (the arbor is the center of the spool, around which the backing and line are wound), but it's still a problem. A tapered leader, after sitting quietly wound onto a reel for an entire winter, a few weeks, even overnight, wants to coil.

A leader like a loose spring won't tell you when a trout's taken your nymph below a strike indicator or off a sinking line. With a dry fly, a coiled leader will make an unnatural pattern on the water, making trout and smallmouths suspicious. And when you want

Bonus-Tip Work, Not *Yank*, Your Tippet, Leader, and Line off Your Reel

Tr-S, Tr-L   Lg-L   Sm-L, Sm-S   Pf-L

Impatience, when getting your line out of your reel, is peril. You find the point of the tippet, yank it—and the tippet buries itself defensively down among turns of fly line. Now it's locked in there in a way that seems to defy reason. Patience is the key. Instead of yanking, you temporarily back off the reel's drag until it's fairly light. Then you rotate the spool by its handle as you *gently* draw off tippet, then leader, then line. Once the line is out of the reel, you can go ahead and start threading it up the guides, whistling cheerfully.

to set the hook on any fly, coils of leader will delay the effect and perhaps take up so much of your rod swing that you won't properly set the hook.

See? A problem.

Same goes for tippets: A coiled tippet can make its own trouble.

So before you fish, squeeze your leader in a straightening gadget (sometimes just two flaps of leather) and pull it through a few times. Or just slide the leader tightly across the pant leg of your bent knee. Do the same with your tippet if it needs it.

And never reel your line and leader and tippet tightly onto your reel at the end of the day. Instead, make a long cast and then reel everything up . . . lightly.

Tip 293 Keep Your Line Straight

Tr-S, Tr-L   Lg-L   Sm-L, Sm-S   Pf-L

Like leaders and tippets, fly lines have memory; that is, after lying curled around a reel spool for months to days, even a few hours, they come off in a series of curls. And even when they seem to straighten under the resistance of retrieving a big fly, like a streamer, that memory's still at work; it makes the line tangle as it hangs below your hands or lies on the water or the floor of your boat. Curly fly lines *love* to tangle.

The simple solution is to go down the line every yard or so (that's roughly a meter, if you're the metric sort), and give the line a firm stretch. That usually does it.

Some lines are particularly stubborn—one, I had to loop around a tree every year and put nearly my full body weight against it to make it even half-behave. All the clear lines I've fished like to coil in cool or cold air temperatures. I try to avoid clear lines when it's chilly out, fishing standard sinking lines but compensating for their visibility with long leaders. Floating lines seem to coil least, but coil they will.

A curly full-sinking or sink-tip line also does a lousy job of telling you that a fish has taken your fly deep in a stream or lake, a situation requiring that you feel the take. So make sure your fly lines are straight before you fish. Really, just do that.

Tip 294 Consider Getting a Fish-Finder

 Tr-L   Lg-L   Sm-L   Pf-L

A fish-finder, an electronic sonar device with a display that tells you all sorts of things—such as where the fish are, how deep the water is, if the bottom is level silt or boulders or beds of waterweeds—is really a tool for fishing lakes. I've seen a fish-finder used in a huge smallmouth river, but to nearly all fly fishers, it's for lakes.

But in a lake, it's marvel. I got mine 20 years ago—and according to my lake-guru buddy (and coauthor on another book) Brian Chan, the newer fish-finders are considerably more miraculous than mine. Still . . . when I first took my finder out on a small trout-and-largemouth lake I'd already fished for over two decades, I was amazed. Everything that had so long been a mystery to me was right there on the screen, plain to my eyes.

There were surprises and resolutions. The lake was twice as deep as I'd guessed, a surprise. The end where I always caught trout but was never sure why was a big shoal, a resolution. Once I had my finder going, surprises and resolutions came in a flurry.

It's hard to locate shoals and drop-offs and deep weed beds in any but the clearest lakes without a fish-finder. Go out to dinner a little less often, ask for a few bucks for your birthday, save up, do some research to find a good model, and then buy yourself a fish-finder. Trust me: You deserve one.

Above: A fish-finder screen in action. See the fish symbols?

Right: A simple fish-finder—small, light, easy to transport—that clamps onto the transom or side of a boat or inflatable craft. There are other designs offering various advantages and options.

Tip 295 Match Your Tackle Not Only to Your Fish

You're about to fish a lake of perfectly acceptable cutthroat trout, 10- and 11- and, rarely, 13-inchers. You thought it would be fun, for a change, to catch them on that 7-foot rod and its 3-weight line, a rod so supple it loads comfortably on a 10-foot cast.

It's going as planned: This is a lake where the trout love to come up as the sun drops, and it's dropping, and they're up. Ringed wavelets appear on the slick water 100 feet away. You take up the oars and slip quietly toward what is now a line of rises. Get too close and you'll spook the fish, nervous up exposed under flat water, but you must get the fly out there ahead of the next rise. You pick up the rod and try to fire the fly out with only one backcast—*oops!* This rod doesn't want to do that.

So you make a bunch of false-casts, finally work the fly out there. The fish, of course, is gone. That's pretty much the way the rest of the evening goes.

What you've done is essentially what Sean Connery's character, Jim Malone, accuses the gangster who's come to kill him of doing in the movie *The Untouchables*: you've brought "a knife to a gunfight."

You always need to consider what you'll need your tackle to do before choosing it, regardless of fish size. A 3-weight makes sense for a stream of smallish rainbow trout— but what if you end up fishing weighted nymphs with a strike indicator and split shot? To a 3-weight outfit, that's just cruel. And inefficient possibly to the point of ineffective. That same 3-weight setup may seem right for a wide desert river full of fun little small-mouth bass, but what if they insist on a heavily weighted crayfish fly?

Get it?

Tip 296 Here's the Skinny on Waders

Tr-S,Tr-L   Lg-L   Sm-L, Sm-S   Pf-L

The basic tools of fly fishing remain pretty simple: a rod, reel, line, flies, etc. But the *options*? They've exploded. Take waders.

When I was a kid, there were boot-foot waders and hip boots—the end. Now, you get to choose among breathable stocking-foot waders, breathable boot-foot waders, neoprene waders, neoprene hip boots, breathable hip boots, breathable *half*-waders . . .

My view: Breathable waders are standard these days, and rightly so—air circulates through the fabric to release perspiration yet water can't get in. Stocking-foot waders are also appropriately standard—wading boots go over the wader's soft feet for a clean fit.

Boot-foot waders, waders with built-in rubber boots, are a bit clumsy and really catch currents with their wide ankles. However, if currents aren't generally quick and you won't be moving a lot (for example, on a rich trout stream where rises are clustered and you mostly stay put and fish), boot-foots get attractive—putting them on and taking them off is a snap.

Neoprene waders, once all the rage, keep you warmer than breathables do (though you can bundle up under the breathables), but hold all your sweat in and get hot.

Hip boots are fine *if* you know just how deep you'll wade and it's not very deep—fish new water and you'll go in over one or both hip boots before you're done.

In water that's not too cold and air that's warm to hot, wearing just wading boots and heavy pants, "wet wading," can be . . . heavenly.

Tip 297 Here's the Whole Hopper-Dropper/Dry-and-Dropper Deal, at Least as I See It 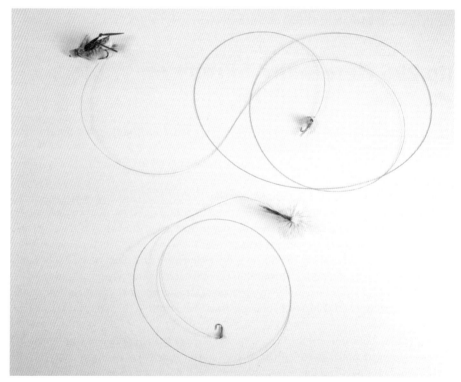 Tr-S,Tr-L

To some, "hopper-dropper" and "dry-and-dropper" both refer to any rig with a nymph hanging below a dry fly, two completely interchangeable terms. But I see these as two separate terms, each referring to a basic rig—and fishing approach—related to but different from the other. To me, a hopper-dropper rig is a big, stout, buoyant dry fly, perhaps one that imitates a full-grown grasshopper, but perhaps not, with a heavy but smallish nymph as a trailer.

Hopper-dropper fishing is pretty much standard indicator nymph fishing in my view, with the indicator switched out for the big dry fly. The generously weighted nymph is fishing deep.

Dry-and-dropper fishing (again, to me) means a modest-size to even small dry fly with a considerably smaller unweighted (or only slightly weighted) nymph for a trailer, and not much tippet (only a foot or two) between nymph and dry. The little nymph is fishing not far down; the dry fly serves as a little indicator (when it's not the fly chosen by a trout).

At the top of the photo is a hopper-dropper rig; below it, a dry-and-dropper rig. SKIP MORRIS

Either way, the dropper tippet should be at least one size lighter than the main tippet to the dry fly, so a lost nymph doesn't also mean a lost dry, and should be tied to the *bend* of the dry fly's hook.

I fish hopper-dropper rigs in streams as I'd normally fish with a strike indicator, covering water, trying to keep the nymph near the bottom, sometimes getting as many takes of the dry as of the nymph. I fish dry-and-dropper rigs in streams to trout showing at the surface but mostly ignoring dry flies, usually during a hatch. Sometimes I'll fish dry-and-dropper rigs, usually with twitches of the dry, to trout showing at the surface of lakes.

Tip 298 Fishing Lakes Usually Requires a Watercraft
Tr-L   Lg-L   Sm-L   Pf-L

Some lakes (and ponds and reservoirs—standing water) have open, solid shorelines that allow you to fish on foot . . . provided the fish are close enough in for that. Some lakes have docks from which you can cast for trout or dabble a fly in the dock's shadow for panfish and maybe a bass if you're lucky. But fishing most lakes—and ponds and reservoirs and any and every other kind of still body of water—requires some kind of watercraft.

If it's a lake where there are no alligators or cottonmouths to bite (or bite off) your ankles, you can consider an inflatable U-Boat or kick-boat or some other craft propelled by swim fins at least part of the time. If, however, there are nasty, biting things in the water, go with a boat.

I fish regularly from a boat for trout, largemouths, smallmouths, and panfish all the time, often way out from shore over shoals or along the outer rims of weed lines. And when I do, I'm typically, at some level, aware that my boat is getting me into far more fish than I'd catch without it. On many lakes, I'm aware that without my boat I couldn't fish at all.

A boat can be a significant investment. But if you expect to fish lakes much, it's a wise one. (One-man rowing pontoon boats are more popular than ever, and a fine choice, but I still prefer a boat.)

Tip 299 Here's How to Fish One Dry Fly All Day
Tr-S,Tr-L   Sm-S   Pf-L

Fishing one dry fly all day: I did exactly that recently. On a lovely creek in the Rockies holding more and bigger wild cutthroat trout than it had any right to. A passable pool was giving up 15 or 20 strikes for a dozen 10- to 14-inchers landed. All on one dry fly.

The hatch was of mayflies (let's skip the scientific Latin and just say it was a large mayfly, okay?). The fly was my own Morris Emerger, a respectable floater, especially for a fly that settles its back end into the water. Those big-jawed cutts really chewed the air and floatant out of the fly, letting in icy creek water. After three fishing hours of wading around boulders and climbing over trunks of fallen trees, I had landed about 50 trout. Trout were plenteous; any seasoned fly fisher could have done it.

But all on one dry fly, 50 trout—how? Here's how.

A lightweight one-person boat can serve the fly fisher honorably, and just one person can load it on or in and off or out of a car or truck without strain.

These days the inflatables—U-Boats, float tubes, pontoon boats, whatevers—can be decked out with rod holders, anchors, fish-finders, and more.

I started by working a paste fly floatant (more a gel, really) into the fly. Then, once it began sinking, I made a few quick false-casts to snap out most of the water, squeezed the fly in the cotton fabric of my shirt (I've seen fly fishers carry cotton handkerchiefs for this), and then shook it in a container of desiccant floatant. (I find that desiccant likes to stick to even a little leftover paste floatant.) From then on, whenever the fly started sinking: false-cast, squeeze, desiccant.

That's it. *Fifty* trout. Could have been 50 smallies up feeding on a hatch, or 50 bluegills. This system for keeping a dry fly up really works.

And here's a tip-within-a-tip: Rinse your hands off right away after using desiccant. It'll dry your hands sore.

The floatants I use: paste on the left, desiccant on the right

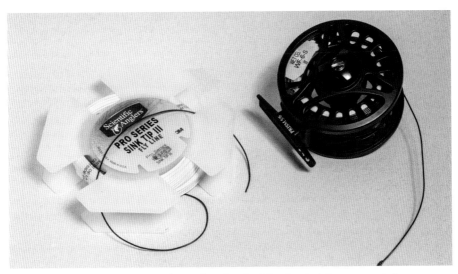

A sink-tip line on the left, a full-sinking line on the reel on the right—I use both line types regularly.

Tip 300 Understand Sinking Lines, Get One (at Least One), and Then Learn How to Cast It Tr-S, Tr-L Lg-L Sm-L, Sm-S Pf-L

In trout-lake fishing, sinking lines are often required—use one, or just reel in and go home. Sure, there's a lot of fine lake fishing on top, sometimes for rising trout. And there are ways to fish fairly deep in a trout lake with a floating line. But it's the sinking line that on trout lakes so often saves the day. Same for largemouth and smallmouth bass lakes. Panfish lakes too.

On streams I'd hate to miss out on all that streamer fishing sink-*tip* lines provide for trout. And for smallmouths.

Full-sinking lines are mainly for lakes. I usually fish a type III line (a fairly fast sinker) for trout and bass and panfish, though I fish a clear sinking line (a slowish sinker) nearly as often. When you troll or cast and retrieve full-sinking lines, they want to stay down, since they lack a floating section to continually drag them back up.

A sink-tip line does have a floating section—a floating section that, in fact, takes up most of the line. A sink-tip line is typically for rivers. The front part of the line goes down to the fish while the line behind, the part near you, rises to avoid tangles with shallow boulders and such. (Which line? I've found a type III with a sinking tip section of around 20 feet a versatile choice.)

When casting either kind of sinking line, full-sinking or sink-tip, you'll need to pick up the tempo of your strokes, because these lines are thin and drop sooner, after a back or forward cast, than do thick floating lines. You also need to work sinking lines nearly in before you can pick them up for the next cast—but that's fine, because fish often grab a sunken fly at the very end of a retrieve.

Tip 301 Stop Occasionally and Do a Tackle Check Tr-S, Tr-L Lg-L Sm-L, Sm-S Pf-L

In a day's fishing, reels and rods and flies can get messed up. When they do, you need to know about it and set them right, otherwise you may run into all sorts of unnecessary grief.

Ferrules loosen. This allows their rod sections often twist until your line has to spiral around the rod to follow them. The result: Your line shoots poorly and resists when you try to manage it. Worse, if that section comes off at a critical point in your casting stroke, the male or female ferrule may split or break. So check your ferrules now and then. If one's loose, align the rod sections, then push the ferrule ends firmly back together with your hands close behind them.

As you fish, your reel's drag adjustment lever or knob (or whatever) will get bumped (notice I didn't say "may" get bumped), and if that changes its setting, you could have a problem. If a big fish runs, it may (1) break off against a too-tight drag or (2) overrun the reel against a too-loose drag and break off when the line tangles on the spool. So check your drag now and then as you fish. (And get a reel whose drag stays put.)

It can take far less than this streamer of waterweed, caught on a fly, to put off trout of even modest caution.

Your fly? Check that too—all kinds of mischief can go on there: tangles with leader or tippet, a twig or scrap of waterweed caught on the hook, the hook's point bent or broken. (And is the hook's point sharp? See tip 302.)

Tip 302 Keep That Fly Sharp

Check your fly now and then, or a fly you're about to tie on, for sharpness. To see if my fly's hook point is sharp, I slide the point across my thumbnail. I hold the fly so its point is roughly at a right angle to the flat of the nail and apply light pressure to the hook. If the hook catches on the nail or scratches a white line across it, it's sharp.

If the hook doesn't catch or scratch (or scratches my nail only grudgingly), it needs to be sharpened. Then I work a sharpening tool (a *hook hone*) across the sides and inside of the hook's point, stroking from behind

Scriiitch—okay, it's sharp.

the point. (Some anglers do all their sharpening *toward* the point.) When I figure the hook is sharp, I make a very few *light* swipes *toward* the point, to remove any burrs.

A fly's hook can lose its entire point when it whacks something on a backcast or the hook can bend out on a big fish or a snag, and then it's shot. When you fish a fly with a dull or damaged hook, you're wasting fishing time.

A fly can just unravel—something else you'll notice when you check your fly closely.

Tip 303 Match Tippet to Fly Size

Tiny flies and fine tippet, medium-size flies with medium-thick tippet, big flies with truly thick tippet—these are the best combinations, in my experience, at least 90 percent of the time. But there are exceptions.

Let's say mayflies matching a size 14 hook are hatching. Then 5X tippet will be just right for your size 14 imitation. But what if the water's clear, the current's lazy, and the trout are well-fed angler-wise browns? Then you may need to tie that size 14 onto 6X, even 7X. You may break off two trout for every one you land on that skimpy filament, but that's just . . . life, or at least the fly-fishing part of it.

But what if the current's choppy enough to hide your tippet? Then you may be able to get away with 4X for your size 14.

The chart to the right of my standard recommendations is mainly for trout in streams and lakes, but it generally applies to the smallmouths and panfish too. The thing about largemouth bass, though: You nearly always need heavy leaders and tippets (if you use tippet at all), because largemouths fight dirty. For them, 3X counts as extremely light and 0X as about typical.

FLY SIZE	TIPPET
26 to 22	7X
20, 18	6X
16, 14	5X
12, 10	4X
8, 6	3X
4	2X
2	1X
1, 1/0	0X

After 0X, tippet manufactures go to "02X" or such, or just the breaking strain in pounds.

Tip 304 Here's How to Avoid and Fix Twisted Tippet Tr-S, Tr-L Lg-L Sm-L, Sm-S Pf-L

Some flies seem designed after windmills. The old Fan Wing Royal Coachman with its great white duck-breast-feather wings: perfect example. When I was a kid, it was a hot pattern. I liked it, tied it, fished it, came to despise it—it seemed no matter how heavy a tippet I fished, this fly would turn it into a tangle of twists.

Though it didn't fix my fan-wing-fly problem, going heavier on tippet often kills the twisting of troublesome flies. But what if you feel a thicker tippet will give your fly a stiff presentation or be spotted by the fish?

Then go to your second solution to the twisting-tippet problem: Try a different fly. Try to find one without many projecting parts, especially parts that resemble the vanes of windmills (which are usually the wings—sections of large feathers, whole flat feathers, synthetic sheeting cut to wing shape . . .). Some flies *love* to twist tippet, some don't care to. Go with the latter, if you can.

Tip 305 Adjust Your Tackle for Creeks

 Tr-S   Sm-S

I grew up fishing creeks, and still fish them every year. There's real charm in that secluded world of tiny pools and bright little fish, everything small and close, intimate. My creek fishing has been mostly about trout, but in the Midwest, East, and South it's sometimes been about smallmouth bass and panfish. Once, on an Alabama trickle, it was

My current favorite creek rod, a 3-weight. The dinky black reel next to it holds a 4-weight line and some backing. The midsize reel on the right is just there just for perspective.

about spotted bass. Not yet about largemouths, but I understand they can show up in certain kinds of creeks, creeks with lots of slow, deep water. Still, on the whole, creeks are really about trout to me, so I'll talk about trout creeks from here on.

Creeks, small streams—fishing them just isn't the same as fishing rivers or even larger streams. There's tackle: If a creek is open along its banks, even a tenkara rod of over 10 feet may do. But a creek edged with trees or high brush calls for a short rod. In *Tactics for Trout*, author (coauthor, actually, with me and Rick Hafele) Dave Hughes says, "I specifically like 7-foot, 3- or 4-weight rods for small-stream fishing in tight circumstances." I agree—that length really helps avoid tangling a rod's tip with tree branches. I now go a little longer, 7 ½ to 8 feet. Rods under 7 feet? For me they make dapping difficult, and dapping is often a big part of creek fishing.

A creek rod must flex comfortably with only a few feet of line out the tip—on a creek you're often casting little line, mostly tapered leader. Right now my favorite all-around creek rod is an 8-foot 3-weight that I fish with a *4*-weight line. The rod's supple with a 3-weight, *sweet* with a 4-weight and 12-foot casts.

Long leaders and tippets are trouble on most creeks, and provide no benefit. A 7 ½-foot leader and a couple of feet of tippet are usually just right. A 4X leader with 5X tippet is my creek standard.

Tip 306 Anchors Catch Fish (Indirectly, of Course) Tr-L Lg-L Sm-L Pf-L

I'd catch a lot fewer trout, bass, and panfish if I didn't own and use anchors. I have two real boats—an 8-footer for one occupant and a 10-footer for two—a pontoon boat, and a U-Boat, and I use anchors with them all.

Here are some of the situations in which I drop an anchor (or two): working a shady spot crammed full of bluegills, fishing the chironomid method over a shoal for trout,

Anchors come in many forms—how complicated does a weight on the end of a rope need to be? Here are two of my anchors. Each has served me honorably for a couple of decades.

fishing with the countdown method for trout or bass or panfish, for many kinds of fishing in a good wind—and they go on from there. All of these examples apply to lakes. Yes, you can anchor in rivers, but if not done correctly, it's dangerous. I'm talking here about anchoring in lakes.

Float tubes and most pontoon boats—small inflatable craft—need only one anchor. Boats require two.

Brian Chan (a virtuoso of trout-lake fishing with whom I wrote a book) recommends one 5-pound anchor for an inflatable, two 12-pounders for a boat 12 feet long and under, and two 20-pounders for a boat of 14 to 16 feet.

The standard approach is to drop one anchor (quietly) off the bow, let the wind carry the boat out a ways as you pay out line, then secure the anchor line. Next, drop the second anchor off the stern, straight down, and secure it. This give the bow anchor a good bite and keeps the boat in place in a wind.

In an inflatable, just drop the one anchor straight down, or pay out some line, and tie it off.

Tip 307 Keep Your Rod

Once, over two decades ago, I dashed the full length of a 14-foot johnboat chasing a fly rod. I'd left my dry fly a couple of dozen feet out and a large rainbow trout grabbed it and bolted while I was fussing with an anchor line at the bow. I caught the rod just as its reel was about to clear the transom. From that point on I was careful—that rod, reel, and line were worth a few hundred bucks!

Here's what I've figured out since:

1. When you're not holding your rod, always keep most of it inside your boat, no more than around two feet of it outside.

2. Try to set your rod so it's caught or wedged in, but in a way that will let the reel's spool spin if a big fish hits. Letting the reel hang over a bench seat, for example, can work, but still—if a fish yanks that line tight, the reel can spring up and clear the seat.

3. If you're distracted by something else, don't leave line and fly out there where you might get a take.

4. Consider installing one of those rod-holding devices in your boat or pontoon boat; this is probably your best insurance against losing a rod (and reel, and line), although extracting a rod from such a device can eat up extra seconds and lose a few fish.

In a U-boat, float tube, or such, propelled by fins, you're holding the rod all the time, so, no problem.

Tip 308 Boats Can Be Murder on Rods

 Tr-L   Lg-L   Sm-L   Pf-L

I've advised you elsewhere in this book to bring two or more rigged rods along when you're lake fishing—it's a boon to be able to quickly switch from that sinking line with a dragonfly nymph, which just stopped working, to a floating-line rod with a dry fly when mayflies show suddenly and trout start rising. The problem is, rigged rods in a boat can take a beating.

It's easy to step on a rod, fall on a rod, set an anchor on a rod, bang a rod against the gunnel . . .

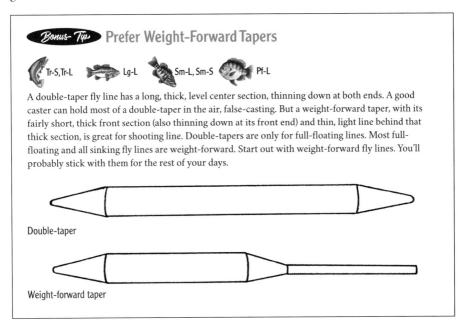

Bonus-Tip Prefer Weight-Forward Tapers

Tr-S, Tr-L   Lg-L   Sm-L, Sm-S   Pf-L

A double-taper fly line has a long, thick, level center section, thinning down at both ends. A good caster can hold most of a double-taper in the air, false-casting. But a weight-forward taper, with its fairly short, thick front section (also thinning down at its front end) and thin, light line behind that thick section, is great for shooting line. Double-tapers are only for full-floating lines. Most full-floating and all sinking fly lines are weight-forward. Start out with weight-forward fly lines. You'll probably stick with them for the rest of your days.

Double-taper

Weight-forward taper

There's no easy solution here, unless you have someone make you a special case to hold and protect your rigged rods when you're not fishing them (which is a pretty good idea). But the main thing is this: Be aware of the dangers.

When you switch places with your fishing partner in your boat, check the rods first, then move them if that makes them safer. Make a habit of looking carefully before setting something down or stepping. And watch those rod tips when you're close to tree limbs and brush along shore.

Tip 309 Here's the Lowdown on Ferrules

 Tr-S, Tr-L   Lg-L   Sm-L, Sm-S   Pf-L

Ferrules, those joints in a fly rod where the open larger-diameter end of one rod section slides over the smaller-diameter end of another, need a little love and conscious care in order to function well and to last. So . . .

First, when you join ferrules together, grasp both the female (large) and male (small) ends up close, only an inch or so behind their rims.

Second, press the male end in *firmly*, but not with real force—push a ferrule together too hard and it may get it stuck. Don't just push the ends together *lightly*, though—a ferrule that opens during a cast can break.

Third, pull ferrules open with your hands well apart, at least a foot.

Fourth, always push or pull ferrules *straight*, along a single line, to open or join them. And never twist the ends of a ferrule as you join or part them.

Fifth is out of vogue, but I still rely on it. Lightly stroke the base of a common candle a few times down the male parts of your ferrules to leave a thin sheath of wax all around them. This will make them easier to open later, and reduce wear. But again: Wax *lightly*.

Tip 310 Take Time Unwinding a New Leader   Tr-S, Tr-L   Lg-L   Sm-L, Sm-S   Pf-L

There you are with a flat little plastic bag in your hand containing a new tapered leader. So far, so good. You open the bag, remove the leader. It's coiled. So you look it over until you find the butt (which may or may not have a loop knotted into it) and see that it's wound around the coils. You carefully unwind the butt of the leader. Now you see that the fine point of the leader is also wound around the coils (which it sometimes is, sometimes isn't), and you carefully unwind that.

Now you straighten out the leader, coil by coil (probably starting with the butt end), until it's all free and fairly straight (you might have to stretch it a bit to truly straighten it). Well done!

Or you could pull the new leader out of the package and just start yanking hard at it (as I always did back when I was a hasty kid dying to get on the water and fish). Then you'd get a leader so tangled you have to throw it away or spend a long time untangling it.

But, of course, that's entirely your choice.

Tip 311 Here's What to Do about Wind Knots  Tr-S,Tr-L   Lg-L   Sm-L, Sm-S   Pf-L

Knots that creep into your leader and tippet as you cast, "wind knots," may or may not matter much. If I get one up high in a tapered leader and it's become too tight to open, I usually ignore it—the leader up there is so much stronger than the tippet that the weakness created by the knot probably doesn't matter. Of course, if I can work it open, easily, with the point of a large hook, or some other needlelike point or just by pushing the ends of the knot together, I'll do it.

If the wind knot's in the tippet—especially if it's a really *light* tippet—I work it out if I can, replace the tippet if I can't.

You'll find that as your casting improves, wind knots occur ever less frequently. I just checked three rods I keep rigged for local fishing (and fish a lot) and couldn't find one wind knot. To be honest, I was surprised—I'm certainly not above making a wind knot. But this does make my point: I'm a very good caster (not a *great* caster—I know some great casters and consequently understand the difference), so for me, wind knots are uncommon. When I started fly casting as a boy? I made wind knots the way a convenience-store clerk makes junk-food sales: steadily, all day long.

So avoid wind knots by casting smoothly and well, and undo them when you can. Replace hopelessly knotted tippets, and leaders. If a tippet is knotted tightly near its point, cut just above the knot, if that leaves sufficient tippet to do the job. But if a wind knot sets itself well up into the thick part of a tapered leader and won't budge? Eh (shrug), live and let live, I say.

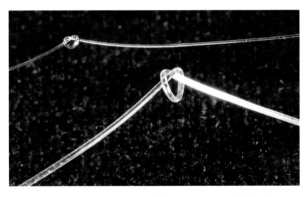

Wind knots: the top one in tippet and the bottom one in thick leader. Neither knot is yet too tight to easily work open. But casting and fishing will soon tighten both beyond hope.

Tip 312
Polarized Sunglasses Catch Fish

Tr-S,Tr-L   Lg-L   Sm-L, Sm-S   Pf-L

In lakes, in colored water or down deeper than the human eye can see, fish-finders identify fish and present them as symbols on their screens. That can provide lake fishers a big advantage. River fly fishers sometimes scoff at fish-finders—too mechanical, too high-tech they say, to suit the elemental poetry of their cherished sport. Then those scoffers don their polarized sunglasses and go back to chucking their flies out into clear rivers.

That . . . doesn't add up. Ever check out what goes into making a polarized sunglass lens? I have. Talk about high-tech . . .

If you're a fish-finder scoffer, do a little reading. You may wind up scoffing less.

Enough on that debate. The point here is that for fishing streams, polarized sunglasses are simply miraculous. (Not just sunglasses, *polarized* sunglasses.) With them, your eyes can cut through that glare on the water to see right down to the cobble and ledges and details of a streambed, showing you all the best places to try your fly.

What a blessing!

Sometimes, you can spot fish. And in the shallower water of a lake you can spot fish, breaks in weed beds, sunken logs . . .

Of course, the water in that stream or lake must be clear, or at least fairly so—polarized sunshades can't work miracles (not quite). But just taking out glare opens up water to the eye in an amazing way.

As big a boon to fly fishers as . . . well, the fish-finder.

Tip 313 Bring a Net That'll Handle Your *Biggest* Fish   Tr-S,Tr-L   Lg-L   Sm-L, Sm-S   Pf-L

You think, My average trout from this stream is about 14 inches long, so I'll bring a net just the right size for landing a 14-incher. My, how *logical* of you. Practical though? Not so much.

I own all these nets, and have owned others that I've retired or given away. I've gone through so many nets, in part, because I kept underestimating the size of the trout I'd catch—they seemed, and seem, to keep getting bigger. (Mind, I'm not complaining.) Two nets, one for average to large trout (its opening around 15 to 17 inches in length) and another for out-and-out big ones (an opening around 21 or 22 inches long), is probably enough for most fly fishers. SKIP MORRIS

What if you hook a lunker?

Last fall was heavenly: rainbows and cutthroats (occasionally brown trout) rising on low, clear creeks and streams and rivers for hours each day to a parade of several different hatching mayflies. The trout ran almost consistently 10 to 15 inches. But over our 10 fishing days I hooked and landed two 18-inch rainbows, one on a river, one on a fork of that river that was really a stream. If I'd carried a net just for 10- to 15-inchers, how would that have gone with the 18s?

Poorly . . .

But all went fine—I landed them both—because I'd brought a large-enough net.

Don't go nuts—don't carry a salmon net, that could hold the family dog, to a tiny creek of little brook trout.

Hook a fish too big for even your big net? It happens. Find another way to land it, unhook it, and free it.

Nets are most commonly used in trout fishing, but they can be handy for largemouths and smallmouths and panfish. And kinder all around—no sore jaws for them, no fin stabs for you.

Tip 314 Here Are Two (Make That Three) Reasons to Replace Your Old Net

 Tr-S, Tr-L   Lg-L   Sm-L, Sm-S   Pf-L

Some older landing nets have mesh bags that taper down in a steep triangle to almost a blunt point—that's murder on trout, a potential (and I don't mean this metaphorically) back breaker. Older landing nets also have mesh bags made of twine or some sort of woven material, which welcomes flies to get stuck in the fibers.

Smooth, fiber-free, fish-odor-resistant, fly-snag-proof rubber landing-net mesh on the left; woven, fly-snagging, odor-collecting mesh on the right. Not all rubber mesh is translucent-white, and can run considerably finer than what you see here.

So, consider replacing your old net with a new one that's got a *fairly* shallow bag mostly level along its bottom, a bag made of rubber mesh—flies won't snag in it and that protective slime on fish won't be easily scraped off by it to hide among fibers and grow ever more . . . aromatic.

Tip 315 Use Fly Patches and Fly Driers Correctly Tr-S, Tr-L Lg-L Sm-L, Sm-S Pf-L

As a kid, I often stuck sodden flies into the little scrap of wool-on-the-hide sewn onto my fishing vest. I wasn't sure why, but I'd seen it done and felt it made me look like a real fly fisher. In time, I decided the point of this business was to dry the flies. So I kept sticking them there. And losing them. Turns out, pin-on patches of wool or squares of rippled foam are really just for holding a fly while you prepare to tie it onto your tippet—a truly handy system—but not a good place to leave a fly for long.

You *can* leave flies in a "fly *drier*," a little ventilated canister or box. Big flies, tiny flies, flies for trout or smallmouths or whatever—a fly drier is designed to hold on to them as you push through stream-bank brush or bump an oar against your chest or whatever else you might cook up to knock flies off a wool patch.

On the left is the old-fashioned wool fly patch. On the right is one of the many variations (there really is no standard design) of the fly drier.

Tip 316 Water Vapor Is Evil

 Tr-S, Tr-L Lg-L Sm-L, Sm-S Pf-L

You can immerse a fly rod in *fresh* water (not salt water) for a long time without much harm. But put that rod into a wet case or bag and close it up more or less airtight and in short order it'll look so decayed that it'll make a fine prop for one of the many postapocalyptic movies that seem to keep popping up on streaming services.

Same goes for a wet reel in a closed-up pouch and a moist to sopping fly in a water-tight (therefore airtight) fly box—rust, rot, the evil of wet vapor made tangible.

So just . . . don't put stuff away wet, especially not so it's sealed up.

Tip 317 A Wet Line Weighs More Than a Dry One Tr-S,Tr-L Lg-L Sm-L, Sm-S Pf-L

Here's yet one more fine reason to support your local fly shop so it'll survive: A fly shop will actually *encourage* you to take several rods out and cast them before you pick one. (Once you do pick one, please consider not running home to order it online after the fly shop people gave you their time and insight and their rods to cast.)

And here's the real point to this tip: When you are test-casting any rod on dry grass (or, if you have no other choice, on dry concrete which is rough on lines), remember that the line you're casting is also dry and therefore lighter than when it's wet.

The weight difference between a dry line and a wet line is just big enough to matter. Consider that when casting a rod to evaluate how it will perform on your target lake or stream.

Tip 318 Graphite's Great, but Fiberglass Still Has Appeal Tr-S,Tr-L Lg-L Sm-L, Sm-S Pf-L

These days, nearly everyone seems to fish graphite fly rods, and I feel they're wise to do so—for a general-purpose rod, and in most cases a specific-purpose one too, graphite's great. Graphite makes a rod light weight, carrying hidden power that comes blessedly into play when you push for longer casts.

Then there's bamboo. It's Victorian-period elegant and rods made from it have an earthy feel to the way they sail out a fly line, a feel bamboo aficionados love. But bamboo rods are very expensive, somewhat fragile, and probably best left to those aficionados (unless you catch bamboo fever, and I may yet). Bamboo is considerably heavier than graphite, so contemporary bamboo rods tend to run 8 feet and shorter.

This leaves fiberglass, "glass," rods. They seemed almost to disappear after graphite really took hold, but they're back; several rod companies now offer glass.

I spent a decade of my life designing graphite rod-shafts (working directly with the factories) and altering premade glass shafts. I know (even if it's knowledge 20-some years old) graphite and glass. So, glass is heavier than graphite but not as heavy as bam-boo. Glass doesn't suddenly stiffen up when you push it (which, as I mentioned earlier, graphite does). So glass, in my opinion, is really at its best in shorter rods (8 feet and under) with light lines (5-weight and lighter) and for short casts, the sort of casts you make on creeks and small streams or along the edges of rivers. (Glass rods *can* handle rivers and longer casts, however, and some like its toughness in longer rods for heaver lines and brute fishes.)

Bottom line: Get graphite and forget about glass until you've fly-fished for quite a while, but after that do consider whether glass might suit you and your fishing.

Tip 319 Why a Four-Piece Rod, Why a Five-?

Four-section rods, a rarity not so long ago, are now the standard. I just paged through a catalog from a big fly-fishing mail-order house and made a rough count: Of the more than 200 rod models from several manufacturers, running from short and light to long and heavy, nearly all were four-piecers. A very few had two, three, or five sections.

As I've stated elsewhere in this book, I spent a decade designing and altering fly rod-shafts, making a living making rods. That, along with my own fishing, convinced me that I'm a four-section-rod man. A four-piecer is ultra handy for real travel (or really, any travel), fitting easily into the tiniest car trunk and staying out of the way in a boat or even a one-occupant pontoon boat.

I truly never could detect a difference in feel or response between my two- and four-piece rods back in my rod-making days. So extra ferrule weight in a four-section rod? Eh.

I love my *five*-section rods too, especially for flying—I can fit them, case and all, into my big suitcase or slip them into a big pouch on my carry-on case and stuff it all in a plane's overhead bin (though I have to remove the rod cases from the carry-on to get them into the bin). Are my five-piecers a smidge heavier than the four-piecers? Perhaps. But I don't notice it when I'm fishing them.

Three-piece rods? I personally don't find them much more convenient than two-piecers. One-piece rods . . . interesting. Supposedly the most sensitive of them all. Maybe, but also the least convenient.

Tip 320 Cast a Rod Before You Buy It If You Possibly Can

Tr-S, Tr-L　　Lg-L　　Sm-L, Sm-S　　Pf-L

I designed (and I mean sent the factory diagrams showing exactly how I wanted the graphite sheeting cut and selected the tapered mandrels on which the shafts were formed) graphite fly rods for a decade as my profession—a *lot* of fly rods—which led me to this conclusion: Fly rods are personal. You date until you find your spouse, vary the pepper and the salt and try fried and boiled and scrambled eggs until you find what suits you, and you listen to all sorts of music to see what pleases your ear. So it just makes sense to take a rod out (with the blessings of a fly shop or on a test loan from a friend) and try standard and slack-line casts, long casts and short, to see if it's really the rod for you before you buy it.

Bonus Tip Keep Your Split Shot in Place

Tr-S, Tr-L   Sm-S

Split shot slip. You can stop their slipping by tying a plain overhand knot in your tippet and crimping the shot on just above it. When casting makes those shot slide down the tippet, toward the fly, they stop against the knot. It works.

If your fly shop does you the courtesy of letting you cast its rods, consider doing your fly shop the courtesy of buying the model you like not online, but there.

Tip 321 Long Tippets Have Advantages

Tr-S, Tr-L

Tippets of 3 feet or longer can make a mess of things in the tight confines of a creek, and offer no advantages I know of in fishing a streamer or bass bug. But with a dry or nymph on a substantial stream or a river? Whole different matter.

With a dry fly on a stream, a long tippet drops to the water in waves of slack, allowing the fly a long natural drift. With a weighted nymph in a stream, the fine, constant diameter of a long tippet—finer than any part of the leader behind it—is easy for the nymph to draw down, and half the battle in stream nymphing is often just getting the fly deep before it's swept to the end of its drift.

In trout-lake chironomid fishing? A long tippet is a huge advantage—same deal as in stream nymphing: The fly gets down and fishing faster. For chironomid fishing, go with a tippet of at least 4 feet, longer is common. (I once saw lake-ace Brian Chan catch two trout on a *27-foot* tippet. But I'm not recommending that . . .)

A long tippet for low-water smallmouths, for shallow largemouths and panfish? Sure, maybe . . . but I haven't yet felt the need.

Tip 322 Forget or Lose Your Hook Hone or Don't Own One? Do This

Tr-S, Tr-L   Lg-L   Sm-L, Sm-S   Pf-L

Small stones in streams are often smooth, polished by I-don't-know-how-many decades of rubbing against each other in currents. If they're fairly flat, they can make good hook hones. (See tip 302 for details on sharpening a fly hook.)

A lake probably won't hold such stones, but there's a good chance you'll find them in the mouths of streams that feed the lake.

The stone can serve as a crude hook hone—but it will do.

Tip 323 Try a Big Strike Indicator on Lakes 🐟Tr-L

For chironomid fishing in trout lakes, I've been going with ever-larger strike indicators because (1) a big indicator packs enough buoyancy to bounce atop every wavelet and animate the deep fly, rather than pass partially through waves as a smaller indicator might; (2) a really big strike indicator is easier to see out there in the chop than is an average-size indicator; and (3) against the resistance of all that buoyancy, the trout often hook themselves on the take.

These big-indicator advantages apply to fishing nymphs in streams too, but are beyond canceled out by one big *dis*advantage in particular: Nymphs below indicators in streams already drift suspiciously faster than the current, but big indicators drag them along even faster. Lakes, though? No current, no problem.

There may be times when normal-size indicators outfish big ones on lakes, perhaps because the smaller indicator resists less, thereby making it easier for a trout to take in the fly. So carry a range of sizes. Still, on the whole, big indicators and lakes, good strategy.

Big strike indicators are clumsier to cast than are smaller ones. But casting them gets easier with time.

On the far left is a strike indicator about the size of a small blueberry; continuing right . . . yikes! That monstrosity on the far right I use only for fishing lakes.

Tip 324 Eventually, You May Want a Vest, Bag, or Box for Every Type of Fishing (or Not)

 Tr-S, Tr-L   Lg-L   Sm-L, Sm-S   Pf-L

I fish a lot. It's part of my job (though I would even if it weren't). And I often bounce from one fish or type of water to another—a trout creek today, a largemouth lake tomorrow, then a trout lake the day after that . . .

So it's a real boon that I have a fully appointed vest I can grab on my way out the door when headed for a trout stream, a tackle box ready to go for trout lakes, a chest pack with everything I need to fish a smallmouth stream, and so on.

An expensive boon, however. I have two pairs of forceps, a couple of hook-removing tools, various tapered leaders and spools of tippet, and a lot more in *each* setup. Not to mention the cost of a vest *and* a hip pack *and* a tackle box, and the rest.

It's all worth it to me—but then, much of this stuff I get at pro prices or for free as a member of several pro-staffs. Good thing, because as a fly-fishing writer, I'm poor.

Before I ask, I need you to know that there's no right answer, but here's the real question: Is it worth it to *you*?

Tip 325 Get Your Stuff Back

 Tr-S, Tr-L   Lg-L   Sm-L, Sm-S   Pf-L

I've left the following at pullouts along streams, at boat launches, and at other assorted places: fly boxes, nets, reels, wading boots, rigged rods, unrigged rods. Most anglers (fly fishers and others) are honest. I know a guy who (cognitively adrift during his hippie years) dropped his wallet and had no idea until the angler who found it gave him a call a couple of days later.

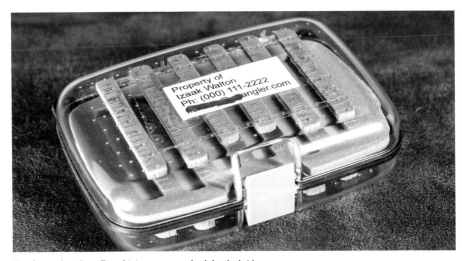

Here's your box, Izzy. Found it in some grass back by the bridge.

That's why I make labels with contact information, and then attach them to my fly boxes, reels, rods, wading staffs, etc. (not sure what to do about boots and waders) with heavy clear packing tape. These days it's wise to give out as little info as possible to strangers, so chose what you put on the labels carefully. (On fly boxes, to make finding flies easier, you can add the theme: "Caddis," "Terrestrials," "Crayfish and Streamers," whatever.)

Tip 326 Rebuild a Leader

Occasionally an expensive tapered leader (they're always expensive, by my standards) grows short before its time, before it's knotted up and hangs stubbornly onto its curls. Do you just cut it off, then, and toss it out? Not on my fly-fishing-writer income you don't. And maybe, regardless of your income, not on yours either.

Look, some fly fishers *build* their own leaders, end to end, from several stretches of level mono, the heavy stuff at the butt, working ever lighter to the tip. So why not *re*build yours? It's easy: Just tie in a section of tippet of a thickness that makes a good transition from what remains of the leader down to the tippet. Or you can rebuild the leader with not one but two sections, working down in thickness, if that makes a smoother transition. Say, a 9-foot 3X leader that's been cut back 3 feet, rebuilt with 1½ feet of 1X, followed by 1½ feet of 3X.

There—I just saved you the cost of some new leaders. My pleasure.

Tip 327 Here's How to Come Back Home with All the Stuff You Left With

During my years as a traveling musician, I lost a lot of goodies while on the road. I'd play a month with a band in Phoenix, then have two days to drive to a six-week gig in San Francisco, leaving behind perhaps a pair of shoes, a bottle of shampoo, a shirt . . .

I was rooming with a bass player when we got moved across the parking lot to another room because some big group had rented out our whole section. My roommate walked his stuff over while I was at breakfast. When I gathered up mine I found he had left the following: two shirts, a pair of pants, three phonograph albums (still the days of vinyl), a belt, and an electric razor. He was new at playing on the road, so as I tossed his shirts onto his new bed I said, "John, we all go through this at first, but you need to get good at collecting all your stuff or you'll spend half what you make replacing it."

On fishing trips, I've left clothes and alarm clocks and such in motels and lodges—and it's always a real pain getting them shipped back—and fly boxes and nets and such along rivers and at pullouts. But through all that, I've learned.

I've learned never to put my clothes in closets or drawers in motel and lodge rooms, to always keep everything I brought out in the open and not in corners hidden by little refrigerators. I've learned to check a room thoroughly—pull covers and sheets off the bed, look all around under the bed and dressers, check behind the shower curtain—*three* times before leaving.

And I learned to look all around my car—and on top of it—*three* times before driving off from a pullout or boat launch, using a flashlight if it's getting dark.

Overcautious? I think not.

CHAPTER 10

STAYING SAFE OUT THERE

Tip 328 Just . . . Wear . . . Glasses

Tr-S, Tr-L   Lg-L   Sm-L, Sm-S   Pf-L

So . . . important. Clear prescription glasses in the fading light of sunset, sunglasses (prescription or not) at midday, or, if you don't have prescription glasses of either kind, inexpensive safety glasses from a hardware store—all are potential eye and eyesight savers.

Of course, no glasses can protect your eyes when you're not wearing them.

When you cast, or are even near someone else who's casting or might suddenly start doing so, wear glasses. Even if you're practicing casting out on a lawn with only a tuft of yarn tied to the point of your tippet, wear glasses. Hooks, and lines and leaders and tippets and the knots on or in them, can scrape, cut, or stab your eyes.

But not when you're wearing . . . glasses.

Tip 329 Being a Wiener Beats Drowning

Tr-S, Tr-L   Lg-L   Sm-L, Sm-S   Pf-L

If I'm drifting a river in a boat, I prefer to wear a life jacket, a "PFD," not only when fast or rough water comes up but the entire time. Doing so, however, seems viewed by some as slightly . . . wienerish. But I'd rather float wienerishly (yes, that's an adverb; no, don't look it up) than sink bravely.

Wading in a stream, few fly fishers wear PFDs, but perhaps they should. Fall when you're thigh-deep in swift water and perhaps hit your head on a stone and, well . . . not

This life jacket is also a fishing vest—just makes sense, wearing a fishing vest while fishing, right?

Bonus-Tip Arms Spread Wide Add Stability

Tr-S, Tr-L   Lg-L   Sm-L, Sm-S   Pf-L

Though I consider a wading staff a must for wading streams (and for those rare times I wade in lakes), some fly fishers always wade without one; some forget to bring theirs; and some, if they carry the sort that jumps together when drawn, forget to slip it from its holster. Whenever there's no staff, spreading both arms out to the sides, and pointing the rod out in line with the arm holding it, can really help stabilize the wading angler.

good. I suppose the decision to wear or not wear a PFD while stream wading depends on your medical conditions or lack of them, age, balance, swimming abilities, and how strongly you object to sinking and staying sunk.

And it depends on the type of PFD. Most of them look just the way life jackets have looked as long as I've been around: big, bright, and bulging (and to some, wienerish). These days, however, there are flat, inconspicuous ones that inflate when you pull a cord or just when their sensors detect water.

For drifting rivers, Carol and I use understated PFDs with pockets for fly boxes and such—essentially, buoyant fishing vests.

Tip 330 Poke Around Before Stepping In

Tr-S, Tr-L   Lg-L   Sm-L, Sm-S   Pf-L

Your wading staff really helps you stay upright in stream currents—that third point of contact makes you far more stable than do only your two feet. But it has another use: checking water depth. If you're about to step off a bank and wade into a trout or small-mouth stream or just wade a step deeper, unless there's good light and clear water, you'd better poke your wading staff down there to measure the depth first. Also, to make sure the streambed's not bottomless soft silt. You can reach out ahead with your staff to see if there's a drop-off coming up. During those rare times I wade in lakes, I use my staff to guide me there too.

Without a wading staff, you can use a dead tree limb lying on the bank. (I really feel we should all carry and *use* some kind of staff whenever we wade.) I hesitate to suggest you use your rod tip for gauging depth—that's an excellent way to break that tip.

Tip 331 Wade Wisely

Tr-S, Tr-L   Lg-L   Sm-L, Sm-S   Pf-L

I spent my late teens training in gymnastics, my early teens training in judo—the former hones balance through handstands, the latter hones a different kind of balance through trying to toss someone onto the ground while also trying not to *get* tossed.

Balance is the heart of wading. Yet after all that early training I still occasionally fall in a stream. Have all along. No one gets away with wading carelessly, and everybody gets a little careless now and then. Even wading calm lake edges requires attention.

Be safe, wade wisely: move carefully and slowly, wading staff both in hand and planted on streambed.
SKIP MORRIS

So here's what I've learned, from other fly fishers and from experience, about wading safely:

1. Carry a wading staff and *use* it. That third point of balance provides amazing support. My staff folds up into a holster but leaps to assemble itself when I pull it out (it's called a Folstaf)—that quick assembly is very handy when I've forgotten to get it out and things get suddenly hairy.

2. Mostly, make a tripod of your feet and staff by keeping the staff generally out in front of you.

3. Plant one foot, shift it to make sure it's secure, do the same with your staff, and only *then* move your other foot.

4. Wear boots with grippy soles. Felt soles (banned in some states) handle average wading; metal studs, often with felt, grip better and really cut through slime.

5. Consider what's downstream before you wade out—a nasty rapid, a drop-off, a *waterfall*? Don't bet your life you won't go down.

6. Wade with a friend, especially in strong or deep currents. Hold hands or wrists; one uses a staff, the other holds the rods. Two wading—slowly—adds stability.

7. Trust your instincts. If looking at the water you plan to wade gives you *any* doubts, logical or intuitive regardless: Do . . . not . . . wade.

Bonus-Tip Never Risk Your Life Over a Fish

 Tr-S, Tr-L   Lg-L   Sm-L, Sm-S   Pf-L

It's obvious: Someone who risks injury—even death—just to catch a fish is a fool. I've been that fool. Especially in my youth, I made dangerous choices in order to reach some promising side channel, or to get above a waterfall. The list of my foolish and risky fishing acts is fairly, and embarrassingly, long. Do . . . not . . . follow my lead. Instead of writing this book right now, I could be occupying a wooden box in the ground.

Tip 332 Protect Yourself from the Sun

 Tr-S, Tr-L   Lg-L   Sm-L, Sm-S   Pf-L

Too much exposure to sunlight can cause problems much worse than sunburn. And fly fishers get more sun than most people, in part because water reflects it.

Even in winter, I protect my hands, arms, face and neck, *everything*, from sunshine. Sure, sunshine is more intense some times of the year than others, but it's out there every day, even on cloudy days, up to its mischief.

How much sun exposure is healthy? The American Cancer Society website offers lots of information on that and on controlling your exposure in general.

I wear long-sleeved shirts with high ratings for sun protection, always long pants, sun gloves (fingerless lightweight gloves), and a wide-brim hat of dense fabric. I also wear one of those masks—fabric tubes, really—that covers my throat, face, ears, and neck. Yes, I look like a hold-up man, look sort of silly in general, but I can deal with that—my mother loved sunbathing and wound up with most of a nostril carved off thanks to skin cancer.

Fishing, walking, jogging, swimming, water skiing, snow skiing, whatever—use good sense in protecting yourself from too much sun exposure.

Tip 333 Consider Tying All Your Flies on Barbless Hooks

Tr-S, Tr-L   Lg-L   Sm-L, Sm-S   Pf-L

Fly fishers often refer to fly hooks whose barbs have been smashed down as "barbless." Of course, the barb, that tiny shard that angles out just behind a hook's point, is still there, smashed or not. What I want to talk about is hooks that come from the factory with no barb, like a sewing needle bent to a hook shape.

Truly barbless hooks do seem to protect fish a tad better than hooks with pinched-down barbs, but that's not mainly why I prefer them—I like how they slip easily out of *me*. I've hooked myself in the lip and the finger past the barb and have seen worse.

Smashed-down barbs still grip flesh. Try backing one out of a trout's or bass's jaw sometime and you'll see. Then imagine that that trout's jaw is your earlobe . . .

If you actually *like* getting a shot from your doctor, you have problems I can't begin to address. But I think (almost) everyone feels a certain relief when the plunger is all the way down the hypodermic's barrel and the needle is slipping painlessly back out of the arm (or out of, wherever). That's how a barb-free hook comes out of a fly fisher: It just slides out.

If you tie your own flies, no sweat: Just tie on truly barbless hooks. If you don't tie, good luck. Maybe your local fly shop can recommend a custom tier.

Fly hooks made without barbs cost more—the manufacturing process becomes more complex without a barb for the machinery to catch. Your decision:

At the top of the photo is a barbed hook, barb intact. On the left, the same model of hook with its barb smashed down. On the right is a true barbless hook, no barb to smash, never was one.

some extra bucks spent or a barbed hook stuck deep in your flesh. And, of course . . . there are the fish to consider.

Tip 334 Protect Your Neck and Ears

 Tr-S, Tr-L   Lg-L   Sm-L, Sm-S   Pf-L

If you want pierced ears, fine, but there are better way to get them than stabbing them with a big streamer fly. Look, even solid, seasoned casters mess up a fly cast now and then. A cast gone wrong can send that fly almost anywhere and with some real momentum.

That's why you must always—*always*—wear glasses when you cast or are anywhere near others who are casting or might cast. But glasses won't protect your neck and ears. A wide hat with brim bent down in back and a shirt with its collar turned up will: Turn that collar up high, and wear a hat.

So what about your front—your throat and face? Glasses again, of course. Your top shirt button buttoned and the front of your collar up. That's about it. As far as I know, no one's yet making a fly fisher's fly-proof face shield. Helps a lot to just be careful with your casting.

Tip 335 Bring All the Clothing You Might Need, in Layers If Possible

 Tr-S, Tr-L   Lg-L   Sm-L, Sm-S   Pf-L

There are many fishing situations in which weather can change suddenly and drastically: any time in spring, anywhere powerful winds are known to rise up at random, always at high elevation . . . You go out in only a light-fabric shirt, assuming the warm sunshine will hold, the air will remain still, and then get caught in a cold blustery downpour and end up, at the very least, uncomfortable. More likely, miserable. At worst, hypothermic.

Or you go out in only a heavy sweatshirt and, once the day warms, sweat.

Carol and I have learned to bring layers we can put on or take off as conditions change. We carry or store these garments however we can: in the back of our fishing vests, in small backpacks, in a cooler in the boat, or, if it's nearby, in the car.

We keep rain jackets always at hand—even a flimsy one keeps us dry, and makes an excellent windbreaker.

 *Bonus-Tip* Communicate Before Passing Behind a Caster

 Tr-S, Tr-L   Lg-L   Sm-L, Sm-S   Pf-L

Someone is planted on the bank of a stream or lake, casting, and you want to walk through behind them. Better let them know first, or you could wind up with a fly in your shirt, or in your ear. Just stop and wait until the caster stops casting, smile, and say calmly, in a voice loud enough that you're certain you'll be heard, "Passing through behind you" or "May I pass behind you?" Once they've given you the nod, *then* go on ahead with a "Thank you."

CHAPTER 11
THE PRACTICAL FLY FISHER AND PHILOSOPHER AND . . . WHATEVER

Tip 336 Fish Hate Rules

 Tr-S,Tr-L   Lg-L   Sm-L, Sm-S   Pf-L

No one really knows why, but as soon as you, or I, or *anyone* makes a rule about fish behavior—bluegills like shade, largemouth bass like long pauses of a hair bug or popper while smallmouth bass like shorter pauses, and so on—the fish will break it, at least occasionally.

So as convenient as it would be if fishing were predictable, it is, in reality, *un*predictable. Imagine you come to a trout river that's dead low, under a bald sun, in scorching midsummer, early afternoon—*horrid* fishing conditions—yet you hook one trout after another on a dry fly. Now imagine you come in early afternoon to a river at perfect height, with dense, still clouds overhead, during the very best part of the Salmonfly stonefly hatch—everything's . . . ideal. So as long as you present a proven imitation of the Salmonfly in the right places, you'll catch trout, right? How could you *not* catch trout?

Trust me: you could not. In fact, you toss your Stimulator up close along classic banks that drop off to perfect depths with currents just right for trout, banks lined with grasses and tree branches that dangle clumsy love-distracted stoneflies out over the water to drop onto it, and . . . nothing. You fish all this wonderful water for hours without budging a single fish.

Look, fish may hate the rules we anglers make, but certain behaviors keep fish safe and well fed—and our rules are based on those behaviors. All very logical, but the fact is, sometimes fish rebel. So trust in the rules—because far more often than not they'll help you catch fish—but when the rules fail, try something else, something *outside* the rules.

Put another way: Keep an open mind, and when the rules don't work, open it wider.

Tip 337 Everyone Gets Skunked

 Tr-S,Tr-L   Lg-L   Sm-L, Sm-S   Pf-L

I fish fairly often (thanks to my profession, of which writing this book is a part) with fly-fishing authors and guides and just devoted, deadly fly fishers. Guess what? I've seen many of them get skunked. I've seen others struggle to catch only one or two fish amid swarms of them. Getting skunked is no point of shame. It's life. At least it is for a fly fisher.

What's "skunked" mean? It means getting shut out, shut down, thwarted, shellacked—it means not catching any fish.

New fly fishers, in my experience, often feel that when they catch no fish, they're doing something wrong or not doing something they should be doing. They're often right about that. But sometimes they're wrong—the fish simply won't be caught, by *any*one. It just . . . happens.

In this book are all kinds of tactics you can try on cagey or moody fish to coax them into taking your fly—and they're tried-and-true tactics that often work. Soak them up, use them. But also accept that when fish won't be caught, they won't be caught. And that any day on fishing water is always a good day. Besides, a good skunking makes, or keeps, you humble. Humility's good; this world always seems in short supply of it.

Tip 338 Come Prepared, and Brace Yourself: Alaska Fishing Is Crazy

 Tr-S,Tr-L

If you've been dreaming for years of fishing the vast, harsh, pristine wilderness of Alaska—and vast, harsh, pristine wilderness describes nearly all there is up there—you need to know what you're getting into before you drop the required big bucks for the trip. And when you go up, you need to be prepared for wildly different fishing than you'll find in any of the lower 48 states or southern Canada.

The last time Carol and I fished up there, we swung big, jointed "flesh flies," flies that imitate the meat torn by river currents from the rotting carcasses of spawned-out salmon, to hook rainbow trout up to 11 pounds, trout with power and stamina that seemed almost impossible even for their size. So, we presented them flesh, flesh swimming across the current. Swimming flesh: I *told* you—it's crazy up there.

Trout this size—trout, not steelhead—aren't common in Alaska fishing, but are hardly rare either. Of course, hooking a brute like this requires the right stream, at the right time. (Landing it requires the right tackle and the right skills.)

That's a "flesh fly" at the top of the photo, a fly designed to suggest a shred of meat from a rotting salmon carcass, like that salmon carcass below it. In some Alaskan rivers, trout gobble this way-past-expiration-date sushi every year. Imagine how big a fish could grow eating all that protein . . .

Yeah, those trout were gulping big chunks of salmon meat.

On the Alaska trip before that one, I waded a wide, shallow river tossing oversize salmon-egg imitations to watch Dolly Varden char (char are nearly trout) go after them by slamming through swarming salmon ten times their size in the clear, thin water.

The point: If you're going to fish way, way up north, you need to do your research. And not just on the fishing—you need to know how to fish safely up there too. There are scads of bears, extreme tides, and, in general, extremes of everything (mosquitoes included).

If you're ever going to hire a guide, Alaska would be the place to do it, especially for your first days, or at least first day.

Tip 339 How You Fish a Fly . . .

Tr-S, Tr-L   Lg-L   Sm-L, Sm-S   Pf-L

I've come up with only a few original sayings worth repeating. Among those few, this is my favorite: How you fish a fly is *at least* as important as which fly you fish. Sometimes I skip the italics.

Let's say you've tied on the perfect imitation of the chironomid that's currently hatching on your lake. The fly captures every detail of the pupa: its size, taper, color, shine . . . But you give it no action, letting it hang motionless while the real pupae squirm all around it. Your perfect fly is perfectly . . . ineffective.

Or you give the fly too much action, scooting it along like a frightened little fish. Again, ineffective.

Or you fish it only 3 feet down while the trout are grabbing the real pupae just off the lake bed *12* feet down. Again: perfect fly but no takers.

It's rarely enough to just have a good imitation—you have to present it in a convincing way, an effective way, and you must put it where the fish are.

Even when you're not imitating anything with your fly, how you fish it can be critical. An impatient retrieve for largemouth bass, for example, will usually bring only follows—not takes—of your popper.

Here's my saying, put another, more direct way: You'll catch more fish (probably far more) with a just-passable fly fished right than with an ideal fly fished wrong.

Tip 340 A Fly in the Air . . .

 Tr-S, Tr-L   Lg-L   Sm-L, Sm-S   Pf-L

Guides and old hands at the fly game like to say, "You can't catch a fish on a fly that's up in the air," and they're right. False-casting feels good, and done well it's graceful and pleasing to both caster and spectator. The problem: It keeps the fly up in the air.

To catch fish, a fly must be in or on the water. So, don't false-cast more than necessary.

It amazes me how much time some fly fishers, especially newbies, spend with their flies airborne. Or just somewhere that's not in or on the water. They fiddle with their flies, adding floatant that isn't yet needed, changing patterns when the one they have on is working, even sitting with fly in hand wondering what to do next. Here's what to do: Get that fly to the water.

I'm not suggesting for a moment that you devote the remainder of your life to maximizing fly-in-or-on-water time. There are plenty of situations—a trout rising in a difficult spot, bluegills showing in the shade back under an outstretched tree limb—in which some time to consider and to make even a few false-casts for practice is wise. I *am* suggesting that you calmly keep reminding yourself to try to keep that fly where the fish can get at it.

Tip 341 Get to Know Your Home Waters

 Tr-S, Tr-L   Lg-L   Sm-L, Sm-S   Pf-L

My absolute lifetime-favorite fly-fishing writer, Roderick Haig-Brown, titled section three of his book *Fisherman's Spring* "The Home River." That's probably how the more general term "home waters" got started.

My home waters include trout lakes; largemouth, bluegill, pumpkinseed, crappie, and yellow perch lakes; trout streams; salmon and steelhead and sea-running cutthroat-trout streams; surf-protected salt waters . . . Well, you get it: It's fishy around here.

But two decades ago I lived near Portland, Oregon, and my backyard fishing options were few. I dug into them until I found a creek of small cutthroat trout just a half hour's drive away and a park pond an easy walk from home with worthwhile spring bluegill fishing. Eventually I joined a fishing club with a trout pond I could drive to in 20 minutes.

But, all that effort for one good pond and a couple of okay fishing spots—*ugh*, right?

Bonus-Tip Check the Fridge

 Tr-S, Tr-L Lg-L Sm-L, Sm-S Pf-L

Yes, this *is* a fishing tip, or at least a practical one for the fly fisher. Most of the motels and lodges traveling fly fishers stay in have refrigerators. And what do most people do when confronted with an unfamiliar fridge? They crank up the cold, to 10 out of 10. If you fail to check the setting, your veggies, cheese, and that fancy leftover dessert freeze overnight. So check the fridge when you first move into your new lodging, adjust it to a modest setting, and then check your food after an hour or two.

No—wrong. Exploring near home was its own reward. When I did find something, I saw it as a real treasure.

Look, your best fishing usually comes with *really* knowing a particular piece of water: its structure, its moods, how it changes through the seasons, that sort of business. Streams and lakes, creeks and gravel-pit ponds you can visit often, near your home, will be a lot easier to figure out than far-off waters.

There are other advantages to fishing close: it's cheap (no motel bills, no airfares, little gasoline burned, no out-of-state fishing licenses); it's handy (no planning, just go); and you can fish when the weather, water temperature, and the rest are right.

Tip 342 If You Want to Fish Your Home Waters, You May Need an Open Mind

 Tr-S, Tr-L   Lg-L  Sm-L, Sm-S   Pf-L

If you live in western Montana, you're probably within an hour's drive of some fine, classic trout-stream fly fishing. Most of us, however, don't live there. Most of us North Americans live in parts of Arkansas and Saskatchewan and California where the nearest decent trout stream—the classic fly water—is hours away. Same goes for trout lakes.

You can sniff around after largemouths or smallmouths or such panfish as bluegills and green sunfish. They're marvelous on a fly rod, but they may not be close by either. In that case it's time to ask, What is?

My wife, Carol, and I live on the east side of Washington State's Olympic Peninsula amid good trout, largemouth, and bluegill lakes and passable trout streams (which is why we travel often to prime trout streams and to smallmouth waters). If we lived instead on the west side of the Peninsula, we might have no lakes handy, and no real trout streams that didn't require real time and some backcountry hiking to reach. Definitely no smallmouth streams.

But if we did live on the west side, we would have rivers around us carrying runs of big, powerful salmon and steelhead, and of spunky sea-run cutthroat trout. There are surf perch along the beaches over there, and probably other intriguing fishing options in both salt and fresh water. None of this is classic trout-stream fly fishing, but it's all amazing.

My advice: If you don't have trout or bass or panfish near home, or you're just the curious sort, chase down the kinds of fly fishing you *do* have within an easy drive (flounder, carp . . .). You may be surprised at the fishing opportunities you discover. And eventually, delighted.

Tip 343 Consider These Strategies If You Bring Extra Rods

 Tr-S, Tr-L   Lg-L   Sm-L, Sm-S   Pf-L

So you've decided to bring an extra rod or two in your boat for lake fishing or along to a stream. But what lines and flies will you rig them with?

My first step in making that decision is to consider what flies I'd normally expect to fish in this particular water at this particular time. If a Western March Brown mayfly hatch is likely on a stream, I'll bring a rod with a floating line and an emerger imitation of that mayfly. My second rod might carry a floating line and an indicator nymph rig with an imitation of the March Brown nymph, or just an attractor nymph. A third rod? Probably a sinking-tip line and a streamer just in case.

Stream or lake regardless, I usually bring at least one floating line and one sinking line (full-sinking for lakes, sink-tip for streams).

I might go out on a trout lake with a floating line on one rod set up to fish a dry fly, another with a floating line for chironomid fishing, and perhaps a third with a full-sinking line and a dragonfly nymph imitation for trolling or working the countdown method over a shoal.

I might go to a smallmouth bass stream with a floating-line rod rigged with a popper and a sink-tip rod rigged with a crayfish pattern.

There really are no hard rules here. You mostly just bring what makes sense and hope that once you're fishing it still makes sense. Then you change things—flies, rigs—if it turns out they don't make sense.

I concocted this medieval contraption myself: a length of bright yarn bound to a clothespin. It helps me find rods I temporarily set aside along a stream I'm fishing—they can really hide out in grasses or forest. I clip the clothespin (by its notch) onto the upper part of a rod and then set the rod in a safe place—pretty easy to later find that pale fluorescent-pink yarn among shadows and dark tree trunks.

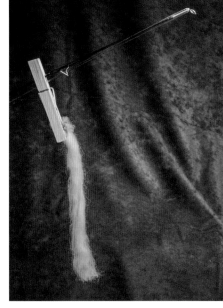

Tip 344 Fish Know When You're Not Looking Tr-S,Tr-L Lg-L Sm-L, Sm-S Pf-L

I know: It's crazy to think that fish wait for you to take your eyes off your dry fly, your strike indicator, or your floating hair bug—and only *then* make their move. But it sure seems they do.

I've watched new fly fishers miss one smallmouth, one trout, one bluegill after another by glancing off to see what bird just called behind them or gaze at clouds. When they look away, a fish takes; when they look back, it's all over, no sign that anything happened. They have no idea. But I do. I've seen this . . . *so* many times.

I then tell them (usually they don't believe me until I give up a few details), and they do better—specifically, they hook more fish. Sometimes considerably more.

So expect fish to take your fly whenever you take your eyes off your fly or indicator, and then—don't take your eyes off your fly or indicator. (You know . . . I might adopt that as one of my sayings.) The fish really will grab your fly once they tire of waiting for you to look away.

Tip 345 The Phrase "Fly Fishing Is Easy" Is a Lie Tr-S,Tr-L Lg-L Sm-L, Sm-S Pf-L

A few years ago I was asked to write an article about fly fishing for an elegant, expensive magazine clearly aimed at the rich. The article was very general—it had to be, with such a vast topic squeezed into 2,000 words. Reading the piece now, I see that I implied anyone could just stroll into fly fishing and start catching fish. And I now believe that although my intentions were honorable, I lied.

Look, no sane person expects to play like Oscar Peterson after a half dozen piano lessons or swing around on the rings like an Olympic gymnast after completing an introductory gymnastics course at a community college. Why, then, do new fly fishers often expect to haul in fish after fish?

The reality is, you're going to get about as much out of fly fishing as you put into it. Go out fly fishing once or twice a year and ignore it the rest of the time and, sure, you'll improve a little here and there, but not much.

If you want to get a real command of this sport and catch ever more fish and find ever more pleasure in fly fishing, you need to get serious. Read books and magazines and websites on fly fishing, practice your casting, and *fish* at least fairly regularly. You'll improve gradually, unevenly, but on the whole you will improve.

You have a fascinating journey waiting before you. I'm a little jealous.

Tip 346 Don't Fuss, Don't Fret—Just Fish Tr-S,Tr-L Lg-L Sm-L, Sm-S Pf-L

A mistake I rarely see experienced, dedicated fly fishers make: spending half their time messing with tippets and flies and whatever other distractions they can find. It's easy to let this stuff draw you off course—trying to pick out that perfect fly for the fish and conditions, deciding which strike indicator will be just right, tying that knot with a perfect-size loop . . .

Look, getting the details right in fly fishing can count for a lot, often for the difference between catching and not catching fish. So respect that. But fussing and fretting are different from paying attention to details: Fussing and fretting are mostly about indecision, if not genuine fear, the fear of making bad choices.

All fly fishers make bad choices. That's never going away. You just try, once you identify them as bad, to follow them with better ones. You don't have to nail the details right off; you get to them, often, through a process.

So instead of fussing and fretting, take the time to decide where to fish and how to fish and what fly you'll try next and the rest, but no more time than reasonably required—then *fish.*

When you first take up fly fishing, everything you do will be slow. That's just you being human. And it can take quite a while to get the hang of this complex sport. But your rigging-and-fly-selecting-and-the-rest time should eventually start diminishing from one outing to the next.

Make it a habit to occasionally ask yourself this: How much of the time from when I hit the water to when I reeled in to go did I spend actually *fishing?*

Tip 347 Details Count

 Tr-S, Tr-L Lg-L Sm-L, Sm-S Pf-L

At the very beginning, fly fishing seems to carry magic—you feel you can just pick out whatever fly catches your fancy, rig it up in whatever way you like, and toss it out anywhere, anytime, and catch those hungry fish that must be swarming in whatever water is near.

It can be almost like that, sure, but it almost never is.

For all the different kinds of fly fishing, you have to get the details right in order to succeed, so pay attention to those details. Learn where trout and bass and panfish hold in lakes and streams—a lot of water will hold few, if any, fish. Fish leaders and tippets of proper length and diameter for the fishing at hand so that you'll have a shot at fooling wary brown trout in slow, clear spring creeks but won't break off big deer hair bugs when you set them on largemouth bass. If there's a hatch of mayflies matching a size 18 hook, fish an imitation tied on an 18—not on a size 12.

The list of important details keeps going . . .

How to rig and where and how to effectively fish for a trout, bass, or panfish in a particular kind of water—that stuff's spread all through this book. So you have the information. The point is, getting one critical detail wrong can often kill your fishing, but if you get the most important ones right, your odds of catching fish, well, *soar.*

One more thing: Focus, and trust your feelings. If trout are rising but refusing your dry fly, consider what might be wrong—too short a leader or tippet, a poor choice of fly, a dragging dry fly, something else? Let that question settle into your subconscious. The answer might then rise up, seem to materialize all on its own.

Tip 348 Never Try to Outfish . . .

Tr-S,Tr-L   Lg-L   Sm-L, Sm-S   Pf-L

A couple of decades ago a guide cautioned me: Never try to outfish someone on their water. Over the years since, I've come to see his point. (Actually, he said, "Never try to outfish a *man* . . . ," but that's a silly restriction considering all the top-notch women fly fishers out there.)

Where trout hold in a particular stream, which parts of a lake the smallmouths prefer—these and a thousand other fishing variables differ from one water to the next. Bottom line: The more and longer you fish a particular water, the more successfully you'll fish it.

So how do you compete on water new to you with someone who fishes it all the time? Answer: You can't. At least not without pulling off a lucky trick or just dumb luck.

There's an easy way out: Don't try to compete. Instead, encourage your fellow anglers when they fail, applaud them when they succeed, congratulate them when they land more fish than you land, and mean it. We're all, or all should be, brothers and sisters in this grand adventure.

Tip 349 Don't Leave Fish to Find Fish

Tr-S,Tr-L   Lg-L   Sm-L, Sm-S   Pf-L

Action just out from the boat launch, at the end of the long narrow lake, had been steady. Every few minutes, one of our indicators would go down and a plump 1- to 2-pound trout would fly up in that spectacular Kamloops rainbow leap of legend.

I eventually suggested to Carol and our friend that we run up to the head of the lake where another Canadian friend had reported "phenomenal fishing" the day before. It was a long run. When we got there . . . nothing. Zero fish.

Finally, we got back to our first spot, but now it was dead too. As we were loading our vehicles to leave, I commented to my friend on what a bad suggestion I'd made. He said, not in a reproachful but in a gentle way, "Well, my dad told me a long time ago, 'Never leave fish to find fish,' and I tend to go by that."

Neatly put, Dad. This little drama took place over two decades ago, and for two decades I've tended to go by that too.

That's the day-trip kind of not leaving fish; there's also the long-term kind. A month ago, in late September, Carol and I fished a Montana creek stuffed with oversize cutthroat trout. After a long day there, I suggested we try a river for a change.

Her eyes grew huge and stared into mine for a long moment (I don't recall her blinking even once). Then she said, "Are you *nuts*? How often do we find creek fishing like this?" We've been together nearly three decades, so I knew she meant no insult. And besides, sometimes I am nuts.

So we fished that creek the following three days and it stayed great. Then we finally *did* need a change. The next week the fishing in the creek dropped off by about 85 percent, probably because the trout moved down into the main river for the winter. We'd done the right thing: kept returning to good fishing.

Tip 350 Keep Fishing Notes, and Here's a Trick for Keeping Them During Trips

 Tr-S, Tr-L   Lg-L   Sm-L, Sm-S   Pf-L

You say, "It was here . . . wasn't it?"

Your fishing partner replies, "It was *around* here, but the water was deeper." And you think, It *was* deeper, but maybe that's because we were here in the spring. Or was it fall?

And there you and your buddy are, relying on your (like mine) pathetic powers of recollection for the details that will get you back to the same spot and the same mayfly hatch that were amazing two years ago. Or was it three years ago?

This messy, ineffective sort of process plays out all over the world every day. The problem is obvious: faulty memory. So what's the solution?

Fishing notes.

I confess that I don't go back through my notes often, but when I do, they sometimes *really* help. Thanks to my notes I know, for example, that if in mid-September, on a certain Montana river, I park in the third pullout downstream from a certain bridge and walk upstream an eighth of a mile, odds are strong that fishing will be exceptional.

Of course, strong odds are no guarantee—fishing and fishing water can change, year to year, month to month, week to week. But come on . . . fishing—and *guarantees*? Ha! That's a good one.

Still, fishing is at least fairly predictable, so fishing notes are often invaluable for finding the right spot at the right time of day or year, bringing the right flies, choosing the right strategies . . .

Here's the trick that's mentioned in the title of this tip. How do you keep notes on out-of-town trips without writing them on paper you then lose? Email. If you can write them in an email and send them to yourself, you can later print, hole-punch, and slip them into a ring binder.

Tip 351 When the Fishing's Hot—Keep Fishing  Tr-S, Tr-L   Lg-L   Sm-L, Sm-S   Pf-L

A childhood friend and I had arranged five days on an Idaho cutthroat trout stream. He was taking up fly fishing again after a couple of decades off. I'd never stopped. The first three days were cold and blustery, and the frequent rains were sometimes so hard they were loud. Those first three days were also . . . amazing.

Bonus Tip See Your Fly in Action, in Your Mind

Tr-S, Tr-L   Lg-L   Sm-L, Sm-S   Pf-L

It always helps me fish a nymph or streamer fly more effectively if I picture in my mind what it's doing down there. If I can see (figuratively) that nymph turning in the current or lurching above a weedy lake bed—*as* I'm fishing it—I just seem to catch more fish, be it trout, bass, or panfish. A sort of heightened sensitivity kicks in. Try it.

Mayflies started showing around 11 o'clock each morning and kept on hatching until dark. The cutts, probably working back upstream after another icy winter spent down in the big lake, were bunched up and feeding everywhere on the hatching insects.

On our first day, after three hours of getting rain blown into his face, my friend asked me how I was doing. In fact, I was cold and wet, despite my waders and rain jacket, but I was just fine, amid all those bugs and rising fish. I told my friend, "We could leave, get warm and dry, but I'm happy to stay as long as the fishing holds up." Then I added, "I rarely find fishing this hot, and it could go cold at any minute—I suggest we dig in as long as it lasts." He considered, then agreed.

And that's what I'm telling you: Dig in—that is, keep fishing—as long as hot fishing lasts. Always stay on it until it's done, if you can, whether for trout, largemouth, small-mouth, bluegills, or any fish.

Oh, that cutthroat stream? It kept kicking out mayflies and trout for those first three miserable, magnificent days. The sun came out on the fourth day and the wind died down. So did the fishing.

Tip 352 Get to Know Your Fishes

To understand the fishes you seek to catch, you needn't study college textbooks on their biology (though, sure, go ahead with that if you like). But some off-the-water time with fly-fishing books or websites or both, that explain the habits and natures of those fishes, will, undoubtedly, pay off in more fish hooked, more fun.

Trout, for example, hold in certain parts of a lake—shoals, bays, drop-offs—and feed best in spring and fall when water temperatures are comfy. Largemouth bass like standing water but will tolerate slow currents, whereas smallmouth bass love a quick bouldery river.

Knowing such details as these and developing a sense of what specific fish species like and how they behave guides you to put a plausible fly into a good spot in all that water, and then fish it convincingly at a proper depth.

Plus, learning about fish gets fascinating. The more answers you find, the more questions, often intriguing ones, pop up: What conditions does a trout require in order to successfully reproduce? At what water temperatures does a largemouth bass feed best? What do smallmouth bass mainly eat in streams? When does a rainbow trout spawn? When does a brown trout spawn? And so on, and so on . . .

Tip 353 Waters with Multiple Species Offer Benefits

Most of the lakes near my home hold largemouth bass, some hold bluegills or pump-kinseeds as well, some hold yellow perch, one holds crappie, and nearly all of them hold stocked trout. The climate here is mild; summer air temperatures rarely top 70 and winter lows typically stay above freezing—just warm enough in the hot (well, what we call hot) months to satisfy the bass and its kin but cool enough to suit the trout.

The presence of the bass and panfish here, outside their native range, creates controversy. Should nonnative fishes inhabit our lakes (even if our lakes lack spawning streams for trout)? Could these nonnatives spread to lakes where trout do spawn, and gobble up trout fry?

Controversy aside, when fishing my local lakes, I never know for certain what I'll catch. That *is* a kick.

And sometimes, when the trout fishing's off, I'll turn to the warmwater fishes and the action picks right up. Or it can be the other way around.

Multiple fish species sharing the same water is pretty common, and often natural. I've caught two rock bass per smallmouth in a Michigan river and loved hooking both fishes. In many places I've found largemouth among all sorts of panfish. I've felt my line go wild when a 7-pound steelhead rocketed off with the nymph I was fishing for trout.

More than one fish species in a given water provides options, which can keep the action up, and welcome surprises.

Tip 354 You Must Both Do and Study in Order to Grow Tr-S, Tr-L   Lg-L   Sm-L, Sm-S   Pf-L

The sort of person who sees everything through the intellect, who lives in thought, is likely to turn to books and magazines and the internet in order to learn to fly fish. The sort who just jumps in, whose natural inclination is to skip all the preparation and go straight to the doing, will get a rod and some flies and, before understanding fly fishing at all, head for a stream. Both sorts should think twice.

You can't, in my experience, grow as a fly fisher unless you balance book (or internet or video or all three) learning with doing. If you just read and memorize, your skills and instincts will improve at a crawl—you need to fish more. But if you rush out and try to wing your way through all the intricacies of fly fishing—and there's a heap of them—you'll develop all sorts of inefficient, ineffective habits. Fly fishing's been evolving for literally centuries. Its current state-of-this-art is all written down, waiting for you to start reading about it.

So read a chapter in a fly-fishing book, then go fishing with your new information in mind, read some more, fish some more, read . . . Seek a balance. Improve. Enjoy.

Tip 355 Could the Problem Be . . . You?

 Tr-S, Tr-L   Lg-L   Sm-L, Sm-S   Pf-L

What I'm going to tell you will seem unrelated to this tip or even to fly fishing for a while, but have faith . . .

When I got the guitar chair in my college jazz big band, I was already irritated with my sound. It felt a tad harsh, and was uneven—some notes in my solos came out too loud, others too soft. A range of volume is musical, but only when it dramatizes the stories the notes are telling. This was random.

I tried different strings, various picks, then switched the guitar I was playing for another I owned that I'd been ignoring. No improvement. I'd just come off two years on the road with a popular band that played funk and other '70s dance music, and my bank

See the fly smacking the water in the lower left of the photo? Whose fault is that? Clue: It's almost certainly not the rod's (or the line's, or the leader's, or the weather's, or the stock market's . . .).

account felt comfortably plump. So I did some research and then bought a new amplifier, a real jazz amp. No improvement.

Finally, I considered the obvious: that *I* was the problem. From that point on I practically took up residence in a department practice room. After a few weeks of daily, careful, patient practice my technique improved. I kept at it, it kept improving.

Within a year, problem solved. The notes became even, round, neat, with each coming off at just the volume I intended.

Point is, I've watched fly fishers do what I did: buy more stuff as solutions—ever longer rods to fix low backcasts, ever more expensive reels to stop breaking off fish, new flies, heavier tippets . . . But were their rods, flies, tippets, or whatever else the problem? Often, I'm convinced, they were not. Often, the fly fishers themselves were the problem. They needed to work on their casting, presentation, fish playing, whatever.

Moral: Make sure shortcomings in your knowledge or skills aren't what's messing up your fishing before you go bankrupt blaming your equipment.

 **Get In and Out of the Way**

Tr-S, Tr-L   Lg-L   Sm-L, Sm-S   Pf-L

Quickly pull (not reel) in your line when someone in the boat with you, or even nearby in another boat or along a stream, hooks a fish that's going to take some serious playing. Normally, this means a big fish or a strong fish (or, of course, both). It's just courtesy—and could avoid tangled lines and a lost lunker.

Tip 356 Watch and Wait for a Glory Day—Then (If You Can) *Fish*

Tr-S, Tr-L   Lg-L   Sm-L, Sm-S   Pf-L

It's summer and, perhaps after some hot, bright, slow fishing days, there comes a quiet day when the clouds all bunch together, dark-edged, looking surly but holding in all their raindrops—and the fish go mad! That's a Glory Day.

Example: July, a Canadian lake I'd come to know well. Fishing kept declining as the water continued warming day after scorching day. Only nymphs would catch a few trout. Then came a Glory Day—I could throw a dry fly almost anywhere and a trout would charge it. For hours. All of it ended in thunderclaps and a downpour sizzling onto the water.

Another example: an Idaho stream. During the heat wave the cutthroat trout fishing was fair only in the mornings and evenings. Then, a quiet, gray Glory Day—one plump golden cutt after another.

Final example: a local largemouth lake on a Glory Day—every time I hit one on that lake, I'm shocked yet again by how many bass it really holds.

Summer, usually, the air muggy and still, somber light filtering through bulging clouds—the fishing may flop, but it could be phenomenal. I've had Glory Days on streams and lakes while fishing for trout, on lakes for largemouths and bluegills. Honestly, I'm not sure if Glory Days inspire smallmouths.

A Glory Day may hold until dark, or end when sunshine starts peeking through or with a violent thunderstorm—whenever there's any danger of lightning, a common component of a thunderstorm, get off the water and get safe.

So while there are no guarantees that Glory Day conditions will trigger hot fishing, it's a fair bet they will. If all the variables for a Glory Day fall into place, take that bet if you possibly can—go fishing.

Tip 357 Regardless of Anything Else, Bring the Critical Stuff

Tr-S, Tr-L   Lg-L   Sm-L, Sm-S   Pf-L

Just before I head out for a speaking gig, Carol always stops me and says, "Okay, let's take stock. Do you have all the PowerPoint shows you need and backup DVDs? Do you have your tying kit and the materials you'll need? Do you have a copy of the contract? Do you have your airline ticket?" (I still print mine out rather than trusting a phone to hang onto it.) And so on, until we've made certain the basics—the things I *must* have if I'm to do my job properly—are packed.

She goes through the same process when it's her gig. (She does a show on photography for the fly fisher.)

Wise woman.

We once drove all the way to eastern British Columbia to fish lakes and, though we brought all our tackle and flies, oars and anchors and oarlocks, we forgot . . . the boat.

The *boat*, we hadn't noticed after three days of driving—the entire bloody boat! Thankfully, our friend had an extra.

The point is, whether for an afternoon's or a month's fishing, check just before you go to make sure you've got *the basics*, the critical stuff you just can't fish without.

Tip 358 Destination Water Off? Change Water Tr-S, Tr-L Lg-L Sm-L, Sm-S Pf-L

Anglers have a tendency to fall in love with a stream or lake and then remain utterly faithful to it. But fishing isn't marriage; there's no ceremony, no vows are taken. In fishing, stay single and play the field. So if that spring creek of legend is plain off—all your strategies and tricks have failed and even the local hotshots are at a loss—let your eye wander.

A couple of years ago I headed off with Carol and a friend to a river that was supposed to be a real sleeper—lots of trout, few anglers. It was lovely but, unfortunately, we found it fast asleep. We worked it hard with dry flies, nymphs, even streamers, and caught only a few small trout and a couple of passable whitefish. After a day and a half of that, and hearing in the fly shop that nobody was catching much, I pulled out the map. There they were: the crooked lines that indicated feeder creeks. So I pulled out my fishing guidebooks, which I'd put in the car just in case (there's a good tip right there: bring the maps and guidebooks), and started reading.

The rest of the five days we fished a small river that fed the main one, and found a few trout, but mostly we worked the creeks—and they were splendid! Lots of wild westslope cutthroat trout and a few brookies and rainbows. We had a blast.

Keep an open mind on a fishing trip in which you've invested time and effort and money. Go for smallmouth if the trout won't bite, or bluegills if the largemouth bass are sulky. Don't let yourself get hitched to one water.

Tip 359 Chase Down the Gaps in Your Fishing Tr-S, Tr-L Lg-L Sm-L, Sm-S Pf-L

This tip, even amid a profusion of tips (artfully written, wise, stunningly practical tips, according to the author), stands out. Fly fishers, in particular *new* fly fishers, miss, lose, or fail to move fish because only a few rungs in their fishing ladder are weak or faulty or missing altogether.

For practical reasons we'll ignore rigging for now: leader and tippet length, leader and tippet diameter, added weight, dropper flies—all that sort of business (though important business it is, indeed).

First, then, is casting. Are you casting far enough to reach the fish? Are you casting too far, so your line drops over the fish and spooks them? Are you using slack-line casts when they're needed? Stop. Consider. Then, if a change is needed, start working on making that change.

Second is presentation. Is your dry fly dragging when it shouldn't? Is your streamer swimming too quickly? Stop, consider, fix the problem.

After these come hook setting (too soon, too late, too hard . . .), fish playing (too light, not letting the fish run . . .), and fish landing (jabbing with the net, trying to lip a large-mouth bass too soon . . .). Again, in each case, stop, consider, fix.

It's worth saying again (if in a different way than before): This tip you particularly must heed. I've seen newbie fly fishers, and even some pretty experienced ones, land only a fish a day amid ample fish begging to be hooked and landed—all because one element of their fishing was wrong or lacking. One problem rung.

Don't just keep doing what's not working. Be attentive, analyze, consider what you might be doing wrong or inadequately or not doing at all—it's likely the very thing that's held the rest of the process hostage. Fish consciously.

Tip 360 Fish Creatively

 Tr-S, Tr-L   Lg-L   Sm-L, Sm-S   Pf-L

Fishing a Montana creek last summer, I had little time left to explore the interesting water leading downstream to a bend—my wife, Carol, and our friend Brian were fished out and ready to go. But they kindly gave me their blessings to try that last stretch—provided I kept the trying brief. Since I was working downstream, a soft-hackle made sense. So I swung one a few times and got some hookups.

Then I realized I could simply hold the rod tip out over the center of the flow and let the fly dangle well below me as I walked slowly down the shallows. I was no longer *swinging* a soft-hackled fly—I was just streaming it continuously downstream. Tug, tug—the trout kept grabbing. I kept walking and smiling, tickled at the success of this silly approach. I hooked several trout this way, and then a real yank shook me from my reverie. A tough, fast 13-inch rainbow, as it turned out, spun line off my chattering reel, had me trotting to catch up.

See what happened? I got a little creative, tried something that made sense to me, a technique with no name. And it worked.

So, you spot a trout holding tight along a high cutbank on your side of a large river. Tough, perhaps impossible spot for a real cast. Go ahead, then—dap your dry fly—even if dapping's supposed to be for creeks. If the trout won't come up, tie on a nymph, skip the indicator, flick the fly upstream a little, and let it drift and sink a foot or so: essentially, dapping a nymph with no indicator—who does that? Apparently, you do. Turns out it works. Now I'll leave it to you to figure out how you're going to land the fish from a high bank.

There are all kinds of odd situations in which I've hooked fish by crazy means. Conventional was useless; crazy was the only solution.

Trout, largemouths, smallmouths, panfish—always be ready to combine established fishing techniques, or create new ones, if doing so makes sense or just feels right.

Tip 361 Try a Third-Day Escape

 Tr-S,Tr-L   Lg-L   Sm-L, Sm-S   Pf-L

That's what I call it: After two days of difficult fishing, slow fishing, or both, I reward myself on the third day, if I can, with fishing that's quick and easy. If the difficult fishing is a spring creek or hours of casting for only a few big smallmouth bass, the easy fishing might be a real creek full of hungry little cutthroat trout, or maybe a productive bluegill pond.

Not to knock the fascination of cagey spring-creek browns or the thrill of hooking big smallmouths, but that third day can be truly liberating. Try it.

Tip 362 Have You Soaked Your Wallet Yet? Of Course You Have! Here's How to Not Soak It (or Your Car Keys) Again

 Tr-S,Tr-L   Lg-L   Sm-L, Sm-S   Pf-L

Since we all eventually take a plunge (I still go down every so often), a wallet is a problem for the wading angler. Once it's soaked, you have to take everything out, spread it all out so it can dry, and then wait. Could take a while. And the ink on that big check you forgot to deposit may run—now you get to see if the bank will take it.

Wouldn't it be nice if you could just leave your wallet at home? I do. Here's how.

I put my driver's license, fishing license, maybe my credit card, and a few bucks in a watertight sandwich or snack bag, and then carry the bag fishing in a *zippered* pocket

God bless modern sandwich and freezer bags.

(in my fishing vest or shirt or pants)—a pocket, in any case, from which the bag cannot escape. No wallet and nearly no bulk or weight, everything protected from a dousing.

But plastic bags are slick. So I don't just put the bag back into my wallet, where it might work its way free; I take out everything and return each item to where it belongs. The next time I go fishing, I take it all out again and put it into a new bag.

I also put my car keys in a plastic bag (in two bags, actually, a sandwich bag inside a heavier freezer bag, both sealed)—the car key, once a cheap metal doohickey, has become an investment.

There are now commercially made bags for protecting car keys, fishing licenses, and such, some designed like miniature river-rafting dry bags—but whatever you decide to use, use it.

Tip 363 Start Packing Early for a Fishing Trip Tr-S, Tr-L Lg-L Sm-L, Sm-S Pf-L

If you're anything like me, I'm sorry . . . That's because I'm pretty addlepated and have, overall, a lousy memory. These character flaws make the already formidable task of packing for a fishing trip even worse.

But I've developed a system, and it really helps. At least a week before the trip, I start The Pile. I start it where it won't bother my wife or our houseguests and where no one will trip over it, in an isolated place. One day I pick out my fishing shirts, underwear, socks, and pants, and toss them onto The Pile. Perhaps the next day I gather my tackle and add it to The Pile. Fishing guidebooks, waders, wading staff, maps . . . It all goes onto The Pile.

Of course, I sort through everything before The Pile gets it. I go through my fishing vest, checking to see if the right flies are there and if I need tippet, floatant, whatever. If I do need tippet (or whatever), I have time to pick some up. If the next day I pick out my clothes and find I need to wash some, I have time to wash them. Time to consider, time to find things, time to prepare. Time: *That's* the point.

On it goes like this until the day I pack it all up—when I often notice other things that are missing. It might be wiser, and certainly a more organized process, to make a thorough list and check each item off as it goes on The Pile, but I'm neither that organized nor that wise.

Tip 364 Do Some Checking a Few Days Out for a Trip Tr-S, Tr-L Lg-L Sm-L, Sm-S Pf-L

My wife, Carol, and I are supposed to be fishing in Montana at this moment. We left town a few days ago under clear skies and a brilliant sun. When we neared Snoqualmie Pass, we noticed a light fog enveloping the mountaintops. As we continued down the other side of the Cascades, the fog—which we now recognized as smoke—held and then stretched over the next 150-plus miles to Spokane, where we had arranged to spend the night. Spokane was worse: The tall buildings had turned gray near the highway, and the downtown area faded off into a great pale wall.

Did we get online that night and do some investigating? Absolutely. Turned out, much of western Montana was, and in fact still is, ablaze.

Our loss of a couple hundred bucks and a lot of driving is nothing—is *meaningless*—in comparison to people evacuating their homes, even losing them.

Still, I wish I'd done a little checking just before we left town.

Had we not seen all that smoke along the way, we'd have continued on only to waste more time, more miles, more money. This sort of thing really does happen—not only fires but flooding, fish kills, drought, heat waves, and more can turn fishing upside down long after you've arranged your lodging and made all your plans. Sometimes they hit just before you depart.

So, in the last days before a fishing trip, nose around a little, make a call, check the internet. There's always the chance you'll need to cancel your plans and make new ones, or just wait things out.

Tip 365 Learn, Explore, Experience, Improve—but Don't Fret

 Tr-S,Tr-L   Lg-L   Sm-L, Sm-S   Pf-L

I wish someone had long ago spoken the words above, the title of this tip to me. In my teens I strove to become the best gymnast in the world. Did I? Nope, nowhere close. After that, the top jazz guitarist. Nope again. The best fly tier? I'll say only that I got a lot further with that than with gymnastics or guitar.

With each of these passions, and a few others, I started out right. I dabbled, grew increasingly fascinated, and wound up with an insatiable urge to learn everything knowable about gymnastics or fly tying or whatever, and to push my skills at this thing beyond their limits.

All that's just fine—every day I could devote to, well, whatever, was a day of the purest joy. A few years down the line, though, it would always turn dark. I'd worry—was I really devoting enough time, improving rapidly enough, trying hard enough? Essentially: Would I ever be as good as I wanted to be?

The stress of all this self-imposed pressure made me grind my teeth together, made my muscles tense and sore, made my stomach hurt. It could have been worse—people, even if indirectly, *die* of stress.

And what good did it all do? None. In fact, it sometimes soured what had been heavenly, made me jittery and irritable, twisted my perspective, and that's just for starters.

Okay, I needed to share that. Thanks for listening. But there is a point: Learn as you fish and as you read about fly fishing, improve your skills, but *don't push yourself*. (Well, push a little maybe, but never a lot.) Explore fly fishing with calm, patient focus and you'll likely find ever greater joy in our magnificent sport, and improve at it in the quickest possible way.

LEARN THE LINGO

140 FLY-FISHING TERMS

1. ACTION, ROD Designates not how stiff or supple a fly rod is, but specifically the *way* a rod *bends*. A "fast-action" rod flexes mostly in its upper third, feeling nearly rigid below that. A "slow-action" rod still flexes mostly up high but noticeably way down, even to the grip. And a "moderate-action" rod, the most versatile, falls between actions fast and slow.

2. ADULT, INSECT To fly fishers, an *aquatic* insect that has hatched from the water into the air, freeing its new wings during its hatching, is an "adult" insect. (Though mayfly adults are usually called "duns" and "spinners.") In the human sense of the word, most fly fishers are adults too, but rarely behave like them.

3. ANGLER Just means "a person who fishes," a fisherman (or sometimes now "fisher-woman" or "fisherperson").

4. AQUATIC The term means "of water," but is used among fly fishers to describe insects that live in streams and lakes: "aquatic insects."

5. ATTRACTOR Any fly that doesn't imitate something—an insect, a fish egg, a little fish, whatever. Attractor patterns can get crazy, and can work.

6. BACKCAST The fly-casting stroke that throws the line back, behind the caster.

7. BACKING A strong level line much finer than fly line, running between the fly line and the reel. Backing allows fish (among the fishes addressed in this book, mainly trout) to make long runs—without backing, the fish would take out all the fly line and then break the tippet.

8. BACKSWIMMER, WATER BOATMAN Similar-looking and similar in behavior, these dark, shiny, teardrop-shaped insects can swim rapidly (thanks to their two long paddling legs), fly, or scurry across the surface of water at any time. They live mainly in lakes and never hatch but do go on swarming flights.

9. BARBLESS Often used to describe hooks whose barbs have been smashed down, to protect fish, to follow fishing regulations, or both. Truly barbless hooks come with no barbs whatsoever.

10. BAY An indentation, tiny to massive, along a lake (or saltwater) shoreline.

11. BELLY An arc formed by wind or current in a floating fly line floating on the water. Also describes an action, as "Let the line belly in the wind."

12. BELLY BOAT Another term for "float tube."

13. BIRD'S NEST A tangle of line, leader, tippet, or any two or all three, on the reel. (There's also a popular nymph fly called the Bird's Nest.)

14. BRAIDS When a river, stream, or creek divides into three or more smaller flows of even slightly comparable volumes, these flows are called "braids." Braids typically rejoin at some downstream point.

15. CADDISFLY An insect that grows underwater into a larva, transforms into a pupa around hatching time, to hatch, finally, into a mothlike adult.

16. CASTS *Crash:* The author's (my) slack-line cast made by aiming the forward stroke low so that the casting loop hits the water before it can run off the end of the line. It's a cast for big dry flies.

Haul, double: A short, quick tug on the line at the end of each casting stroke, to increase line speed.

Haul, single: Essentially, the double haul but with the tug on only the back or forward stroke.

Parachute: A slack-line cast for downstream presentations.

Pile: A slack-line cast made by a high forward cast pulled down to the water.

Roll: For situations where a backcast is blocked by trees, a hillside, etc. The forward casting loop is formed only slightly behind, or even in front of the caster.

Reach: A slack-line cast made by lowering the rod to one side or another after the forward casting stroke is completed.

S (or lazy S): A slack-line cast made by waggling the rod tip, after completing the forward casting stroke, to throw waves into the line.

Shepherd's crook (or negative curve cast): A slack-line cast made by casting sidearm and under-powering the forward stroke, so that the line lands in a loop.

Standard: That's as close to any as the common name for the simple straight-line cast from which all other casts evolved, and which is used more often than any other.

These aren't the only casts, but they're plenty for trout, bass, and panfish fishing.

17. CHIRONOMID The name denotes a mosquito-like insect, running tiny to large, when it's in lakes. In streams it's always tiny and there it's called a midge. (See **midge.**)

18. COVER A boulder, lily pads, broken currents, a log—anything a fish can hide under or hold near for protection in a stream or lake.

19. CRAYFISH Looks like a little lobster, lives in some streams and lakes, and is *beloved* by smallmouths and sometimes eaten by largemouths, panfishes, and trout.

20. CREEK Flowing water, smaller than a stream.

21. CRIPPLE An established term referring to insects that tried to hatch but ran into problems and now are stuck on or in the water. A politically correct term may eventually replace "cripple." I use the term "failed hatcher."

22. CZECH NYMPHING Drifting a two- or three-nymph rig below (or not too far out from) the rod tip, with no strike indicator.

23. DAMSELFLY A slender, swimming nymph that prefers lakes but does fine in slow currents, lives among weeds, and climbs out to hatch into a slender flier sometimes olive, often blue.

24. DEAD DRIFT Means a floating fly or strike indicator drifting freely with a stream's currents, as though not attached to a leader or tippet at all.

25. DRAG The drawing of a fly or strike indicator off its natural drift on stream currents. Drag is caused by currents pulling on line, leader, tippet or any or all of these. Though often a problem, in some cases (fishing soft-hackled flies, for instance) drag can work in the fly fisher's favor. "Drag" also refers to that part of a reel that adjusts the spool's resistance to releasing line.

26. DRAGONFLY A plump nymph, usually huge (huge for an insect), that lives in lakes and some streams, and crawls from the water at hatch time to emerge from its shuck as an even bigger, swift-flying adult.

27. DROP-OFF Where a the outer edge of a lake shoal turns sharply down into deep water.

28. DROPPER A nymph fly (typically), trailing on a short length of tippet tied to the main tippet or leader, up from the bottom (point) fly.

29. DROPPER-NYMPH RIG A rig of one or more artificial nymphs trailing off short sections of tippet at intervals up from the bottom (point) fly.

30. DROP SHOT A nymph-fishing rig for streams in which the point fly of a drop-per-nymph rig is replaced by one or more split shot.

31. DRY-AND-DROPPER A hazy term often overlapping with "hopper-dropper." To me, "dry-and-dropper" refers to a small to modest-size dry fly with a small to tiny lightweight nymph hanging from some tippet tied to the bend of the dry fly's hook. Hopper-dropper: big dry fly, heavier nymph.

32. DRY FLY In general (and to me), *any* floating fly, regardless of whether it floats high on the points of its hackles, down with its body on the water, or only partially with most of its abdomen sunken. Some see floating emerger flies as a category separate from dry flies.

33. DUN The newly hatched mayfly, free of its shuck, wings out and up. No other insect is described as having a dun stage.

34. EMERGER, FLY A fly, either floating or sinking, that imitates some aquatic insect in some stage of emerging from its shuck.

35. EMERGER, REAL Any aquatic insect at any point in the process of escaping its shuck to hatch.

36. ENTOMOLOGY The study of insects. It's mostly "aquatic entomology," the study of insects that live in water, that matters to fly fishers—though sometimes land insects, such as ants, grasshoppers, and moths, feed largemouths, smallmouths, trout, and panfish.

37. EVENING RISE That period from around sunset to dark when trout often feed hard and rise freely. There can be a sort of evening rise for largemouths, maybe small-mouths, and for some panfish.

38. FALSE-CAST A casting stroke, forward or back, intended to hold the line up above the water, rather than deliver it *to* the water. "False-casting," continued casting strokes above the water, can serve in both fishing and casting practice.

39. FERRULE That part of a fishing rod where two sections overlap a few inches, so the rod can be disassembled for convenience of storage or transport.

40. FISH-FINDER An electronic sonar device with an image on a screen that depicts the contour of a lake bed (or the bottom of a saltwater bay or, sometimes, a big river) and identifies fish down there.

41. FLOAT TUBE Originally, a truck-tire inner tube with a strapped-on seat, later a specially made round bladder inside a fabric shell that includes a seat and backrest and more. Propelled by swim fins. Largely replaced by the U-Boat and pontoon boat today.

42. FLOATING LINE A fly line that floats, end to end. Sometimes called a "full-floating line" to distinguish it from lines that float in their back sections and sink in their front ("sinking-tip" or "sink-tip" lines).

43. FLY LINE A thick, smooth line tapered down through the front and back ends. The weight of the line carries out the lightweight fly behind it. Some fly lines float, some sink, some do both in different sections, and nearly all come in one of two tapers. (See **line, taper**.)

44. FLY REEL, PARTS OF The "frame" is the shell of a fly reel. A reel mounts on a rod by its "foot." Inside the frame is the "spool" that holds the line and backing. The fly fisher turns the spool by its "handle." The resistance with which the line can be pulled out is adjusted on the "drag."

45. FLY ROD, PARTS OF The heart of a fly rod is its rod shafts, together called a "blank." The sections of the rod are joined by overlapping "ferrules." Mounted at the butt of the rod is the "reel seat," which tightens to hold the reel, and directly above it is the cork (or foam rubber or whatever) "grip" or "handle." Often, just above the grip, is a tiny loop or catch for holding a fly, called a "hook keeper." Up the rod, small metal coils (sometimes little hoops set in metal frames) called "guides" are bound on with thread; a different guide on the rod's point is called the "tip guide" or "tip-top"; the big guide (sometimes two of them), the one down closest to the grip and made with a strong frame, is called a "stripper guide."

46. FORCEPS A surgical pair of pliers with long, slim jaws that fly fishers use for extracting flies from fish.

47. FORWARD CAST The casting stroke that throws the line out in front of the caster.

48. FREESTONE Describes a stream (or river or creek) fed by surface water (not springs) that runs free—no dams along its course.

49. FRY A term for juvenile fish, especially ones that school.

50. GRIP Means (1) the manner in which you hold a fly-rod handle and (2) the handle itself. So if you say, "I grip the rod grip using the standard thumb-on-top grip," you'll be technically correct but annoying.

51. GUIDE, FISHING A man or woman who, for a fee, takes clients fishing and helps them catch fish.

GUIDE, ROD
See **fly rod, parts of.**

52. HACKLE A chicken feather that comes in several forms and is used in many ways to make flies. Rooster dry-fly hackles are stiff, long, and expensive, and wound onto fly hooks to make bristly collars. Other rooster hackles and hen hackles are supple and absorbent and make wings, collars, tails, and more on nymphs, streamers, and some floating flies.

53. HAIR BUG Typically, a big fly of thick pocketed hair (such as deer hair) compressed and sculpted into a thick body, perhaps with tails, rubbery legs, whatever. Normally fished for largemouth and smallmouth bass, but sometimes for other species. Little hair bugs are fished for panfish.

54. HOOK, PARTS OF The "eye" is the wire loop to which tippet is tied, at the front end of the shank; the "shank" is the *usually* straight stretch of wire behind the eye; the "bend" is the curve that starts at the rear end of the shank; the "barb" (which some fly hooks lack) is a tiny prong angling off the wire just behind the point; and the "point" is the hook's sharp, well, point. Though not an actual *part* of a hook, the "gape," or "gap," the distance from the point to the shank, the hook's bite, is an important factor in hook design.

55. HOOK, SPECIFICATIONS AND TERMS Wire thickness: "light wire" or "fine wire" is lighter than average wire, "heavy wire" is heavier than average, and "standard wire" is of average thickness. Heavy wire hooks are generally for sinking flies, light wire hooks for floating, and standard wire hooks can go for either.

Size: the higher the number, the smaller the hook, so size 22 is tiny and size 4 is much larger.

Shank length (doesn't affect hook size or the size of the gape): "1X long" means a little longer than the standard shank, "4X long" means long indeed, "2X short" means pretty short, and "standard length" means just what it says.

56. HOPPER-DROPPER A rig with a big, buoyant dry fly (such as a grasshopper imitation) and a smaller nymph dangling from the bend of its hook on tippet. Some consider "hopper-dropper" and "dry-and-dropper" interchangeable terms. To me, a dry-and-dropper rig is the lighter of the two, smaller dry, smaller and lighter nymph.

57. IMITATION Any fly designed, or used, to imitate an insect or little fish or something else fish eat.

58. IMPRESSIONISTIC FLIES Flies that imitate creatures and things fish eat, but imitate them in a loose, general way, often covering a considerable range of insects, small fishes, or whatever. The opposite of realistic flies.

59. INDICATOR NYMPHING Fishing one or more nymphs below a strike indicator. A common method in trout streams. Nymphs are fished in lakes with indicators, but then this approach is usually called "chironomid fishing," even if a fly imitating something other than a chironomid is used.

INDICATOR, STRIKE
See **strike indicator.**

60. INFLATABLE A float tube, U-Boat, pontoon boat . . . in fly fisher's talk, any small (usually one-person) watercraft that inflates.

61. KICK-BOAT A kick-boat is, to me, a seat set with a frame that's mounted between two pontoons and propelled, at least primarily, by swim fins rather than oars. (See **pontoon boat.**)

62. KNOTS *Backing to reel:* A knot to secure the backing to the reel (*duh* . . .).

Blood: Attaches the butt of a tapered leader to a short section of heavy leader (often the butt of a previous leader) which is attached to the tip of the fly line. Can be used other ways.

Clinch, improved: A standard knot that locks a fly to a tippet.

Clinch, Skip's: The improved clinch knot with an extra step that makes it more secure.

Mono loop: A knot that creates a little loop at the end to allow the fly to swing freely.

Morris loop: Like the mono loop knot but (in the author's opinion) easier to tie and offering more control of the loop's size.

Nail: For attaching the butt of a tapered leader (or short stretch of heavy level monofilament that attaches to the leader) to the point of a fly line.

Surgeon's: Also called the "double surgeon's knot," for attaching tippet to tapered leader.

Sure, there are other knots, but these are really all you need for trout, the basses, and panfish.

63. LARVA The stage before the pupa stage of an insect that follows a complete life cycle (larva, pupa, adult).

64. LEADER A monofilament *fly-fishing* leader is normally tapered, either through a manufacturing process (a "knotless" or "pre-tapered" leader) or tapered by levels of ever-finer monofilament knotted together (a "knotted" leader). A tapered leader continues the momentum of the cast, to throw the fly well away from the line.

65. LIE A place in a river or lake (or any kind of water) where a fish will hold or is holding. A trout lie might be the slowed current behind a boulder; a largemouth bass lie might be the shade under a floating log.

66. LINE, FLOATING, SINKING-TIP, FULL-SINKING Fly lines are designed to float or sink or both. A "full-floating" or just "floating" line floats from end to end. The front end of a "sinking-tip" or "sink-tip" line sinks while the line behind it floats; it's a line mostly for rivers, so the line near the angler doesn't get caught up in the shallows. A "full-sinking line" sinks end to end and is mainly for fishing lakes and other standing water.

Full-sinking and sinking-tip lines sink at different speeds, and these are often described by "type"—a type I sinks slowly, for example, while a type IV sinks very quickly.

67. LINE, TAPER A fly line starts out at its tip with a small diameter. The thickness increases, "tapers," gradually down the line. Soon the line is quite thick and this long section is called its "belly." If after the belly the line slims down again and continues that way to the end, it's a "weight-forward" line, by far the most common line taper. If the line continues thick most of the way through, tapering down again at the end as it did at the start, it's a "double-taper" line.

Floating, sinking-tip, and full-sinking lines all typically come in weight-forward taper. Only floating lines come in double-taper. Start out with weight-forward lines if you're new to fly fishing. (See the bonus tip on page 283.)

68. LINE, TO LINE A FISH To "line," in fly fishers' speak, is to drop your fly line over or too close to a fish or so that it drifts over a fish and alarms it.

69. LINE, TO LINE A ROD To "line" a rod is to run the fly line up through a rod's guides, a part of rigging the rod for fishing.

70. LOOP, CASTING When a fly line is cast, a loop (a "casting loop") forms in the line and rolls down it, carrying the line and fly out.

71. LUNKER Angler slang for a big fish.

72. MAYFLY Lives and grows underwater as a nymph, hatches to a "dun," matures into a "spinner." The female spinner returns to the water to release her eggs. Only the mayfly has dun and spinner stages.

73. MEND A curve thrown upstream or downstream in a fly line. Also a verb: "to mend line." Mending avoids drag on a fly or strike indicator.

74. MIDGE Always tiny in streams, but can be much larger and is usually called a chironomid when it hatches from a lake. It's a larva that transforms into a pupa that hatches into a winged adult that looks just like a mosquito.

75. NYMPH, ARTIFICIAL Any subsurface fly that resembles a real nymph or larva or pupa, or seems to. There are both imitative and attractor nymph patterns. Fly fishers may toss anything that's fished like a nymph into the nymph category: imitations of aquatic worms, sow bugs, fish eggs, scuds . . .

76. NYMPH, REAL The immature underwater form of some aquatic insects.

77. NYMPHING Simply means "fishing a nymph-fly in a stream." (Not a term commonly used in lake fishing, even though nymphs are routinely fished in lakes.)

78. PALM The action of pressing the palm of the hand against the exposed rim of a fly reel's spool to increase resistance against a running fish. Of course, a reel's spool must have an exposed rim for palming to work.

79. PATTERN, FLY Refers to either a list of materials for tying a specific fly or to the finished fly itself. A bit confusing, but such is fly-fishing lingo.

80. POCKETWATER A riffle (see **riffle**) studded with exposed boulders. Behind each boulder is a hollow where fish can hold.

81. POINT A finger of land jutting out into a lake (or other standing water). Also refers to the sharp tip of a hook.

82. POINT FLY In a nymph rig carrying more than one fly, the lowest fly, the one on the end of the tippet, is the point fly. In a drop-shot rig the point fly is replaced with one or more split shot.

83. PONTOON BOAT A pair of pontoons (usually inflatable) mounted in a frame with a seat and other features, propelled by oars and often by swim fins too. "Pontoon boat" and "kick-boat" are used interchangeably by some anglers. To me, though, the former is mainly for rowing and the latter mainly for propelling by fins.

84. POPPER A fly with a stout body of cork or foam rubber. If cork, the body normally is painted.

85. PRESENTATION Describes how a fly is "presented" to a fish: delicately, roughly, with or without added motion, from upstream or downstream . . .

86. PUPA The second primary stage of the three stages of some freshwater aquatic insects. The first is the larva and the last is the adult stage.

87. READING WATER To read water is to identify the places in it where fish hold and feed. In your typical lake or stream, fish will be concentrated in certain areas. These areas offer you your best shot at finding good fishing.

88. REALISTIC FLY A realistic fly pattern includes convincing details—gills, pectoral fins, neatly divided tails, neatly pointed wing cases, and so on—that make it imitate a specific insect or creature fish eat (such as a Golden Stonefly nymph or a sculpin). There's quite a range in realistic flies, from mildly lifelike to convincing enough to fool the human eye. Realistic flies are the opposite of impressionistic flies.

89. REFUSAL When a fish has come at a fly and then turned away from it, *refusing* to take it.

90. RETRIEVE Working a fly back by tugging or drawing in fly line, to make the fly swim or dart.

91. RIFFLE A relatively wide stretch of creek, stream, or river carrying a good but not truly swift current over a fairly level streambed around two to four feet deep. Some riffles are broken by a few boulders. Riffles broken by a lot of exposed boulders are really pocketwater.

92. RIVER Flowing water bigger than a creek or stream.

93. RUN A lazy, fairly deep flow in a creek, stream, or river, usually studded with large boulders. A run may follow a riffle and feed into a pool, or just stand alone.

94. SCUD Looks like a tiny shrimp. Lives in lakes and slow streams. Never hatches.

95. SCULPIN A small dull-colored bottom-hugging fish common to creeks, streams, and rivers, sometimes lakes. Trout and smallmouth bass, in particular, eat many sculpins.

96. SELECTIVITY Describes when a fish is fussy about what flies it will take. Common behavior with trout, especially during insect hatches. Selectivity can come into play with both largemouth and smallmouth bass and even panfish.

97. SET When an angler pulls on the line to sink the fly's hook into a fish, the angler "sets the hook," making a "hook set." So the word is both verb and noun to the fly fisher.

98. SHOAL A relatively flat lake bottom angling slowly deeper as it continues away from shore. Shoals typically end in drop-offs.

99. SHOOTING LINE To shoot line is to let go of it after the rod stops at the end of a casting stroke (typically a forward stroke) so that the line can just sail on out.

100. SHUCK The outer skin an insect sloughs off as it hatches from nymph or pupa to winged adult.

101. SIDE CHANNEL A smaller flow breaking off the main river, stream, or creek. A side channel typically empties back into the parent water downstream. Are two side channels of about equal volume a "split" or are they still side channels? Who knows?

102. SIGHT-FISHING Means fishing for a fish you can see—not just its rise or swirl but the fish itself. Sight-fishing often requiring serious stealth, but it's exciting.

SINK-TIP
See **line, floating, sinking-tip, full-sinking**.

SINKING LINE
See **line, floating, sinking-tip, full-sinking**.

103. SLACK Fly fishers use the word to describe waves, curls, or an arc in tippet, leader, or line. Slack allows a fly or strike indicator to drift naturally on stream currents rather than getting dragged around by the line, leader, or tippet that's getting dragged around by the currents. (See **dead drift** and **drag**.)

104. SLACK-LINE CAST Any cast that drops the line, leader, tippet, or any combination of these in waves, curves, or in an arc on the water.

105. SNAG GUARD Usually, heavy monofilament bound partway down a fly hook's bend and behind its eye to loop around the point of its hook, though there are variations. Snag guards are most common on largemouth bass flies, helping to keep them from catching on waterweeds and the trunks and branches of fallen trees. Snag-guard flies are also called "weedless" flies.

106. SOW BUG A small to medium-size crustacean important to trout fishers in slow, weedy streams. Sow bugs never hatch.

107. SOFT-HACKLED FLY A century-plus-old fly design with a simple body and a collar of long, flexible feather fibers. Also called a "soft-hackle."

108. SPINNER The fully mature final stage of a mayfly, be it female or male. Though other insects mature too, none but the mayfly has anything called a "spinner" stage.

109. SPLIT Where a stream (or creek or river) divides into two channels of about equal volume. A term rarely used, in part, because creeks, streams, and rivers rarely divide equally. Can also refer to split shot.

110. SPLIT SHOT A tiny round or ovoid weight, formerly of lead and now of nontoxic metals, with a slit. The shot (one or more) is mounted onto leader or tippet above a knot (the knot keeps the shot from sliding down) by putting the monofilament into the slit and then crimping the slit closed with pliers or forceps. Split shot help sink a fly.

111. SPRING CREEK A creek, stream, or river fed mostly or entirely from springs. Spring creeks tend to run a constant volume and a constant cold temperature comfortable for trout. They're usually rich in insect life.

112. STOMACH PUMP I've long preferred to call it a "throat pump"—its tube should *never* be forced into the stomach of a trout. That's murder. Worse, actually—torture. A throat pump removes insects and such from a trout's throat so the angler can determine what the trout was eating and match it with a fly.

113. STONEFLY A stout underwater nymph that crawls out of the water to hatch into a stout, winged adult. Stoneflies live only in currents, usually pretty quick currents.

114. STREAM Technically, a flow larger than a creek but smaller than a river. Fly fishers, though, often use the term "trout stream" for anything from a trickle to a big river (as long as it holds trout, of course). I used it in this book mostly to describe all flowing waters.

115. STREAMER A fly imitating, or to at least to some degree resembling, a small fish.

116. STRIKE A confusing term as fly fishers use it—which makes it a true fly-fishing term. A fish taking a fly is a strike (or "take"), and an angler pulling on the line to sink the hook point into the fish's mouth is also a strike (or "set").

117. STRIKE INDICATOR A buoyant little ball or a hank of buoyant yarn—*something* that floats to hold a nymph suspended below it and tell the fly fisher when a fish takes the nymph.

118. STRIP The act of pulling fly line in a few inches at a time, the line slipping between thumb and finger and in through the rod's guides. Each pull is also called a "strip" of the line.

119. STRIPPING APRON A stretch of netting or material, built into many float tubes, U-boats, and pontoon boats, that lies close in front of the fly fisher to hold and control loose fly line temporarily not in use.

120. STRIPPING BASKET Hangs from the fly fisher's waist to catch and control loose fly line temporarily not in use. Normally reserved for situations that require lots of long casts while the caster mostly stays in place.

121. STROKE, CASTING A swing of the rod forward or back to propel the fly line out. The casting stroke that throws the line behind the angler is the "backcast." The "forward cast" (I've also heard it called the "forecast" and "front cast") throws the line out in front of the angler.

122. STRUCTURE Refers to about any sort of irregularity (ridge, drop-off, depression, hump . . .) in the bed of a lake or stream (though the term is used mainly in lake and saltwater fishing), as opposed to flat, featureless bottom. Fish of all sorts tend to gather around structure.

123. SUNFISH A group of flat, ovoid panfish all quite similar, such as the bluegill, pumpkinseed, and green sunfish. Some *pan*fish (rock bass, crappies, yellow perch . . .) aren't sunfish—they often behave like sunfish, though, and even hang out with them. Largemouth and smallmouth bass are *technically* sunfish, but no real angler thinks of them as such.

124. SWING A "swing" or "wet-fly swing" (sometimes, when a soft-hackled fly is used, called a "soft-hackle swing") is performed by casting across the current and then letting the line, and the fly, *swing* back in downstream of the angler. The rate at which the fly crosses the river may be slowed by mends of the line.

125. TAILWATER A creek, stream, or river that emerges from one or more dams.

TAPER, FLY LINE
See **line, taper**.

126. TECHNICAL To fly fishers, this adjective means fishing that's "challenging in a refined way," usually for trout. So "technical fishing" or "technical water" might refer to a clear, slow stream where crafty rainbows demand fine tippets and excellent presentations of tiny flies.

127. TERRESTRIAL To fly fishers, the term refers to land insects that wind up on water.

128. TIPPET Monofilament of constant diameter tied to the tip of a tapered leader to help avoid fly drag, sink nymphs and streamers, and prolong the life of expensive tapered leaders.

129. TONGUE, CURRENT The long triangle of broken water feeding into the head of a pool on a creek, stream, or river. Trout and smallmouth bass often hold alongside and in a current tongue.

130. TOPWATER Means "concerning the surface of water," especially in regards to largemouth and smallmouth bass. "Topwater" bass fishing would be fishing poppers and floating hair bugs, floating flies. The term "topwater" is sometimes used in regards to trout fishing by the same meaning it carries with bass fishing.

131. TRAILER RIG A fly trailed behind another fly on a short length of tippet tied to the bend of the upper fly's hook. A rig normally for nymphs, but sometimes made up of two floating flies.

132. TROLLING Towing a fly around behind a boat or inflatable craft, normally in a lake or other standing water (reservoir, pond . . .) on a full-sinking line. Trolling *can* be done with a floating line.

133. TURNOVER Happens when a lake hits about one temperature from top to bottom. Winds pull at the surface causing the water to rotate, churning up silt and debris from the bed. Turnover usually happens in spring and again in fall, and can really depress fishing as long as it continues.

134. U-BOAT A sort of float tube with an open end, so that the body of the craft is shaped like a U for easy entry and exit.

135. WARMWATER FISHES Fish species comfortable in water warmer than trout prefer. Refers mainly to largemouth bass, smallmouth bass, and panfish.

136. WEEDLESS Describes a fly with a snag guard, or some other feature, that keeps the fly from catching on water plants, submerged stumps, tree branches, and such. (See **snag guard**.)

WEIGHT-FORWARD

See **line, taper**.

137. WIND KNOT A knot in leader or tippet created during casting. Wind knots weaken monofilament, especially wind knots in tippet or in the fine tip of a tapered leader. Some anglers work them open, others ignore them, especially if they're well up the leader.

138. WORM, AQUATIC Looks like an earthworm but lives in freshwater streams and lakes—crazy, eh?

X, FOR HOOKS

See **hook specifications and terms**.

139. WET FLY Usually refers to a traditional sinking fly with a tail, body, hackle, and swept-back *wings*, commonly fished for trout in streams on the swing (just as soft-hackled flies are commonly fished). Some fly fishers will call almost any fly that's fished subsurface a wet fly.

140. X, FOR LEADER AND TIPPET An X designates the diameter of tippet or a tapered leader's point. The larger the number before the X, the finer the monofilament—7X is very fine, while 5X is typical for trout fishing and 2X and 0X are stout indeed.